High Priestess of Schizophrenia

by

Alexandria May Ausman

This book is a work of fiction. Any references to historical events, real people, or real places, are used fictitiously. Other names, characters, places, and events are products of the author's imagination, and any resemblance to actual events or persons, living or dead, is entirely coincidental.

Book cover illustration by Alexandria May Ausman
Editor: Jon M. Ausman

Library of Congress Control Number: 2023914264

ISBN: 979-8-9871098-8-5 (ebook)
ISBN: 979-8-9871098-9-2 (paperback)

Published By:
Ausman & Cousins LLC
1700 North Monroe Street
Suite 11, Box 284
Tallahassee, Florida 32303-0501

For author interviews: ausman@embarqmail.com

Das Kaiser Haus Series

The Collar King Series

The Most Brutal Man in Europe Series

Claus's Revelations (Coming soon)

The Psycho Series

Cemetery Kid (Chapters 1 to 20)
Stop Calling Me Psycho (Chapters 21 to 33)
Motor-Psycho (Chapters 34 to 44)
Delusion of the Collar and the Key (Chapters 45 to 53)
Brutality's Prisoner (Chapters 54 to 64)
Aesthetic Akathisia (Chapters 65 to 74)
Metallic Burden (Chapters 75 to 83)

27 Masters Series

Anita the Benevolent (Chapters 1 to 7)
The Beast and the Witch (Chapters 8 to 16)
High Priestess of Schizophrenia (Chapters 17 to 24)
The Professional Dominatrix (Coming soon)

Book Three Characters: High Priestess of Schizophrenia

Andrea: Mistress Five, an interim

Arodia: High Priestess of the Green Ring

Boyd: a deputy sheriff

Brigida: mother of Andrea

Cherie: a waitress and schoolmate of Psycho

Christian Axel: secret husband of Psycho/Rachel, trainer and original Master

Christine: the second Master, a psychopath, her home burned down mysteriously

Chuck: spouse of Lisa, member of the Green Ring

Circe: the third Mistress, a Priestess of the Green Ring

CJ: a college classmate

Cody: son of Albert and Suzy

Commisso, Dr.: state hospital psychiatrist

Crystal: a schoolmate

Debbie: Psycho's sexual psychopathic and sadistic mother

Delilah: niece of Maiden Mary, caretaker of the nursery

Delleh: a High Priestess of the Green Ring, a 5th Level Initiate

Dennis: the county sheriff

Diane: CJ's live in friend

Dude: a command hallucination, an aggressive anger shard of Psycho

Frizzy: a funeral home co-worker

Ginger: a FemDom, Mistress Ten

Jake: stillborn child of Andrea
James: spouse of Tracy, member of the Green Ring
Jimmy: divorced spouse of Andrea
Johnny: a Summoner
Jon Ausman: the current Keyholder
Julius: a funeral home owner
June: a funeral home master embalmer, Mistress Nine, an interim
Kevin: deceased spouse of Dellah, a 3rd Initiate
Kick Start: a high school classmate
Linda: a deputy sheriff
Lisa: spouse of Chuck, member of the Green Ring
Looper: a disembodied voice, Psycho's narrative hallucination
Marie: Master Seven, an interim
Mary: Maiden to Circe, takes care of Psycho's children
Moore, Mrs.: high school counselor
Nikki Jaimes: a schizotypal, the teenager in all pink
Nikki French: Mistress Six, an interim
Orin: Father of the Green Rings
Pat: a master mortician
Paul: a California Dungeon Master
Peggy: Master Four, an Interim Master
Psycho: a schizophrenic trying to survive
Ralph: a slum lord
Richard: a Summoner
Roary: a High Priest, 3rd Level Initiate, also known as Richard
Ron: spouse of Circe, lives with Mary

Samson, Mr.: a funeral home client
Scruffy: a "fire" dog
Simon Brag: a command hallucination shard of Psycho, her lost inner self
Solomon: Richard's High Priest
Tammy: Master Eight, an interim
Tracy: spouse of James, member of the Green Ring
Vicky: partner of Andrea
Violet: Nikki's mother
Zeppelin: a golden fur dog

Preface

After Psycho finally escapes Christine she falls into the hands of Circe, a practicing witch who runs a shop offering potions, candles, and counseling. Circe is a pursuer of cash, and she trains Psycho as a money-maker.

Psycho, the mother of two, needs a guardian to help her deal with basic needs such as eating meals, bathing, the taking of medications, and surviving. Circe offers such services but wants to use Psycho to raise herself another rank among the Wiccans within her state. To do so she wants to subjugate Psycho.

The battle between the two women results in massive betrayals, treachery, murder by proxy, thirty-day interim Masters. and heroic rescues.

Finally, one appears who knows what Psycho needs and is determined to receive "service for service."

Chapter 17: Interim Master Peggy
The Fall of Mistress Circle

1994 was the year of the Interim Masters and of our rise to High Priestess. We have already been through so much, but we were born for this shit. We just can't seem to get enough. As the New Year begins, we prepare for battle once more. This time it is not for our sanity. In 1993, we had fought that war, only to soundly lose our bid to be sane. We are still reeling from the damage of that epic failure.

This time, we are engaged in a struggle with our Mistress. She has been useless in her service delivery but has taken much in return. Now that she has been effectively rendered powerless, Mistress Circe is beyond angered. She would like to see us pay for our daring to defend ourselves from her abuse. Her plan is to break us down by offering our collar to the highest bidder. However, before this auction begins, she plans to give many people a chance to sample the prize up for grabs.

In a most unusual move seen by any Keyholder to this date, Mistress Circe will use her ability to leash to allow Interims to hold our services in a series of "thirty-day trials" as our Master. Her excuse is that the next holder of our Will can be discovered more safely with this type of arrangement. Mistress Circe still holds our collar and Key, but soon she will find the one who will pay the price she has in mind. Before the most respected of all our Masters, well until Master Jon, we will suffer in the service of six

Interim Keyholders over six months. Our next true submission will be to our tenth Master this very year.

Wow, so we go from third to tenth in only seven months. This is very unsettling. Well, we never expected a life following a Key would be easy. Ready to start the latest dramas? Awesome. Okay then grab your coffee, smoke them if you got them. Bring your ear for gossip, oh, and hip waiters too in case the stories the town's people tell you are total bullshit. Wouldn't want you to mess up those nice shoes of yours?

"This is unforgivable. Give her the collar Mistress. She is the right one for the job. I choose her." **Psycho to Circe regarding Master Peggy's Interim status - January 1994**

"We have met," I said to Pat as I shook Nikki's hand.

He raised his eyebrows. "Oh? Well, that is great. Hey, I have something for Nikki in the car. I will leave you ladies to catch up for a minute. If you would excuse me?" Pat left for the parking lot of the funeral home.

Nikki stood there smiling that weird smile she always seemed to have on her face. She was still dressed from head to toe in pink. In fact, like me, she hadn't changed a bit. It was as if I had traveled back in time. I stood there looking at her waiting for her to tell me why she was smiling like that at me.

"You are still in black? Do you have a Motorpsycho too? How's Zeppelin," she asked sweetly.

I shook my head. "No Motorpsycho yet. Working on it. I heard Zeppelin and Cody are doing great. So, how is Violet and your dad? I have been trying to get out to see you both. I have been just so busy."

She giggled, "Uhm, yeah, I heard. You have been busy taking over churches and burning down people's houses."

My eyes went wide. "What? Burning down houses?"

She stopped giggling looking frightened. "Oh. Psycho don't be upset. Daddy said they say you burned down that guardian's house, oh what did he say her name was, started with a C, I think."

I interrupted her. "I did not. If I had burned that bitch's trailer, trust me, she deserved it. I would also like to correct you in that it was "a" church, not churches. Geez, Nikki. Does everyone have nothing better to do than to start rumors."

Nikki shook her head. "Hey, I didn't say that stuff. Daddy just tells mom and me the stories, is all. I know you are nice Psycho. I tell daddy you are not a witch, and you don't go putting spells on people and stuff."

I rolled my eye at that. "It isn't your fault. I asked for it by bothering to speak to you in the first place. I should have just said thank you for helping me out a few years ago and been done with it. For what it is worth, I am happy to see you have a boyfriend. Tell Violet I said thank you too. Now, I have work to do. I won't be seeing you around if that is okay with you. I don't need the trouble."

She smiled and nodded, not a brain in her head. "Okay Psycho. I will tell her. Bye now." She waved as I took off for the embalming room.

I couldn't believe that poor intellectually disabled Nikki was dating my Master Mortician Pat. I wondered if he was aware the girl was slow. It was not my business, but I did feel some need to protect Nikki from a pervert. She was a pretty girl, but a bubble head. A slick Californian like Pat could mislead her easily.

I swore I was going to keep my thoughts about it to myself. I didn't need trouble with my boss. However, call me stupid, I just couldn't stay silent and allow him to take advantage of her. He came back in closing the door while smiling to himself.

"Nikki is a nice girl," I said flatly while glaring at him.

He smiled proudly. "Damn straight she is. What a beauty, huh?" He walked over and grabbed the embalming hose while I made the incision into the client's carotid artery.

I snorted. "That she is Pat. You are aware she is not all there." I looked up at him hard.

He looked down at the client. "Yeah, I know she is retarded if that is what you are asking. I know what that must look like, but my intentions are sincere."

I laughed out loud. "Oh? You are sincerely planning to take advantage of her? The girl's IQ is barely room temperature on a winter day Pat. Have you met Violet? I am having a tough time believing she would allow you to fool with Nikki at all. What is wrong with you? Don't want bothersome things like the ability to say no getting in your way of using a woman's unit?"

I spewed out before I could think better of it. This guy was my fucking boss. Here I was acting like an asshole for a girl who had never brought me anything but trouble. Okay, she was good to Zeppelin, I must give her that.

Pat stopped trying to insert the hose into the now opened artery, to look at me appearing surprised instead of angry. "I didn't realize you two were friends, Psycho. I just assumed no one saw Nikki the way I do. She is a wonderful person; I can see past her schizoid stuff and low intelligence. I have never met a sweeter, more loving or giving person in my life. As for taking advantage, I would never do that. I promised Violet no hanky-panky till after we are married in July. I am a man of honor. She is wearing my engagement ring. I want Nikki as my wife, not just as a fuck Psycho. I love her more than my own life." He actually teared up as he said this.

I was startled by his revelation. Though I didn't know him very well yet, it was touching to hear a man say this about a woman, especially weird Nikki. Pat was able to see Nikki as the worthy human being she truly was. Even my cold-hearted ass could respect that.

"I apologize, Pat. I thought, well never mind. I am an asshole. It is not my business anyway. I should have butted out." I went back to my job embalming the customer's unit.

He chuckled. "No need to apologize. I told you I didn't know Nikki had any friends. You stood up for the woman I love. That makes you golden in my eyes and you just earned my respect too. I must admit, I was pissed when Julius told me I was to work with you. You know, the rumors about you and all. But, like Nikki, you are a lot more than anyone gives you credit for. Thank you for sticking up for her like that. You are welcome in our home, after we move in together, anytime. As for Violet, she is a great woman. She raised the future mother of my children. What is not to love?"

I sighed. "Okay enough, Pat. If you spin any more sugar, I will get diabetes. Then I will end up on this table next to Mr. Samson here. While a nap sounds like a dream come true, I better stick around for a bit longer. Oh, and I am not Nikki's friend. I just know the family is all."

He laughed. "You look healthy to me. I wouldn't expect you to be a client of mine anytime soon, Psycho. You may not think Nikki is your friend, but she is. Now so am I. Don't argue with me. No one is so rich they can throw away a friend, Psycho."

I shrugged. "Then you should know that I am not only poor, but I am also near homeless and glad of it. Keep your friendship and hers to yourselves. I don't have the energy."

Pat laughed hard at that. "Man, you are as cold as this stiff, Psycho. Well, no problem. Sooner or later you will get tired of hanging out with people who are not going to add anything to your conversations. Nikki and I will be around when you are ready to call on us."

I shrugged. "Boss, I thought you said you had heard the rumors about me. If you had you'd know that there is no one, or thing, on Earth that that doesn't add to my conversations. I am a legion of discussions no matter where I go. Silence is a gift I do not possess."

He narrowed his eyes. "Huh? That's not true. You almost never speak. In fact, this is the most I have ever heard you say."

I chuckled. "You may not hear it, but I am talking non-stop, Pat. In fact, I wish I could shut the fuck up."

He gave an "ah ha" look "Oh you mean you think a lot. Me too. I have racing thoughts myself, so I totally get it."

I started the formaldehyde machine. "No, thinking a lot is not what I mean Pat. I mean actual conversations even though I am not a part of them. They are always going on around me. The corpses, this machine, that wall. They never shut up."

He appeared stunned. "Seriously? Shit. Have you ever been tested for schizophrenia, Psycho? I mean I don't want to scare you or anything but people who hear voices, well they are usually mentally ill."

I stopped the machine so I could glare at this fool giving him my full attention. "Yes, Pat. I have been tested for it. I have been tested by it. I just assumed Julius told you, or the fucking town rumors did. I have schizophrenia,

Pat. You are the one who should be scared, not me. I already know I am insane, but you are only just finding out. How funny that you missed the only rumor out there that is completely true." I laughed as I walked off into the storeroom to grab more embalming fluid.

Pat feeling so strongly for Nikki despite her obvious disability made me start to think again about my own situation. She had somehow found someone to love her. It was absolutely amazing to me.

First, Violet never let the girl blow her nose by herself. How the hell did she even find the guy? Second, Nikki was dumb as a bag of hammers. Yet here she was engaged to be married to this fellow that was ready to defend her honor. It was blowing my mind, okay if I had one.

I had a fucking Key and collar, provided perfect service and was even making my Mistress money hand over fist and couldn't even get her to give me my fucking medications. Something had to be wrong with me, oh yeah, I'm crazy. I almost forgot there.

Okay, so if the intellectually disabled can be loved by someone they didn't give birth to, why not a schizo? Nikki didn't possess any better a "people friendly" demeanor than I did. So, what was it that I was doing wrong? This was a problem that I would need to talk with Simon about. If we could get a person to care about us the way Pat seemed to Nikki, we could get rid of Mistress Circe's collar, and never have to find another, right?

I had decided to keep my job at the F&T for a bit longer. I went to part-time. I was only called into the funeral home when there was a "pick up" or a client that had a funeral arranged for the next afternoon that the day embalmer couldn't get to. If I didn't have work on a client I was expected to come in for at least two hours five days a week and do stock ordering, cleaning, and paperwork for the coroner when appropriate. I was paid by salary, so my hours didn't matter. Only the work being finished was the goal. I really liked the job. There was one drawback. It was depressing as hell.

Pat told me to think of the dead as mannequins rather than the units of people who were no more. That was impossible even for a psychotic. Each person I prepared for their final sendoff tended to get to me a bit. I wondered what their life had been like. If they had gotten everything they had been looking for. I wondered if they would trade places with me if they could. Even if they knew my life was shit and I was a prisoner of the State. Maybe any life was better than no life. This was the question that began to haunt me day and night. It was an interesting change in me. I had spent the last six years trying almost everything to both save and end my existence. Now, I was questioning if death was really the peaceful escape I had imagined it to be. I even started to be glad I had not died, even if it meant being, well nuts.

When I wasn't working, I spent my time with my children and Simon. The Yule Sabbat was coming, and Mistress Circe was starting to bug me again about special service of the collar. She wanted to receive it after the Yule ritual citing "it was required to have ritual sex on the Sabbats."

I told her, "To do it yourself or get that useless husband of yours. We are done. Not interested and never was."

She didn't like that response. When Yule arrived the Sister Coven again was cancelled due to Delleh's health. Apparently, she had gotten better over the summer and fall, but I was in the Snake Pit. I had missed the big get-togethers. Now this one was cancelled.

Mistress Circe was livid. She was frustrated that I had not been providing any services, and she wasn't even getting to show me off to the Queen of Green. I had become a worthless item in her mind. She decided to punish me, she was going to start a "series of probationary" try outs to identify a new Keyholder.

She didn't want to transfer my Key till after the Beltane ritual designed to raise her, and I, a level higher. However, she wanted to make sure I suffered as much as possible till that hallowed day arrived. She called me to a meeting with her in the kitchen on the last day of 1993.

She was sitting there seeming pouty as I sat down, "Psycho, I have called you here to discuss my leashing of the collar option."

I smiled bitterly, "Oh? I thought I revoked all your rights. Did you forget?"

She snorted, "You did indeed. But you did give this one back so that I could find a new Keyholder. You are the one who has forgotten."

That made me raise a brow. "You found someone? I just assumed you would wait till after Beltane, but why call me for a meeting if you have decided to transfer."

She interrupted me. "Not quite so fast, Psycho. I didn't say I had found someone. I said I want to talk about the leash rights. I want to wield it right away. I do have someone in mind, but I want to set down rules. I don't expect you would have a problem with that."

Now she had my attention. "Of course not. Rules are mandatory if you plan to leash me. What the fuck is this about? What game are you trying to play now, Mistress? I am in no mood. I start college in two weeks. If you are jerking me around, I will make you sorry," I growled.

She snorted. "I am already sorry, Psycho. Trust me. I have a woman interested in your collar. I just am not sure she is the right one to give the Key to."

I laughed. "You mean you don't know if she can afford it. Come on Mistress. I am psychotic, not stupid. You want to leash me to the woman to see if you can tempt her into coming up with the price you are asking." I sat back and crossed my arms glaring at the greedy bitch.

Mistress Circe looked at her hands. "So? It is mine to do with as I please, Psycho. What I am doing is perfectly legitimate. While I tempt the potential Keyholder; you can

12

see if the match is good. I think it would work well for both of our best interests."

I frowned. "It would except you are not the one having to fucking serve someone who may not work out. I want to set limits on this bullshit. I say no more than two weeks. I will not provide special services of the collar to any interim you choose. If I haven't submitted, they should not be allowed to bed me. I am not a whore no matter what you think, Mistress."

She cackled like the witch she was. "Oh no, no, no. First you will need to do thirty days to be sure. Next, not providing special services is fine, with one stipulation: If they make it the thirty days, they should be granted a one-time demonstration of this specialty. It is only fair they get to experience all the services if they survive the trial period. Plus you can find out if they are twisted. You wouldn't want to submit again to find out they are like Christine in the bedroom, now, would you?"

I sneered, "Or you, Mistress."

She glared. "You loved it, Psycho."

I rolled my eyes. "Cut the shit, Mistress. You know I didn't, but you have a good point. However, I will only allow it once and only if they make it the full thirty days. I want to be able to end the probation anytime if I find them unmanageable."

Mistress Circe was still fuming over my insult at her sexual prowess. "I want that right exclusive. I am sick of

13

you demanding everything and I get nothing. You won't even do the job of my Maiden and provide consort after a damned ritual."

I laughed. "Should've thought of that before you took away my meds and let me go mad dog. Or while you were beating me for doing a decent job adoring you, or for that matter, taking without giving a fucking thing in return. Don't get me wrong Mistress, you are one of the best fucks I ever had. Too bad it wasn't the enjoyable kind." I stood up ready to punch her in that weak chin of hers.

"Sit down, Psycho. I don't want to fight with you anymore. If you don't want me as your Mistress, fine by me. You can go and serve the Interim Master, and she can see if she does any better. Here is her address. She is expecting you. Now get going. The trial period begins tonight." She threw a piece of paper with an address scribbled on it.

I looked at the paper as if she had just thrown a dog turd at me. "Seriously? You accepted without asking me first. Unfuckingbelievable."

Mistress Circe stood up slowly. "Too late now. If you don't go, she will withdraw the offer thinking we are not seriously considering her. I would pack light if I were you. I doubt she will be the one." She started to leave the kitchen.

"Hey, wait just a God damned second. First, if you think she is not going to be the one why should I bother? Second, what about my kids? I can't haul them to some stranger's house. What if she is a creep or killer?" I grabbed the address trying to decide if I even knew what part of town this woman lived in.

Mistress Circe looked back at me. "Your kids can stay with Mary. I already talked to her. You can visit them until this whole thing is settled one way or the other. As for if she is a creep or killer, you surprise me. You are willing to go there, be alone with a stranger, but you leave the kids out of it. Fucking loon. She may have the money she tells me. She wants to see if you are worth her entire lifesavings first. If I were you, I would make sure to treat her right, or you will still be stuck with me. sweetie." She faked a smile at me.

"Fuck you, Mistress," I growled as I pushed her out of my way headed for the door.

"If you had done that none of this would have happened, Psycho. Oh, you can take the Honda this time, but if there is another time, you will make your own arrangements." She yelled as I started out the door to meet this new idiot who wanted my collar.

I just flipped her off but kept going. I could hear her cackling behind me as I got into the car. She was such a bitch. I really hoped this new person was the one who would fix this entire mess.

I had not been caring for the unit again. I would forget to take my meds, eat, and not bathe since I got out of the Snake pit. If I didn't find someone to handle this shit soon, I was going to be in trouble. I even forgot my probation and therapy appointments. I had been using an alarm clock but often forgot what I had set the fucking thing for or forgot it at Mistress Circe's altogether. I was failing yet again.

Simon would remind me periodically, or I would have already starved to death. I didn't want to play Mistress Circe's little auction game, but it did make sense to check out the candidate carefully this time. I had three horror shows in a row. I was not ready for number four to be a repeat. So, the year of the interim began that very night. I would start the first day of the New Year with Master Peggy.

Master number four
Collar Holder (ONLY-No Key):
Interim Master Peggy: The Fair
Reign: December 31st, 1992, to January 30, 1993.

I pulled into the long driveway of a single level home with huge windows everywhere. I sat in the car looking at this weird house thinking the occupant must really love my brother the sun. I had never seen a house like this one. If Picasso decided to go into architecture, then he built this house. It was definitely a custom job.

I was surprised because I assumed if the woman named Peggy had not been able to afford Mistress Circe's price, then surely, she would live in a trailer house or a shack. I wondered how much my Mistress was asking if this person couldn't afford my collar. A house like this was expensive. I just shook my head grumbling about the stupidity of this game. Seemed that handing over a collar shouldn't be so fucking much trouble, but then again, I didn't think much of myself at that time. It seemed like much ado about nothing to me.

I walked up the weirdly shaped porch to knock, but the door swung open before I could. A woman in her late forties with brown tightly permed short hair and big glasses poked her head out. She was wearing a white sweatshirt and pair of jeans with loafers. She appeared very normal on the surface.

"Ah Psycho, I have been so excited to meet you. I have been pacing for the last hour waiting for you. Welcome. Come in, come in." She reached out and practically clawed my arm pulling me inside before I could stop her.

She then held me still holding my upper arm as she closed the door. "Okay, don't move. I want to see what I am purchasing here. Circe told me about you and what you can do, but she was vague about your description. I thought you would be older or maybe ugly, but that does not appear to be the case. Hmmm, there must be something wrong with you, or you wouldn't have this weird problem Circe told me about. I mean, seems to me a looker like you could get someone to take you in for free. So what is it? Let me have a look. I will figure it out, I am sure." Peggy began to circle my unit.

I started to feel like a damned horse at a livestock sale. She kept walking around my unit pulling her glasses up then down searching me from head to toe. I stood there my head down wondering what the fuck this was all about. I wondered what exactly Mistress Circe had told this person.

"Uhm, pardon me, Peggy? I am mentally ill without a support system, a felony history, labeled violently psychotic, and I have two dependents that I care for. The Collar and Key services are my way of assuring I can meet my court ordered guardianship and medication management. That is what is wrong with me," I said politely but honestly while keeping my gaze to the floor.

She stopped circling. "Oh, you can talk. I thought maybe you were deaf and dumb, or maybe retarded? You seem intelligent enough, that is a plus. Great. Let's get started, shall we?"

She grabbed my right wrist and began to pull me after her. Peggy was five foot six and weighed at least one hundred and seventy pounds to my then ninety-five. I was dragged unable to break her grip but starting to become very afraid. This chick was nuts. I pulled back digging my heels into the carpet as she attempted to go down a hallway just to the right of the exceptionally large living area.

"Where are you taking me? What do you mean get started? Slow down. I don't even know you, lady," I said stressed out of my mind as she continued to try to pull me.

She stopped and finally let me go. I backed away now very frightened of this crazy woman. "Ma'am, I don't know what Mistress Circe told you but there are rules to this arrangement. We need to talk before this goes any further. Please may we sit down to discuss this? I don't even know what to call you or anything."

She snorted then rubbed her hand over her forehead. "Okay, fine. Whatever. I though Mistress Circe said I could do with you as I pleased. She never mentioned rules."

I glared at her already hating this woman. "No Ma'am, I am not a slave. You can't just go dragging me around to do God knows what. Please, let's sit down to discuss this. I will answer your questions and we can come to an agreement. We are together for the next thirty days, so I suggest you take this opportunity to get to know what can and cannot be obtained if you purchase my Key."

She nodded. "Alright, you have a point. Do you want something to drink? I have beer, and Bourbon but none of the light liquors."

I rolled my eyes. Oh shit, this is going to be a long night. "No thank you. I think you need to sit. We have a lot to talk about."

Peggy finally did sit down, and we spoke at length about the situation. She told me that Mistress had pulled a fast one by telling her that I was a mindless fool who does whatever you tell her.

While I was angry the Mistress did that, I was not surprised by it. Mistress Circe tended to be a passive aggressive bitch. I began the protracted process of correcting Peggy's misunderstanding of what it is that I do or don't do. She sat there nodding and listening intently. I noted she drank three beers while I went over the ground rules, services offered, and those expected in return.

She then in turn told me she had been seeing Mistress Circe for spiritual counseling for two years since moving there from Minnesota. She was a closet lesbian who had moved to the town for work. Peggy was a licensed practical nurse at the hospital several towns away. Because of her sexual orientation, she had believed not living in the town where she worked would keep knowledge of her secret relationships from reaching the ears of her homophobic bosses.

The trouble was there were no relationships to be had. Peggy had found that the lesbians in these small southern towns were so quiet she was unable to find any girlfriends. She had become quite lonely and had been complaining to Mistress Circe about it. Then lucky for her, my Mistress informed her she just happened to know of a girl who would not say no to any of Peggy's alternative desires. All she had to do was pay the price. In other words, Mistress Circe had sold the idea to Peggy I was a sexual plaything that she could purchase, keep hidden at home, and solve both her carnal desires and difficulty with finding company. Peggy was terribly upset to find out that was not the case.

I just rolled my eyes at this bullshit. "Okay look, apparently Mistress Circe has given you the wrong impression. I apologize only for your misunderstanding but not for her bad manners. I will leave you to your own. Thank you very much for your time. I do wish you much luck in your romantic endeavors." I stood up ready to leave now that it was discovered this was not going to work.

Peggy let out a yelp, "Hey. Wait a minute, Psycho. Where are you going?"

"I am leaving Peggy. I am not a whore, darling. I told you this is not going to work." I was wondering if this woman had just ignored me or was stupid or what?

"I paid money down. I was told no refund, Psycho." She looked at the floor appearing embarrassed that she had just admitted to paying for what she thought was a "live in call girl."

I snorted. "Too bad for you then. I didn't get paid. Sounds like this is the Mistress and your problem, not mine. Unless you are looking for what I told you I am, then we are done here. You seem to be looking for sex. I am not interested in you as a love interest. You seem like a nice lady, but the special services of the collar are only for a Master. The Master must provide service for that service. Nothing is one sided, Peggy. I already told you all this. So, I will be on my way." I headed for the door.

She jumped up from the couch and grabbed my arm again. "Wait. Wait. Okay, I want to try out for the Key. Let me try for it please."

I shook her off now really thinking this chick had a blown fuse. "What? I just told you…"

She shook her head while interrupting, "I get it, I understand. I can do what you want for the services you

21

provide. It is quite simple actually. Like a marriage where everyone knows their role. I could do this. It makes perfect sense. I will show you that I am Keyholder material. Give me a chance. What do you have to lose? I mean Circe really pulled a number lying like that. That was beyond mean. I almost raped you. I was thinking, well never mind, will you give me my thirty-day trial?"

I looked at the floor. "I won't sleep with you."

She chuckled nervously, "Well, you will if I am the Master, right?"

I nodded, "Yeah that is part of the deal."

She smiled. "Well then, I will just have to learn to be Master. That is the title I want. I don't know about all the rest, but I am a fast learner. You show me what to do, and I will do it. It may even be fun."

I sighed. "Usually is if you are the one on top. The bottom sucks though."

She nodded. "I bet. Yet here we are. So, what next?"

I began the process of attending and demonstrating my various skill sets, and services I could provide to Master Peggy. She was enthralled with them all. She tended to ask for the "hands on" services the most often, such as dressing, massaging both body and feet, and hair brushing. Her favorite was of course bath service and she tended to be a bit grabby, but I kept her at arm's length reminding her I didn't play that shit until collared.

Despite her constant demands she kept her hands to herself. She tended to cop a feel, whenever she could get me compromised. The woman was like a fucking octopus. I would knock off one of her attempts only to be captured by another. By the third day, I already began to think this would not work out. However, I always honor an agreement. So, I kept my misgivings to myself, cursing Mistress Circe at least one thousand times a day.

Other than playing footsy every chance she got, Master Peggy was also a heavy drinker. I had to help her drunk unit to bed every day she had off from her job. I was appalled that this LPN was such a lush. It made me worry about any future hospital visits of my own. I prayed all the fucking nurses weren't like Peggy.

The only bright side was she was not a mean drunk. Just a crying one. I would have to listen to hours of her self-loathing, demands to know why no one loved her, and woes about family members who didn't understand her lifestyle. While annoying as all get out, it was not abusive. I decided by the second week, if this one did get my collar, I certainly had endured worse in the recent past.

I eventually changed my mind about being upset if she managed to purchase my collar. When it came to her end of the bargain, Peggy was spectacular. Under her rule, I never missed a meal, dose of medication, and had never been cleaner. She turned out to be obsessive compulsive regarding scheduling. Likely, this was the biggest reason she was considered a great nurse despite her weekend warrior drinking issues. She would call me at work or come

23

by to make sure I took my pills or brought me my baby food when I forgot it. Peggy took off work to make sure I made all my appointments. In the area of returning service for service this woman was even better than Master Anita had been.

By the end of the second week two things had changed in my life: the semester had begun again, and I had decided Master Peggy was my next Keyholder. The second our thirty-day trial period was over I was ready to submit. I was not interested in her in the carnal sense at all and knew that a submission would bring on that dreaded task of sleeping with my Master, but hell I had dealt with Mistress Circe. I could deal with Master Peggy.

In fact, I already knew it would at least be an improvement from my last three Masters. Master Peggy may not have been a looker or even fun to talk to, but she did appear to be interested in her lover's needs. I was told often enough of what she wanted when she got the Key. The woman never stopped talking about it in fact.

So, at least I would finally get reciprocation for my efforts or so it would appear if she were telling the truth. Since I did not ever expect to love, care about or even be attracted to my Master, getting what I give was the best I could ever hope to obtain when it came to sexual service. That was a somewhat comforting thought. I still refused to give in to Master Peggy's desires to try out the special service of the collar.

To my dismay she had learned from Mistress Circe if she made it thirty days, she would get one shot at it before her probation period was done. I was more than pissed the Mistress told Master Peggy that, but again I was not fucking surprised. Mistress Circe wanted to make my life as hellish as possible. That was fine by me. Quid pro quo, bitch. May 1st was coming soon enough. I would get her back.

By the end of the second week of Master Peggy's reign I began my Spring semester of college and extra courses in the Funerary Sciences. I had told Cherie the day before while on shift that my address had changed. She raised her eyebrow over that but didn't say anything until the next day after she had picked me up.

She rolled up her window then headed for the main road after I had gotten in her car. "Uhm, Psycho, it is not my business, but I need to ask you something."

I sneered at that, "If it is not your business then I suggest you keep it that way, Cherie. There is never a need to stick your nose in my affairs."

She glared at me briefly. "Okay, I am just going to ask it then. Are you gay?"

I snorted at that. "Nope."

She was surprised I answered so quickly but didn't appear angry she asked it. "Aren't you curious to know why I asked?"

I rolled my eyes. "Nope."

"Damn. Why are you always such a smart ass? I asked because a gay nurse lives in the house I picked you up from. I didn't know if you knew that but that is what everyone says. She is from, like, Kansas or something. Anyway, I didn't think you needed any more rumors floating around out there. So, I thought you should know that woman is gay. You may want to not hang out there," she spewed out like a broken sewer line.

I narrowed my eyes at her. "Cherie, shut the fuck up. If any rumors were started it would be from you since you are the only one who would think that kind of crap. I know Peggy and she is not gay. She is anxious, obsessive, and a bit pedantic, but never gay. However, if she were, that is not your business. I would like to thank you for keeping your homophobic drivel to yourself. As it is, these clothes I am wearing are clean. I wouldn't want you getting the shit you talk on them. Oh, and she is from Minnesota not Kansas, you dolt."

Cherie let out her breath as if offended. "Oh my God, you are such an asshole. I was trying to be a friend and help you out, Psycho. People do talk, you know. I hear all kinds of shit about you. I must listen to them say you are a witch, gay, a freak, and I heard you even work at the funeral home. What the fuck is wrong with you? Why can't you just be fucking normal like the rest of us? Why can't you dress right?"

I chuckled. "Uhm, schizophrenia, Cherie. Why the fuck do you even care? What they say about me doesn't have any bearing on you, darling. I don't give two shits what anyone says about me."

She growled, "It matters because if they think you are gay, they will say that shit about me too. I am not gay. I think that is fucking sick. I am afraid everyone is going to start talking about me, like they do you. Have you heard what everyone is saying, Psycho? You have to stop acting stupid and grow up. This is not high school. No one is ever going to want to have anything to do with you."

"If you are bothered by what they say, then stop riding with me, Cherie. I am already court fucking ordered to let the State know when I take a shit. I will be damned if a bunch of backwoods, knuckle dragging, ignorant, fucktards are going to dictate the few freedoms still left to me. I will wear whatever the fuck I want. As for who I sleep with, live with, or hang with, that is only my business. So, fuck off. If only everyone would stop having anything to do with me, then wouldn't I be the lucky one," I yelled, now quite angry with this meddling void.

The bully shut up after that. The rest of the semester would be a chronic replay of the above fight. Cherie and I were getting along like water and oil. If we weren't yelling at each other over lifestyle differences – okay she demanded I change and I told her to fuck off so not really arguing over hers, just mine – w were silently listening to our mad boxes. I was so busy with my classes and courses for my embalming job, I was slowly exiting my job at the F&T. By summer, I would be gone completely.

I was still balancing studying for the upcoming judgment before the panel of elders during my Third-Degree initiation and seeing my children. It was again, becoming a bad time for regular sleeping. I was always running somewhere, nearly late for something. Luckily, my daughter was only three and son only about to turn two. They were so small; they would never recall these bad old days of homelessness. Mary was great to them, and their lodgings were clean, safe, and stable.

I knew I needed to finish my repairs of the yellow shit box house so we could be reunited as a true family unit. I spent the long hours at night working at my house. I had saved a lot of money when I was incarcerated. Mistress Circe had kept my checks for me. I immediately paid off my next several months of payments. I needed to pay back Linda for kindly saving my home when I had been away.

I had called to arrange a meeting with her to cover my debt. She had laughingly said I could work out the payoff in trade. I, of course, told her no thanks. She told me to meet her that afternoon when she got off work. I did as she asked but stood at her car in the jail parking lot. I refused to meet her inside. I had seen that jail enough for a lifetime. While I was waiting on Linda, I saw Dennis come out off shift to head home. He teased me, asking if maybe I was there to race him.

"Here to practice, are you? Beware, I have been working out." He pretended to be ready to run after me.

I chuckled somewhat bitterly at that. "Nope, just came by to see if you had any rooms for rent. Asking for a friend. I had heard you were being considered for the Olympics in the 500-yard dash, Dennis. Any truth to that rumor?"

Dennis frowned at that. "Speaking of rumors, one day when you aren't busy, I heard one that I need to discuss with you."

I perked my ears. "Oh? Well, I assure you that I have been an incredibly good girl. No kicking in doors and taking over churches or beating people up, I swear it."

I was now a bit nervous. Dennis had never been interested in anything he heard about me since the Julie bullshit. I wondered what was so bad he needed to ask me about it.

He opened his car door. "It has to do with that pretty, silver necklace I have seen you wear since before I can remember. A little birdy told me, there is a story behind it. I would like to have your side of it. So would Boyd." He nodded, looking sour then pulled out and left me standing there shaking in my boots.

"Shit, someone told the cops," I thought as I saw Linda finally coming my way.

"Hey baby, you don't know how many wet dreams I have had that started out with you waiting for me by my car," yelled Linda playfully.

"Oh, well you old romantic. I would have suspected I was waiting by your bed in your dreams, but hey, I suppose

29

a ride is a ride," I teased back still trying to shake off the creepy feelings I got knowing Dennis and Boyd may have discovered the secret I was keeping.

She laughed. "I can only imagine, Psycho. What's up? Are you looking for a date?"

I laughed as I took out the money, I owed her. "Well now I feel downright dirty handing you this cash, Linda. I have never had to pay for it before. You are one expensive girl. Hey, should you be working this close to the cops? Aren't you afraid they will arrest you?"

She laughed again. "Nah, I have an in with the police officers around here. Hey, Psycho, someone told me they saw you spending time together with old nurse, Peggy the other day. Do you know her?"

I rolled my eyes. This town was nosey. Seemed you couldn't belch without everyone knowing what you had for dinner.

"Yeah, I know her, so," I said suspiciously.

Linda shrugged. "Ah, just that she is a Sister you know. If you hang out with her too often don't be surprised if she puts the moves on you. She likes them young and cute. They don't come any cuter than you baby doll." She winked at me.

I chuckled. "Are you jealous, my Goddess? You have nothing to worry about, I swear it."

Linda looked around to see if we could be heard. "Hell yes, I am jealous. If you are carrying on with her, I want to know what she has that I don't?"

I shrugged. "I said you have nothing to worry about. That is because, my Goddess, you and I are never going to happen. As for Peggy, that isn't happening maybe either. I don't know. It is too early to tell."

Linda's eyes went wide. "Seriously, Peggy has a shot, and I don't. That is fucked up, Psycho. Look if this is about money, I make just as much as she does."

I glared at my dear Goddess. "Offending me is not the way to convince me to sleep with you, Linda. In fact, it is a sure-fire way to end our association. I already told you once, you are too good for the likes of me. You need not go slumming. You could have someone of quality. I suggest you just leave it at that. Thank you for the loan. I hope you understand I hope not to see you anytime soon. Unless it is at the store or on the street in passing. I need to get going. I am late for ritual preparation."

Linda growled, "I wish you would stop referring to yourself as scum, Psycho. You are a beautiful and intelligent girl. I would do almost anything to have you for myself. Until I can get you to see me as more than just a friend, I would like to ask a favor."

I smiled then teased her, "Uhm, no. I told you I am not going to sleep with you, Linda."

Linda snorted. "Stop being cruel, Psycho. I don't like hearing it and you know it. Besides, I wanted to ask you to talk to Circe about letting me join the Coven. I have asked her several times. She keeps turning me down. Maybe she will listen to you. She is your guardian after all."

I was startled to hear that Linda had asked several times. "She keeps turning you down. Does she say why?"

Linda shook her head no.

I nodded. "Tell you what, Linda. If you can wait until New Moon in May, I will get you in."

She looked surprised,. "Really? That would be so awesome. Wait, why new moon in May?"

I broke out in laughter. "Because the Coven will belong to me come May 1st when I become the High Priestess. I will initiate you, Goddess. The circle is where you belong."

She stood there with her mouth open for several moments. "You're kidding. You are going to be a High Priestess? How? Oh, my Goddess. This is amazing. I am so proud of you Psycho."

I laughed. "Yeah, thank you, Goddess, Look I really have to go. I am not HP yet. See you in May, first New Moon. I will grant you the white cord if you are sure that is what you want."

She danced around as if she had just won the Superbowl. I took that to mean yes, she did. I left quickly after for my lessons with Mistress Circe. Master Peggy's interim period was ending the next day. I wanted to know what the chances were that my Key would soon have a new owner.

I found Circe in the shop setting up new displays of her most recent candle batches.

"So, Mistress, what about Peggy? Is she the one," I asked without bothering to pussyfoot around.

Mistress Circe didn't even turn around to look at me, "Maybe, I have another bid already. She is to start her trial period tomorrow night after Peggy's ends."

Her greed never ceased to amaze me. "Seriously? I agree with Peggy. Give her the Key, Mistress. There is no need to seek any further."

Mistress Circe chuckled as she turned to look at me. "This new one is offering more money than Peggy. Peggy can try to match the price, but until then you will go to this address and start the trial right away." She pushed the address at me.

I looked at it irritated, but then upset. "No fucking way, Mistress. I refuse. I know this one." I threw the paper back at her.

Mistress Circe's face twisted into a demon. "Oh yes you will, Psycho. She told me she knows you. That is why she is offering so much. You will go or so help me I will keep your collar for good. Let's see how long you can last without that assistance you need remembering what fucking day of the week it is."

I shook my head. "No, Mistress. This woman fired me from the nursing home when she found out about my son. I worked under her. She was my boss. Andrea is not eligible for the collar."

She glared, "There is no rule about being fired when they are not a Keyholder, Psycho, and you fucking know it. Andrea is offering big money for that stupid Key of yours. Goddess only knows why since she knows you. She must not have paid attention to what an asshole you really are. For whatever reason, she adores you. Go figure on that one. You had better get over it. I know the person business. In a small town you are more likely to know the candidate somewhat. Now, that is the end of it. Get out of here and finish off your time with Peggy, then go to Andrea. No more arguments, I mean it."

"I will have to take the Honda. I still don't have a ride." I smiled assuming that would end it since she had said she wanted her car back.

Mistress Circe chuckled. "Nice try. Keep the Honda another month. See you around, Psycho. Don't do anything I wouldn't do."

I guffawed at that. "As if I could think of anything you wouldn't. As you wish Mistress, you fucking asshole."

She started cackling at that like she always did.

I picked up the paper still grumbling. I couldn't believe my bad luck. I had just assumed that Master Peggy would be my next Master. Instead, I was going to have to serve my old boss Andrea for a fucking month. I started to wonder if maybe Linda or Dennis or even Boyd would be next. Mistress Circe was starting a bidding war. I should have figured out she would pull that shit, the greedy bitch. As it was, the time to end my service to Master Peggy had come. I was somewhat upset to have to say goodbye but that is the way it goes. I had just started to respect and even like her as a person.

I pulled into Master Peggy's driveway for what was looking like maybe the last time. I went to open the door but just as the first time I had arrived, the door open and I was pulled inside by the amorous woman. She was dressed in "bedroom attire." I just stared at her dumbfounded.

"Uhm Master? Bit cool for\ that outfit, isn't it?" I was not sure what to say to the scantily clad Master.

I had realized what I had forgotten. It was the end of her thirty-day trial. It was pretty obvious she was calling in her special services of the collar one time right. I had been dreading this night for the entire thirty days. Yet, it was promised to her if she did her job. Master Peggy had completely done the service of a Master. So, I would have to do mine, completely. Oh well, that is just the way it goes.

Master Peggy was quite wanton after having been without a lover for a couple of years. To be honest, so was

I. She was a very generous in bed. I have no complaints for a change. She kept her promises, all of them. The sexual congress was not one sided as it had always been. She was maybe the first satisfying experience since the very beginning of my career with the animal act in my childhood. She used her privileged service all night. I didn't complain. I needed the relief myself. She was able to keep my attention and never failed to return the pleasure she received. I was very satisfied with this final check on her abilities to wield Simon's Will. She was not twisted, cruel, nor into fetishes or thudding. It was her complete equality of service for service that caused me to be a bit more than upset that I was not submitting to this woman the next day. Instead, I was packing up and heading to the next Interim Master. This was beyond stupid I thought. Since Master Peggy was absolutely suited for the role of Master.

Poor Master Peggy was so impressed by my adoration that night and service over the thirty days that she didn't want to give me up. She tried to block me from leaving by throwing herself across the front door. When that didn't work, she cried and begged me to stay with her. If I had any feelings, they would have been hurt to have to leave her like that. However, I was not her lover, girlfriend or even her friend. I am something else entirely. My job was complete, and I follow my Key. I said goodbye and even allowed her to hug me, though I did have to pry her off to get away.

In case you wondered, kissing is never permitted even during service of the collar to a full Master/Mistress. Not because it keeps me from attaching, but because the shock is horrid.

NOTE: *I of course, had taken my Key from the Simon Jar. Mistress Circe still did not know it. However, the key was still technically hers. I never betray my collar, no matter how much I wanted to on this one. I was more than angry to be leaving this Master, but that is just the way it goes. My lifestyle does not permit me to get too attached to any Master/Mistress's. If I did/do, well ask Master Jon what happens. He knows, since with him I did get attached finally.*

I have to say that Master Peggy was a good person. Other than her drinking a bit too much I could not cite fault. She was just a lonely, mid-aged woman who knew how to equally share the loads of shit life throws at everyone. Master Peggy would have made an excellent Keyholder. There is no doubt in my mind had she been granted my collar, she would have eventually gotten my Loyalty Dog too.

However, this thirty-day trial and one night of fair adoration was all there ever would be between us. When the time for auction came, she was outbid. I happen to know she did offer her life savings. Sad to know that by the way, flattering but sad. The one who would outbid them all is still to come, and the price she paid must have been extreme to have beat out Master Peggy's enormous number. I know Master Peggy's because she told me, but I never learned the amount that won my Key from Mistress Circe.

I would never see her again and have no idea what became of her. I hope she met some beautiful woman who was wonderful to her. She deserved to be treated right. I rarely say that about anyone in my stories, so if I do, you know I mean it. She is forever known in my memories as Master Peggy the Fair.

Well, that was fucked up, wasn't it? We finally found what we were looking for, but Greed reared its ugly head once again. Damn that witch Mistress Circe. Oh well, that is life for us. Sometimes we win, but usually we lose.

Chapter 18: Interim Master Andres & Secret Discovery
The Fall of Mistress Circe

It sucks to be us. We would say you have no idea how true that last statement is, however, if you are still here reading you now have a clue that we are telling the truth. For example, our life just got harder in February of 1994. How could that even be possible? Our Mistress Circe is trying to pull us to her will using her leash on us. She has set us up as the whore she has accused us of being all along. We are passed from household to household until she believes she has punished our insolence enough, and until her pockets are filled. If she can't have us to herself, she will make sure to make us worthless to those who would, or will she? Her little plan may backfire. Some could view this situation as enforced prostitution of our reputation; others may see it as good advertisement. We shall see. For now, we have a lot to do. Mistress Andrea is calling us, again.

If that were not enough to keep us hopping, we are preparing for our initiation into the Third Level of Wicca with the Ritual of the Three Mysteries and The Great Rite. Our black cord will come at a most unexpected price. Our need for revenge on Mistress Circe will protect us from any indignity that must be suffered. Once we have the power of the Triple Crown, we can finally destroy all of Mistress Circe's dreams, just as she managed to do to ours. As High Priestess we will accomplish our vengeance, but we will find we accomplished so much more.

So, ready to live life in the schizophrenic fast lane? Awesome. Grab your oil, scourges, oh and leave your clothes at home. You will have to be Sky Clad for this chapter. That's right beauties, come just as you were born, don't worry, no one is looking at your unit like that, okay maybe that guy over there is. What the fuck did Delleh just say? Uh Oh…

Well, guess it just sucks to be us. See everyone below since we are always at the fucking bottom.

"It all makes so much sense now. I had wondered all this time why such an intelligent kid would hang out with so many, pardon my language, dumb asses. I don't know if I approve, but I have to admit it is damned clever."
Dennis to Psycho – March 1994

I drove through the darkening backroads as my brother the sun set in the western skies. The crying and pleading voice of Master Peggy echoing in my Looper. I gritted my teeth while I gripped the cracked steering wheel tight. I watched my knuckles go white from the pressure of my attempts to hold back my anger at this latest indignity. I was heading to the address Mistress Circe had written out that would lead to a new thirty-day probationary Master. It simply didn't make any sense. Master Peggy was the correct candidate. Mistress Circe had to be doing this for more than money. Sure, she was greedy, but this little bidding war she was setting up was not usual behavior for the impulsive Mistress. I realized there was much more to this game of hers than just getting the highest dollar possible for my Key.

Cherie had been complaining louder and louder on our rides to school. Linda had already heard the rumors about my association with Master Peggy. People were starting to openly question my sexual preferences rather than just the usual assumption that I was a whore at best and a twisted fuck at worst. Even Linda was being much more open and forceful in her attempts to get me into her bed. Mistress Circe wanted the town to believe me to be openly lesbian. That was only part of it.

She was also selecting normals who fit a certain category. Female, middle-aged, not very attractive, semi-professional, lonely, and that were single for more than three years. These ladies were everything that would curse a woman in a small southern town in the early 1990s to single status. They could afford to support themselves, were no longer childbearing, had no real charisma, and were not beautiful. Males in the changing south of the time would have felt emasculated by a lady who did not need his support. The good old boys also wanted to keep their "pretty but dumb" gals barefoot and preggers. My Interims were not the kind of lionesses that would tolerate these puffed-up lions trying to run the Pride. Now, how that affected me is that these kinds of ladies had no lovers, boyfriends, or otherwise tended to gravitate toward the tight knit social structures of other women like them. They also would brag to each other anytime they had anything that helped to stroke their very kicked around self-esteem. So, in a sentence, they would brag to other gals of their special relationship with the young pretty Psycho who appeared to adore them. However, they were keeping their sin of paying for this privilege out of their coffee talks. Therefore, it seemed I really did love them, rather than the truth of the situation.

This tendency to boast brought about several problems for my already uncomfortable situation. First, my very weak support system, think Cherie and Linda, was hearing of my so-called affairs. One was being punished for associating with me, the other was getting her feelings hurt. Second, it was assuring that I could easily end up in an endless parade of needy, clingy, lonely, neglected ladies all bidding for the collar, while taking their number to hold the precious thing for thirty days.

I groaned aloud as I realized on that drive, I may never get a new Master. I may end up forever rented out but never bought. This was yet another weakness in the Key rules we had not thought of. I mentally told Simon to fix this error.

In the meantime, I would have to find a way to put a stop to Mistress Circe's attempts to passive aggressively punish me in this fashion. It was too late to stop this one, but I would be damned if I would leave this loophole open for a future asshole.

The ideas on how to put an end to this horrid situation spun like silk inside my shattered mind. I knew none of them would help stop this latest nightmare leash, but I needed to somehow slow this bitch Mistress down. I pulled up into the driveway of the house, that allegedly belonged to my old work boss Andrea, determined this would be my last Interim. I looked through the veil of night to see a large cabin like chestnut brown home sitting in the backdrop of the forest. It had a screened in porch that lined the entire front part of the house. I took a deep breath to steady my nerves. I really hate to be so remote when meeting a collar holder for the first time. Even though I had known Andrea professionally, you can never be sure what anyone would do when there is no one around to hear you scream.

As I got out of the car, the sound of the screen door slamming shut caught my attention. I looked toward the house just as a bright light shown in my eyes, blinding me. I put my hands up against the offending spotlight to protect my sensitive peepers.

"Who the fuck goes there," I heard a woman's voice yell out.

I tried to look around the glare to see if maybe I had stupidly pulled into the wrong drive. I saw a shadowed faceless female outline. I could not make out her details. The shot gun, however, that I could see very clearly. This person was about to blow my ass away.

I cowered immediately to my knees trying stupidly to cover my head with my arms as if that would stop the shot. "Oh shit, hey, whoa, stop. I am looking for Andrea. Do not shoot please. I will leave. Don't shoot."

"Psycho? Is that you," I heard the woman say.

I stayed down. "Yeah, unless that is a problem. Then no, it is not Psycho." I had decided I was whoever the fuck this woman wanted me to be if it kept me from becoming a statistic.

"Get off the ground and let me see you in the light. I am looking for Psycho. If you aren't her, you are a fucked asshole," screamed the woman.

I shook all over thinking, "Oh fuck, am I Psycho? Oh, please let me be Psycho." She had me so scared I couldn't even remember if I were. Not kidding. Don't judge me stupid unless you have had some crazy bitch holding a shotgun on you deep in the woods while shining a flashlight in your eyes. Believe me you get pretty dumb when that scared.

I stood up trying not to piss my pants. I very slowly put my hands on my head. I just assumed, like Dennis and Boyd, this was a safe way to show I was unarmed and not aggressive. The fear of that gun going off had me nearly run away screaming terrified. I had just embalmed a fellow who offed himself with a shot gun. It was quite a horrid mess. It had to be a closed casket funeral. I am saying I was a more than a bit sure this was not going to be fun if she pulled that trigger. I assumed it was going to hurt like hell.

The woman ran the flashlight over my unit stopping at my face. I squinted my eyes trying not to cower again while submitting to her investigation of my identity.

Then the light dropped. "Oh shit, Psycho. You scared me. Get in here. These woods are dangerous at night," she yelled still standing on her porch.

Shaking my head, I said, "Andrea? Look you put down the gun, and I will come over there but not till I am sure you aren't going to blow my fucking head off."

The shadow woman laughed out loud. "Yeah it is me. You are late. You were supposed to be here two hours ago. The gun is down, come on, Psycho, get in here."

Fifth Master (Collar-No Key)
Interim Mistress Andrea: The Reborn
January 31st to March 1st, 1994

I walked toward the dark figure cautiously still shaking in my boots from this most unexpected welcome. "I apologize. I got stuck at my last job."

I wasn't lying. Master Peggy had done her damn best to keep me from leaving. I had to trick the needy thing by pretending to be agreeable to stay the night. When she headed for her room, I took off like a shot. Mean, I know, but I didn't want to have to hit the lovely lady. She knew what it was when we began the situation. So, I did what I had to do when she tried to redefine the agreed upon end of our contract.

The dark faceless Andrea led me into her cabin. Inside I walked into a large living area that I immediately noted not only had custom made furniture, everything was made from the log house building material, but dozens of pillows of every size and shape. They were strewn about the various couches, love seats and chairs. Andrea apparently liked it extra-comfy.

I was still looking about the room when Andrea, who was laying her shot gun back against the wall near the front door, approached and began stripping off my long black coat. I pulled back in absolute horror.

"Excuse me. I don't know what Mistress Circe told you but that ain't happening. Get off me," I yelled, still very irritated that I was going to have to serve this RN from my nursing home job in every way. I would be damned if I would sleep with the bitch too.

Andrea jumped back appearing startled. "Oh. I was just trying to take your coat so you could get comfortable."

I growled at her while holding my coat closed tightly. "I would be comfortable if I were driving off right now. Why did you rent my collar, Andrea? What were you thinking? Did I do something to offend you when I worked for you? I told you I didn't mean to lie about my pregnancy. I needed the work that badly. I thought you said you understood, but then Mistress Circe tells me you are bidding to hold my Key. Is this punishment for something I have done to you? Hmmm, I am all ears."

Andrea looked at me strangely as she brushed her medium length red hair out of her eyes. She sat down on her couch and sighed loudly. I stood there glaring at her waiting for her response.

She was a tall woman at nearly five foot nine, with medium length fire red locks. Her face was covered with freckles of flame. She was rather frumpy but not terribly heavy. Her heavy jawline and ample bust spoke of her

46

Germanic heritage. Her mother was a native of Berlin, and her father had been a rouge Irishman. Andrea had many of the worst stereotypical attributes of her parents' homelands.

She was broad like the Germans but had the bulbous nose of the Irish that turned red with even a hint of alcohol, excitement, or temperature change. She, like Master Peggy, was unattractive, middle-aged, and lonely. However, unlike Master Peggy, Andrea classified herself as straight and had just divorced her long-time husband three years before due to his adoration of the local dime store cashier. She had not been able to date successfully, and in time I would again find that terms like straight, gay, or other are often loosely defined by availability and environmental conditions.

She looked at me appearing genuinely sad, "I have just been so lonely since Jimmy and I divorced. I started seeing Circe for spiritual counseling right after I left him. So, one day about two weeks ago, I came in early and was waiting in the living room for her to finish her session with Peggy. Circe had been talking with Peggy about, well, your collar. I overheard that she was trying to get Circe to give her a Key or something. Anyway, I got nosey and asked about it and Circe told me the whole deal. I thought about the idea of having someone around that couldn't leave me, well I know it sounds stupid but, damn it is stupid, isn't it?"

I shook my head. "Not as stupid as following a fucking Key like a loon."

She laughed hard. "Yeah, I knew about the schizophrenia, but wow this is beyond crazy, Psycho."

Finally feeling a bit more relaxed that Andrea wasn't going to try to rape me I chuckled. "Hey, watch who you call crazy, Andrea. I mean you rented me, didn't you? That makes us both insane in my book. So, I guess you had better tell me what Mistress Circe told you. She tends to stretch the truth." I took a seat, leaving my coat on, in the loveseat across from her.

Andrea informed me that Circe told her the same shit as Master Peggy. I just groaned realizing that I would have no end to "Leashes" if everyone thought they were getting a mindless whore. Damn that witch. I was really going to make her pay for this attempt to bury me. I had been seeking revenge for her attack on Simon. Now, the old bitch had made it personal.

I spent the next two hours clearing up the misconceptions and giving the scoop on what Andrea had truly leashed. As Master Peggy before her, she had paid money down. My Mistress's greed was boundless. I gave her the same option as I had the one before her. She could follow my Key rules or I would be happy to go back to Mistress Circe's house and promptly kick her ass. Either way, I no longer cared.

NOTE: *I had just declared war on this dried-up old excuse for a High Priestess. There was now no limit to what I was willing to do to make sure her dreams, business, and reputation were crushed beneath my platforms. Good thing I felt that way too. It was going to take doing "just about everything" to get that bitch.*

Andrea decided, like Master Peggy, to try her hand at playing the role of Keyholder. She selected the title of Mistress Andrea. Her interests in me were much more mundane in that she loved an exceptionally clean house. I spent most of the thirty days under her collar reign on my knees scrubbing the hard wood floors. Don't get me wrong, like all the Keyholders she loved the personal services I provide such as wake up, dressing, bathing, messaging, and bedding service (just tuck in, no special services of the collar). However, she really hit my domestic abilities much harder. She loved to eat, so like Julie I had to cook constantly. Her passion was unique and delicate home-made desserts and candies. To her extreme pleasure, I had been well trained in a wide variety of culinary delights. She told me after her reign she gained at least twenty pounds with me around.

Mistress Andrea was relatively boring in conversations, loved watching TV (which I can't do to this day) and was generally lazy when not at work. Her other genuine problem was that of her lost motherhood. She had only been pregnant once in her life. The result was a still born son born one month too early. After this worst nightmare any mother risked, she was double grieved when they discovered early-stage ovarian cancer. She had to have a radical hysterectomy rendering her bid for children moot forevermore. This double tragedy began the long descent of her marriage of high school sweetheart Jimmy to the rocky bottom of divorce. He never forgave her for losing his son, then going barren, so she told me. Jimmy you're a fucking asshole for saying that to her. I hope your balls withered; you prick. Just for the record.

They had taken a photo of her holding her dead child just after his birth. She would stay up late at night forcing me to look at the macabre photo with her while she cried on my shoulder. My Mistress would beg God to tell her why he cursed her with so much unhappiness. I did feel bad for the poor woman. Her only dream had been to be a mother. That was never to be.

So that was the answer to her wanting my collar and offering more money than Master Peggy could afford. Mistress Andrea wanted a replacement for her lost imaginary children. She turned out to make a Great Mistress indeed. Like Master Peggy before her, she made sure I ate, bathed, and took my medications. The only place she failed was in my appointments and medical situations. During her reign I developed one of my infamous kidney infections. Mistress Andrea didn't take me to the emergency room when I informed her one night, I had a fever. Instead, she put me to bed and tried to baby me. The next morning, I began to piss blood. Sepsis had set in overnight. I required several shots of the powerful Rocephin to save my life and three days in the hospital to boot. Mistress Andrea also did not show up to pick me up when I was released. I had to call Linda, as Mistress Circe refused to do it even though the bitch was my fucking guardian.

This set me up for a most uncomfortable discussion with my Goddess about my latest girlfriend. That of course

50

is what Linda assumed Mistress Andrea was since she was unaware of the Collar and Key delusion.

Linda gently helped me into her car as I got out of the wheelchair in front of the hospital discharge doors, "Thank you Goddess. I didn't know who else to call."

Linda just nodded then got into the car taking me back to Mistress Andrea's home as I requested. You could have cut the tension with a knife in that cab for the first leg of our long journey to the forest where my Interim Mistress resided. Finally, Linda could take it no longer.

"Okay, Psycho, I want you to be honest with me, no teasing. Do you think I am pretty?" She kept her eyes on the road without affect as she asked that question.

I looked at my Goddess. "No, I don't Linda. You are the most beautiful creature on Earth. Pretty is not the correct term for what you possess."

Linda closed her eyes and blew out her air as if punched. That confused me a bit.

"Then why, Psycho? Why not me?" She started to tear up.

I felt my heart fill with ice as I realized she was thinking I was dating Mistress Andrea and she was not good enough in my eyes.

"Goddess, I have told you a thousand times. I don't want to be a notch in your bedpost. That is all I can ever be to you. You could get any old whore you wanted. You are

51

better than that. I simply am not. You deserve better than I can grant you. It has nothing to do with your beauty, your personality, or your ability. It is me, not you." I looked at the floor sighing as I admitted the truth to her.

Her eyes went wide. "Psycho, stop talking like you are just a whore. For that matter stop acting like one. You have jumped three beds in three months. From Circe to Peggy, now to Andrea. What the fuck are you doing to yourself. You are good enough for me. Any woman would be lucky to have you." She went red-faced while yelling. She almost drove off the road as she lectured me.

I just shook my head. "You think you know so much, Goddess. You don't know anything at all. It is best you never ask me about my personal situation anymore. You are not my mother or lover, and I am starting to think, not my friend either."

She became angry. "I am your friend, Psycho. How can you say that?"

"It is my understanding that friends don't judge without proper information. You are making many assumptions about things. As it is, it is my business not yours what I do, who I live or sleep with or don't. I warned you to stay in your Heavens running the world and leave us mortals to our imperfect lives. You will fall if you keep on trying to reach down," I said sternly in a schizophrenic speak warning.

Linda let out a yelp, "I don't understand you. I just want to love you, Psycho. Why won't you let me."

I softened my irritation with my Goddess when hearing her admit the truth as she perceived it. It was of course, not the truth. Lust and love are two different things. Linda would no doubt ravage my unit till I begged for mercy from her pleasures. However, I already knew she would never make sure I didn't destroy the very thing she thought she wanted to worship for life. Lust will wane, and then I will lose her forever.

NOTE: *Truth was I believe with all my heart that I was the one in love with Linda or whatever I am capable of anyway. My compassion for her was as strong as it was for my children, Zeppelin, and close to that of my Simon. I wanted her to be happy always, honored, worshipped for the true Goddess she is. Those are things I could never give her completely. I am schizophrenic. My emotions are incomplete, and my reality is irreparably busted.*

The only way I could show her my love was to let her go before I hurt her. No matter how bad I wanted to run away with her, hold her, adore her, I would never dare. Sadly, I hurt everyone eventually. I cared too much for my Goddess to subject her to my demons.

Now you know the hardest part of the reality of my relationship with Linda. I adored her. She could never return it and because I couldn't stand losing her, I always kept her in the Heavens. I never wanted her to discover the truth: that she didn't love me at all. I needed her to believe that she did, and I needed to believe that she did too. I have survived all the cruelty I have known by living in delusions. Linda's love was a delusion I refused to break, no matter how hard she tried to get me to.

I smiled at her bitterly. I felt my chest ache as I turned her offer down. "My Goddess, you already own the only thing I still had left to grant to anyone. You hold my trust. Please my love, don't break it. It is very fragile and cannot be replaced. It was a hard gift to part with, but you managed to steal it somehow. I have never tried to retrieve it because I know you will take wonderful care of it. No matter where I go, I know who owns it. I would ask you to always remember, you can't steal twice what you already have. Love and trust are the same thing Goddess, in fact, the latter is so much harder to obtain, and so much easier to lose. Understand I am saying I trust you Goddess, always."

Linda shuttered, then began to cry. I kept my eyes to the floor, not offering to comfort her. This was something she needed to hear and deal with, or our relationship would be lost forever. I instead cursed Mistress Circe for forcing me to hurt her. It was beyond cruel making her watch her fantasy be defiled by what she perceived to be lovers more worthy than herself in my eyes. I could never tell her the truth. If she knew there was a way to possess me, she would stop at nothing to get it, and I already told all of you, I never wanted to lose her. Owning my Key and Collar almost assured me I would hate her for it.

*The reasons for my almost universal hatred of every Keyholder, no matter how kind they are or not, that will be explained in time. For now, just understand that is the nature of the relationship forged by my enforced service

*to another. **Trying to justify love for a Master would be harder than you can imagine. If you think about it, it makes sense. If it hasn't yet, don't worry, I will get around to telling you soon.***

Linda was still silently weeping when she dropped me off at Mistress Andrea's house. She peeled out leaving me standing there sighing at this latest uncomfortable standoff with my weak support system. Mistress Circe had to be stopped. At this rate I was going to be truly without anyone to aid in even the simplest of functions very soon. I had developed a plan to end her terrorism through her Leashes, but I knew it would only hold for a bit.

Still, I had to do something. The two Interims were both good selections. I was fearful that if Mistress Circe continued to offer to rent out the collar, eventually I would get a really bad ride. I had decided to square off with the greedy woman using my only real leverage, as soon as I could, to end this latest guest Mistress.

Mistress Andrea's reign was about to end, and I had already lost three days of work and school over her lack of medical attendance. This Mistress had been overall very adequate. I could live with her holding my collar without fear. This little issue could be resolved easily, I assumed, since Mistress Andrea was a reasonable, non-psychopathic person.

One error in judgement didn't disqualify her as a good key candidate. Not unless it was a big one. Not taking me to the hospital with a heavy fever for a few hours was not that big since she did take me once the fever wouldn't break. Her not picking me up, also no big deal. In every other area she seemed capable and willing. I felt confident either Mistress Andrea or Master Peggy would be fine picks for my next submission. Now, I had to get Mistress Circe to stop her shit and sell the fucking Key to one of them.

When I went inside the house, I found Mistress Andrea sobbing. What was with all the women crying around me that day?

"What is wrong Mistress," I asked as I came through the door. I mean, shit, I was the one who nearly died of septic shock. For what the fuck was she crying.

"You are going to leave, like everyone always does. Jake left me, Jimmy left me, my Mom Brigida is old. She will leave me too. Then I will be all alone Psycho. Please, stay with me. Don't leave just like everyone else," she sobbed loudly.

I rolled my eyes where she couldn't see me do it. "Now Mistress, we discussed this. I must go. You want my collar you must take it up with Mistress Circe. That is the rule of the Key. It is hers, not mine, to give."

I sat down on the love seat across from my blubbering Mistress. "You are going to leave tomorrow then? Wasn't I good to you? I didn't abuse you or take advantage. I would love you and give you and your babies a good home. I would love them too, like my lost Jake. Please Psycho, tell Circe to let me take the Key."

I nodded. "Oh no worries, darling. I do intend to have a little talk with the witch. However, until then you need to pull yourself together. I mean it is up to you Mistress, but do you want to really want to spend the last few hours with me crying?" I looked at her smiling, "I could make you a souffle or maybe crepes?"

She stopped crying and looked at me hard. "No. I want something else to comfort me this time."

I shrugged. "Okay, what is your wish Mistress?"

She stood up then smoothed out her nurse's scrubs, she often wore them even when not working. "It has been thirty days. Circe told me I was entitled to something called special services of the collar if I finished my trial period. I have completed it. I want you to give me this one now."

I almost choked. "Huh? Uhm, Mistress, you don't know what that service is apparently. Mistress Circe should have been honest with you. The special service of the collar is…"

Mistress Andrea interrupted. "Psycho, I am not a child. I asked her what it was. She told me what it is. I am telling you I am demanding this service be given to me. If you are leaving tomorrow, then I have the right to ask for it now. I know Circe did tell some fibs but the look on your face tells me this one is no fib. This is what I want, so let's go."

I just stared at her dumbfounded. "But I thought you are straight, right? Mistress I have a deep voice, but I am all female. I don't uhm, have what you need to please you with this special service."

Mistress Andrea began to laugh still wiping her tears away. "You have everything I need to be satisfied. I am straight that is true, but I don't see any fellows around her beating down my door to make me feel special. I do, however, see a young lady who is alleged to have a gift at making someone feel good. Call it gay if you want. I just need someone to touch me and make feel like a woman. So, as I said, let's get going."

Oh well. It is sadly a pit fall of my Key and Collar delusion. I did as the contract dictates. I made the Mistress grateful to be a woman as she used this privilege as her processor did, all night. Just as Master Peggy before, she attempted to be generous as a lover, but since she was straight, she had no fucking idea what she was doing. It was not just her preference in the gender of her partner that was disruptive.

Mistress Andrea was poorly experienced in the art of lovemaking in general. Jimmy must have been a real selfish pig. She had never had an orgasm in her life. She grew up in a strict home and barely knew how her own unit worked. It was like being with a nearly fifty-year-old virgin.

So, she meant well, but in the end, I was left on the side of unsatisfied. She kept apologizing and making promises to learn. Her chronic apologies made the whole thing unbearable and killed any chance I would ever ask her again for a return of the favor if she did end up with my Key.

As it was, Mistress Andrea also would not win the bid for my collar. The thirty-day trial period, and one night of special services was all she ever would enjoy, just like Master Peggy before her.

She did bid an even higher amount than Master Peggy offered, and I was told even called the winner and made an offer after the auction was closed. Alas, my tenth Collar Holder was not swayed, at that time anyway.

NOTE: *On a side note, the night I spent with her caused her to change teams (not kidding) and she became on out in the open Lesbian (the power of an orgasm, huh). She briefly dated my Goddess Linda two years later. She finally settled down with a nice woman from another town five years later. She and her beloved partner Vicky lived in that house in the forest until Mistress Andrea died in 2014 at the age of seventy-two of breast cancer. She had finally found someone who would never leave her. I am glad. She deserved to be loved like that. It makes me smile to know sometimes Karma works in positive ways too. Mistress Andrea will forever be known in my memories as Mistress Andrea the Reborn because that night so long ago, she finally understood she was more than just a failed babymaker.*

I left Mistress Andrea who refused to see me to the door. She was, as usual, crying while wailing that she was unloved, alone and wanted me to promise I would come back. I could not promise her that. If she were unable to wrestle my Key from that old biddy's clawed fingers there was nothing that could be done. At least this time, I didn't have to trick someone to get out the fucking door. I walked out into the sunshine, started the Honda and left Mistress Andrea behind, forever.

I returned to the home of my Mistress and the true Keyholder. She was doing a reading on some poor hapless woman as I came through the door. I expected once Mistress Circe was finished, she would hand me another note with yet another address on it. Well, this time I wasn't going to go. I sat down in one of the bean bag chairs to relax. I was conserving my energy for the battle to hold off the leashes that was sure to begin within that hour.

I had nearly fallen asleep thanks to never having time to rest like I should with work, school, and constant service when Mistress Circe came in demanding me to kneel. I did as she asked and of course she tried to hand me the note I was expecting.

I took it and saw the name, Nikki. "Forget it, Mistress. I will not give this person my service."

Mistress Circe growled. "Yes, you will, Psycho. I already told you that if you don't play ball, I will just keep your Key for good. This is your only way out." She cackled then sat in her own bean bag chair.

I stayed kneeling but smiled looking at the floor. "You keep forgetting I am your only way out too. I will not serve Nikki on your leash. I must have this month and the next to study for the Elders' examination. Otherwise, your Maiden may fail to be raised at Beltane. Then where will that leave you Mistress? Hmmm? You and I both know if I fail, there are no second chances. It is up to you. I can serve Nikki and fail that exam, or not and pass." Checkmate bitch.

She gasped. "You are ready, no way you will fail."

I chuckled. "Want to bet your Elders' cup on that, Mistress?"

She growled like an angry bear. "What am I supposed to tell Nikki? You will interrupt my little bidding war. I want top price for that worthless collar of yours."

I interrupted rudely. "Not my fucking problem now, is it Mistress? Make up your mind. I have work and studying and kids to attend to. This is starting to bore me to boot." I yawned for effect.

She reached out her walking stick and poked my unit with it hard. "Get out. I will call Nikki and tell her she will have to wait till after Beltane. Go fucking study, work, or tend your brats. I don't care what you do, as long as it is nowhere near me."

I rubbed my shoulder where she had gored me. "Where am I supposed to sleep?"

She sneered, "Not my fucking problem now is it, Psycho?"

I stood up without being released to do so. I was smiling with satisfaction that I had won, this time.

"Yeah, it is. Do you want that fucking cup? You must make sure I am around to take that black cord, don't you? How awful would it be to get almost to May and have me kicking in the doors at the supermarket, or another church to preach to the horrified patrons? I mean I have never seen anyone invest so much only to leave it in the rain to ruin so close to the end. Then again, I have never seen anyone as greedy as you Mistress. Maybe you would do something so stupid." I started to leave.

"Wait. Stop right now, Psycho," she yelled as I got to the door.

I didn't turn around. "What now, Mistress?"

"You will return to my service immediately. I will resume my duties as Mistress until Beltane. That is the way it is going to be. I have had it with this shit. I have never wanted to see a May Pole so bad in all my days," she said hatefully.

I turned smiling. "I refuse your commands. I will not provide special services of the collar, and I will not provide any services that are hands on. I will neither work as your Necromancer nor make any of your filthy products to rip off an unsuspecting public. You lay a hand on me, I will call the cops. I will offer to cook, clean the house, and attend to the tigers only for room and board until we are finished with Beltane," I countered her demands.

She twisted up her mouth as she considered my offer, finally saying, "You are unfair. You want me to remind you of all your stupid shit, drive my car, and I get nothing but a clean house and fed tigers?"

I laughed. "I pay for that fucking car and the floor is not much of a God damned room or board. It is certainly not worth being with you in your bed. In fact, there is nothing you can offer for any of my services other than the ones I just said. You don't help me take care of my unit, there will not be one to take the initiation. So, up to you, darling. Take it or leave it, Mistress."

She of course took the deal. Mistress Circe had no choice. She wanted to be Queen of the Green, but she had to become a Fourth Level Initiate first (Crone). I was her only hope, and her biggest hurdle in her bid to try to make a run at Fifth Level Initiate (Queen). Any trouble or unfairness to her situation was her own fault. That is what you get when you force the raising of a schizo to High Priestess, then abuse the shit out of them even when they were doing what you asked.

The next two months were beyond busy with constant work, fixing my shit box house, studying for my job as embalmer, my Pathology career at college, and my examination before the panel of Elders to obtain my black cord. I barely slept.

My twenty-second birthday passed without notice. Even if I forgot it, but then I usually did. It wasn't until I was walking back from the funeral home to work on my house one night early in the morning that I was even reminded I had one that week.

Pat had been a clever work Master, and I had learned the basics of my job already. He rarely ever showed up at the graveyard shift to make sure I was there to do my job anymore. I had become a trusted employee. I was down to two days a week at the F&T. Cherie, and I were barely speaking over yet our latest disagreement at my having moved back in with Mistress Circe. She was convinced I was not only a Lesbian Witch but a whore too. This was simply pushing all her buttons. However, she still needed my gas money, so she would bitch, but she would show up every morning to pick me up, nonetheless.

To be fair, most of the town thought what Cherie feared was truth by now. I didn't give two fucks. My collar protected me from the small-minded viewpoints of that town. If I were able to provide obedience and perfect service, some idiot would always be happy to exploit me for their own needs. I could only hope while they did such a dastardly thing, they would make sure my own needs were attended. I was still hopeful that after the Betaine Sabbat was over the greedy Mistress Circe would sell me out to either Mistress Andrea or Master Peggy. After she had what she wanted, I assumed my Key would burn a hole in her pocket.

I had gotten to the funeral home that night to mercifully find no work to do. I had left the Honda parked at the yellow house, so I walked back to breathe in my mother the night. It was nice to be free of books, service, work, and the terrible twos and threes of my toddler youngsters if only for the quick fifteen-minute stroll home.

I was unlocking the door to go inside and paint when the squad car pulled into my driveway.

I turned around to see Dennis and Boyd getting out headed my way. I felt the urge to run, but I knew I hadn't done anything in a long time. Surely, they weren't trying to pin something on me.

"Hey boys, to what do I owe this dubious pleasure?" I tried to keep the shakiness out of my voice, but I was scared.

I could see Dennis smile at me in the inky blackness. "Just stopping by for a chat, Psycho. No arrests, or cuffs, I promise. Can we come in?"

I narrowed my eyes to try to see if he was telling the truth. "You have a warrant, officer? Before you even say it, that smell is the sewers. I don't have anyone moldering in my bathtub, so what is this about?"

Dennis and Boyd both chuckled at my statement. "Look we saw you walking home from work and thought since nothing is going on in town tonight, we'd come by and say howdy to our birthday girl. Twenty-two, I am both pleased and surprised you have made it this far. You see Boyd, our little Psycho is all grown up. Has a respectable job, making the Dean's list at college. I am damned proud, aren't you," said Dennis somewhat teasing, somewhat.

"It is amazing. Who would have thought I," Boyd agreed.

I nodded as the police officers closed in now practically standing on my feet. "Okay, thank you for the birthday wishes. Now cut the shit. What is this really about, Dennis? Walking home from work isn't breaking curfew and I am over twenty-one anyway. What do you want?"

He looked at me, his smile melting away. "We want to talk to you about that silver necklace you are wearing, Psycho. Remember, I told you awhile back I wanted to have a word with you about it."

I felt my toes go numb and my bladder almost let go of its contents. "Huh? My, my, huh? Tonight? Dennis, it is fucking midnight. Can't this wait? I have shit to do. Come back another time when I am not…"

Dennis didn't allow me to finish. "We could. It is not illegal what we were told by the birdy about that necklace, but then again there are rumors. What the rumors say about it isn't legal. Psycho, here is the deal. You can invite us in to give us your side of the story, or I can ask around, get rumors, and maybe arrest you for probable prostitution." He was glaring at me.

I almost choked on my spit. "Prostitution? Are you fucking serious," I yelled out, forgetting the hour and the proximity of my neighbor's houses.

I couldn't believe it. I was about to get arrested over rumors. Holy shit. I really was smack dab in the middle of bubba land if they could actually arrest me because my neighbors were delusionally believing I was selling my ass.

"Keep your voice down. That is why we are here, Psycho. An off the record, friendly little visit for coffee. You can clear all this up by just telling us what story is true. I don't want to spend hours tracking your movements or talking to everyone around you if I can just have your side of this story. I know you think no one listens to you, but you have always shot straight with us. You tell us the truth, there won't be any need for this to go any further, not our visit tonight or our looking to bust you in the act. We need you to explain what this collar business is all about." There Dennis said it.

He did know something about the collar. Now it was up to me to either throw him out as I had the right to do, call my attorney which I also had the right to do, or just tell them the truth and let it go. Since my following the Key is not illegal, it isn't by the way, I believed it best to just clear this up without letting my secret get even further out there than apparently it already was.

"Well, I do have a coffee pot, but it sucks. Come on in fellows before the neighbors see you and think you are some of my paying customers," I said bitterly as I unlocked the door to allow Dennis and Boyd inside.

I had already fixed all the broken windows, replaced the locks, removed the soiled carpets, and repaired the holes in the walls. I almost had the house ready to move into. I had been finishing the painting during that week. I still didn't have any furniture but an old rocking chair and a stuffed chair that one of the neighbors had put out front for the garbage man. I had drug it into the house late one night assuming no one would miss it.

Dennis took the rocker and Boyd took the chair. I stood there angry at this latest indignity wrought on me by an ignorant public with wagging tongues.

I looked at the floor. "Well, what do you want to know. Ask me now, because after tonight I never want to discuss this ever again, Dennis. I mean it. I am not breaking the law. I have the right to my collar and my Key. I don't sell sex for money or anything else for that matter. It isn't prostitution. Come on, out with it."

Dennis looked at Boyd. "Well usually I am the one using that line, Psycho. Here it is. Crystal told us that Julie brainwashed you to believe that she had control of your behavior. She told us that Julie made you believe that the silver collar was her mark of ownership. Like back in the old days, a slave collar. Crystal told us that is how she got you to follow her orders all that time."

I chuckled. "Yeah? And so, you come here over that bullshit? Crystal was telling the truth. I don't see how that was illegal on my part. That was also five years ago."

Boyd looked at me. "It was, yet you are still wearing that collar, Psycho. Why?"

I snorted. "I am just a nostalgic old fool, Boyd baby. Now are we done here?" I said shifting my weight then crossing my arms with irritation at this interrogation in my own fucking house.

Dennis shook his head. "No, we are not. Crystal also said there is a Key that Julie made you believe could be passed from one person to another. She said Julie convinced you it was a piece of you. Like a voodoo spell you follow it no matter who gets it. She said you blindly obey the person with it too. I ignored this as kid's fantasy or even psychotic stuff, Psycho, but then I noticed like Boyd here, you are still wearing that collar. I also noticed you have been moving around a lot lately. Then I hear rumors you are sleeping with several of the ladies here in town. Psycho, what the Sam Hill is going on? I can't bring myself to believe that you are selling yourself over a delusion or whatever this damned collar business is."

Boyd cleared his throat. "We are sorry to have to pry but, Psycho, the big concern here is that you are being abused by someone or worse, traded around town for sex" His voice broke up as he said that.

Well, he was sort of right now, wasn't he? Humm, I would have to think about that one. In truth, I am not a prostitute. The strange delusion of my collar and Simon's Key had created more of a mix of a courtesan, concubine, and/or submissive situation. I am not selling sex, or anything for that matter. My contracts are equal services for equal services or a trade of attendance of daily functioning needs for attendance of daily functioning needs.

· *Courtesan: The term originally meant a courtier, a person who attends the court of a monarch or other powerful person.*

· _**Concubine:**_ _Was a highly coveted honor and concubines were formally recognized in a ceremony much like a marriage._

· _**Submissive:**_ _Ready to conform to the authority or will of others; meekly obedient or passive._

However, with that in mind it was then I realized, Mistress Circe's practice of charging the leashes cash as a down payment for services could be construed as prostitution when I provided services of the collar (even once) since these ladies were not getting to keep my collar, there was no promise of a long-lasting relationship. It is not quite the actual act of selling sex, but she was certainly telling these ladies that is what she was selling me for, until I cleared it up that is.

I made a mental note to threaten Mistress Circe with going to the authorities if she pulled the lying shit with any more potential Keyholders in the future. I would not tolerate her getting me arrested for something I was not doing.

I took a deep breath and in the next few hours told the story of the Key and Collar to Dennis and Boyd. I answered all their questions and tolerated their surprised looks. Finally, they understood the entire process as much as anyone can. I did not have to protect Mistress Circe's name since she was a Master in name only. So, I explained she was the current Keyholder. It was her fault I was going around from house to house seeking a new Master.

I left out the money part only to protect Master Peggy and Mistress Andrea's reputation as upstanding semi-professionals. Dennis and Boyd may not have appreciated the girls having paid cash thinking they had indeed bought a hooker.

Dennis took a breath then very slowly said, "Well, I can say what you are doing is not illegal, Psycho. It is dangerous as hell. Someone may get your Key and kill you someday you know."

Boyd shot a worried look at Dennis. "Why would they do that? If they have the Key, Psycho does what they ask. Why would you kill something that wonderful? It wouldn't make any sense."

Dennis looked at Boyd surprised. "Wonderful for who, Boyd? Psycho here? I think you'd better think again. The only people who would put a damned collar on another human being are monsters, Boyd. They can do anything. Didn't you just listen to her? Boyd, Psycho just admitted that she is getting into relationships where she had to sleep with a person she doesn't even like as part of a bargain to get them to help her with her symptoms and keep her off the streets. Worse yet, it is working. Think Boyd, we used to arrest Psycho almost every day, now almost never. Look at her. She is not a skinny, dirty, angry girl anymore" He snorted, appearing angry.

"I don't understand, Dennis. Why are you angry? I am not breaking the law. I had a problem, you just admitted it. I fixed it, well Julie did, to be honest. I found a way to get the support system required to survive my disease and my own hand." I looked at Boyd who was just sitting there in disbelief at the tale he had just heard.

Dennis stood up suddenly hitching up his pants. "Psycho, you listen to me close. I get why you are doing this I do. I don't agree with it, but I know this is the real world. The world is a cold, uncaring place. I want to believe there is another way, but I know you are right. That is digging into my heart in ways you cannot even begin to understand. If you ever get into any trouble, or anyone of these sickos you call master tries to hurt you, call me. I will make that son-of-a-bitch sorry he or she was ever born." He was yelling and pointing at me trying to make his point clear.

I nodded. "I hear you, Dennis. Do me a favor and never tell Linda about what you heard here tonight please. I don't want her to get involved." I looked at the floor sorry to have to call out my Goddess, but I had to for obvious reasons.

Dennis looked at Boyd and they both nodded. "This will never go any further, Psycho," said Boyd looking sincere.

The officers began to leave. As Dennis went out the door I said, "Hey, Dennis. I know I have been a pain in your ass for years, but I want to say thank you for everything. I should have told you that many times. I hope it is enough that I am saying it now."

I looked at the floor again, hoping he understood why I was saying a general thank you. Dennis had not killed me even when he could have many times. He had saved my life more than a handful of times. He helped me get my very first motorcycle license. Now he was keeping my secret, and not judging me for it. I owed this man with, well, my life actually.

He looked at me, appearing sad. "Psycho, you don't have to thank me for caring about you. I am the one that needs to say thank you."

I was startled by that. "What? Why?"

He frowned. "For not giving up. For not hating everyone. For never complaining, for never using drugs, abusing others, or taking to lawlessness. For pulling yourself up when no one else was there to help you and still today not asking for more than you think you have earned. You have more basic human dignity and tolerance than anyone I have ever known. I am going to remember you in my prayers, but not for your continued success. I am going to pray for the patience and strength you have. You do what you need to do to rise above it all, Psycho. You have my respect and silence. Have a good night. Stay out of trouble, okay?"

I nodded as he left. I watched the car leave and head back down the road. I went and sat on the old rocker and cried like a child. I didn't cry because of the kindness or the honesty in which he said those words. I cried because, beauties, I was tired. I was barely twenty-two and already I was scarred to shit, war torn, and seen more horror than most do in a lifetime. I could see the years to come yawning before me like the many gates of hell, and I wept that I was cursed to enter them all. I couldn't go back and going forward was like walking blind on broken feet. I had both earned respect by battling to stay afloat and become hated for it. Everyone had an opinion about me, but no one offered aid, unless I served them that is.

I will be honest that I considered taking my life again that night. Seriously considered it. Don't be too surprised. I usually think of it two or three times a week. Sometimes more. The experience of emptiness is beyond painful. No matter how strong you may think I am, I have a breaking point too. I hit that wall almost every day and have for going on fifty plus years. My sentence is life for a crime I never committed. It would take a toll on anyone, no matter what you may think. The sun can shine, the birds may sing, a smile from a child may warm your heart, but in the world behind the shattered looking glass, every day is dark, empty, and cold. Nothing can get through unless it is amazingly loud. The only things that are loud are pain and terror. That is my world, the world of the schizophrenic. So, occasionally, I cry and get the fuck over myself. Can you blame me? Too bad it only helps for a minute. That night, I needed that minute.

Life went on after that most bizarre confrontation with Dennis and Boyd at the house. The rest of the month flew by, then April came and went too, almost unnoticed as I struggled to meet deadlines with college coursework, make it to my jobs, take care of my children and finish my studies for the dreaded Elders Panel examination. I was only a week or two away from having the yellow house completely livable as May the first finally arrived. It was showtime at last.

My year and ten months of study would have to be enough to get me through the most rigorous Elders Panel, Third-Level initiation of the Three Mysteries and The Great Rite. I had learned all my invocations of this extraordinarily complex ritual by heart. Still, I was beyond nervous as I donned my black ceremonial robe and grabbed all the items required by a Priestess of my soon to be stature. The red van pulled up with our small family of coven members all abuzz about the impending performance of the first raising of a High Priestess in the Sister covens in over twenty years. No one had ever seen the ritual performed except for the current High Priests and Priestesses. Mistress Circe enthralled the group on the way down talking about how it used to be done in the old days.

Sister Lisa looked shocked. "Did you have to do the Great Rite like that Circe?"

Mistress Circe laughed. "Hell no. They only did it literally back in the old days. Now it is all symbolic. The sword is the phallus, and the cup is the vagina. Now when you put the sword into the challis, the male puts his sword in the cup the female is holding, the actual sword and cup. If they did it the way they used to, there would be a lot less High Priestesses around these days." Everyone started laughing at that.

Tracy, Mary, and Lisa must have asked me a million times if I was nervous. I told them I was scared out of my mind. No reason to lie. I knew I had my lines down, and I knew I had studied as much as anyone could, but there is always that doubt in your mind that at the last minute you'll fail. I was so used to fucking things up and failure. I sort of expected to fail this too.

Amazingly even the long ride didn't calm my nerves. I saw that Mistress Circe was nervous too. She kept asking me if I remembered this invocation or that one. She even pretended to play the High Priest saying his parts from her books.

Tracy suddenly looked nervous as she watched us play our parts for the ceremonial ritual. "But who will be Psycho's consort, Circe? She doesn't have one. This initiation calls for a male initiate and a female."

Mistress Circe chuckled. "There is a Summoner who has no consort either in one of the Sister Covens. I will get his High Priestess to loan him for it."

Mary looked surprised. "But he won't know the lines, Circe."

Mistress Circe looked at me. "They let the helpers read. I had to do that. One of the Sister Covens loaned me a Summoner when I took the Third level. He read from the book while I had to know the lines. It is not too formal once you get through the Elders Panel. That is the hard part. The rest is just well show really. I mean it is spiritual but now it is all for symbolism. Not the way it was back in the day."

I felt comforted by that. If I were to go through this horrible testing in front of a panel, it would be good to know if I forgot a line, at least my partner was having to read his. I was glad Mary had asked. I thought I had to know both parts. Silly Psycho had learned them both, but I never told anyone because I was worried, they'd laugh at my stupidity.

We arrived at Springfields right on time. I was getting out of the van with everyone else when suddenly two Summoners from the Sister Covens came and told me to follow them. I looked at Mistress Circe who told me to do as commanded. I walked behind the large fellows scared out of my mind. I realized the initiation had begun.

Summoners are the male version of the Maiden. They do all the announcing for ritual and circle events. These Summoners had been sent to retrieve me by Mother Delleh herself. I was taken behind the big cabin to a small shed secluded from the main building. They knocked on the door and I was bid entry by the Queen herself. Once inside the Summoners left quickly.

Delleh was sitting cross legged on the floor of this shed. I looked around at all the Wiccan moon and star decorations painted on the walls and ceiling but other than a round pentacle star throw rug nothing else was in this little place.

"Shut the door, Psycho, and come sit with me my daughter," she said sweetly.

I did as she commanded. Sitting on the round rug across from her. My heart was pounding in my chest as the Looper warned of my coming failure to pass the test. Delleh looked heavier and stronger than she had when I first met her. I was told her cancer had gone into remission. May the Goddess be praised.

"You have studied hard I have been told. Sister Circe says you are ready for your crown today. I am hopeful you are." She looked at me to see if I would agree.

"Yes, Mother. I am as ready as can be expected." I looked at the floor in respect to the Mother of the Covens.

She looked at me hard. "You will pass the exam. I can feel it in my heart. Then we will adjourn to the ritual rooms for the performance of your Great Rite, Third-Level initiation. The Crone ceremony for your High Priestess Circe will begin after. You will raise her and take your rightful place on her throne."

I nodded. "I understand Mother. I have studied the proper invocations and words. I know them all by heart now."

She nodded. "That is good because, you and your Summoner are exceptional cases, Psycho. Neither of you have a consort. Both of you are ready for the black cord. Neither of you are third year students in the traditional sense. Because of my illness, we must raise new leaders and a new Elder. It is the way of the universe that the Wheel turns, and the old harvest is reaped, and a new one sown. You and Richard are the first to be sown of the Green Rings in over twenty years. This is a great honor."

I looked down in reverence of her words. "I thank you and my brothers and sisters for finding my unworthy spirit worthy of it."

She smiled when I said that. "You will now be given the answers to the three Mysteries."

My tradition does not allow me to share these three Mysteries. However, it is what she told me after my receiving this gift that was beyond horrifying.

"Sister Circe has spoken to you of the Great Rite," she asked me, appearing to look a bit nervous.

I nodded, "Yes, I have learned it, Mother."

She cleared her throat. "You have learned it from a book. Each Coven has different rules and ways of doing this Rite. We practice The Great Rite as a sexual union. It is the most important part of the third-degree initiation ceremony in our Wiccan/Witchcraft Traditions. The Great Rite is the wedding of the masculine and feminine, the God and Goddess. It is considered a sacred act wherein the gender polarity of the initiate is joined with its opposite, thereby making the initiate whole."

I looked up startled at Mother Delleh while she paused to cough. "Did she just say it is a sexual union with some dude named Richard? What the fuck," I thought wildly. No one said anything about this shit.

"Mother, Mistress Circe told me the Great Rite is symbolic in modern times. She told me she did hers symbolically. She said it was not real." I was starting to panic my eyes were wide with sheer terror.

Delleh shook her head no. "Sister Circe was not raised in our Circle, dearest daughter. She would not know of our rules of the Third-Level initiations. In our circle The Great Rite is actual. You and Richard will perform The Great Rite by copulation. The goal of this formal ritual is to make the act of sex become impersonal, thus removing the mundane personality, and allowing the divine to possess and fill the void. Just like in ancient times, Richard and you are unknown to each other, and would most likely never be intimate again. Richard is_from one of the Sister Coven's Summoners. He will be raised with you as High Priest on this most glorious of nights. The two of you will be magical working partners by this consummation union today. You will have a true consort and he a Priestess for all future Coven events. I embrace you both as the Green Rings newest generation of Coven Leaders."

I thought I was going to pass out. "Mother you are saying I have to have sex with Richard, to become a High Priestess during the Great Rite with everyone there watching."

She chuckled. "Oh Goddess no, daughter. Everyone below Third Level must leave as soon as the Sword is about to enter the Chalice."

I gasped, then said in sarcastic Psycho fashion, "Oh well, okay that is so much better. Only you and seven other people there watching me get ritualistically raped by someone I have never met. I was worried for a second."

Huh? Uh yeah, you read that right. If you missed that ending, you might want to read it again. Oh, and for the record, the entire ritual is done sky clad in front of all the coven members. Hmm, so I am wondering at this point, do I really need to be a High Priestess that bad?

Chapter 19: The Great Rite
The Rise of High Priestess Arodia
The Fall of Mistress Circe

In this chapter we have quite a treat for you. We are about to become a powerful High Priestess in the old religion. As you have read, it will cost us dearly, but that is the way of all things worth having. They are never easy to obtain.

In order to become a leader of pure hearts one must first completely disrobe. You must shuck off all the trappings of the world of the real. Let go of your abstractions of morality, definitions of society, and become your true self. You must find the animal within. The foundation of humanity, the truth of our functions as a race of beings, the act of creation is the purest form of worshiping the creators of all there is and will ever be.

Psycho must choose to become the Wiccan she has denied with a heart unmarked of doubt, fear or hate. She must willingly embrace her destiny. Only perfect love and perfect trust will allow her to receive this most amazing gift of pure compassion for all of humankind. She did not know it, but this was the test that she had been studying for all along. The examination of the Elders was not what it appeared to be. That is the lesson she has already learned well. Just like in her real life, the spiritual meanings of all things are deeper than what the eyes can see. Psycho is already an expert at never trusting what she perceives as reality. Her rise to High Priestess will be as stunning and beautiful as The Great Rite was meant to be.

The Crone Circe is still seeking a new Keyholder. She got what she wanted but unlike Psycho never learned the lessons taught by Wicca. Her greed has blinded her to the realities of the position to which she had lusted. Now, she sits alone and secluded. She is watching angrily as the schizophrenic she intended to control destroys her house of Gold with her message of black. Her circle was always a Loop, but High Priestess Arodia has opened the stagnated. The circle shall swell, filling with hearts of love, equality, and freedom. She has sown the seeds of green into the barren golden ground. A temple of the people will be harvested from the sweat of industry. The High Priestess and her High Priest will unite the followers by their honor of the Old Ones. As prophesized, they shall unite the impoverished Covens and heal the broken heart of the Mother.

In retaliation for her perceived hurts, the Crone Circe will seek out a new Holder of the Key. She hopes to crush the budding flower of progress and steal the throne of Green by humiliating the leader she has created. A new Interim Master is selected from the growing list of those hoping to win the bid. Master Nikki will try to demonstrate she is the woman who should hold the circle of silver.

So, ready to become a High Priestess the old-fashioned way? Ah, then remember, no matter what you see or feel, don't turn away your eyes. It is your sacred duty to watch. You are in the presence of the God and Goddess on Earth.

They have come to show you the arcane visions of the creation of all that is, will be, and ever was. It is okay if you experience pleasure in the act of their copulation. After all, that is why they call it lovemaking. You start chanting, and we will get going. Our rutting Stag is waiting.

"I would have had a heart attack if I were told I had to have sex in front of the Elders with a guy I had never met. You are way braver than me. I guess I will never be a High Priestess if that is what it takes to be one."

Lisa to Psycho during trip home from Beltane Sabbat – 2 May 1994

*Lisa is the future Maiden and High Priestess (in another ten years) to High Priestess Arodia/Psycho.

Mother Delleh just chuckled at my sarcastic statement. "Oh no, my daughter. You misunderstand me. You must accept your High Priest willingly. Rape is not only illegal, but also an abomination in the eyes of our God and Goddess. Everything must be done with perfect love and perfect trust. If you or Richard don't agree with any part of this initiation, it stops immediately. No one should be or can be forced to do anything they don't wish to do. It is not permitted in these Covens to coerce, threaten, or otherwise demand a member to engage in any ritual or spiritual act. Sister Circe should have told you that it is our Coven's practice to perform The Great Rite actual, but that does not matter. Richard was also unaware. He didn't even know he was to be raised today. He was selected out of necessity, and because he is ready for the black cord. He is also

84

without a Priestess, as you are without consort. It was meant to be, or it was not. Only you and Richard can decide that."

I blinked in disbelief at that. "The poor fellow didn't know to study. How did he take it? I mean do I at least get to meet him first?"

Mother Delleh smiled gently. "I am told he was as upset as you are now. You have met him. He was the blond of the two Summoners who brought you to this meeting Psycho. He was sent with an escort to meet you. If he had disagreed, there would have been a knock on the door. Since there is no knock, Richard has accepted you as his Priestess to worship for all his days. He is now in another shed being prepared for this rigorous ritual. He has been secluded as you are about to be for one hour. He has to manually make himself ready to hold his seed till the entire Rite can be performed."

I looked at the ground trying not to laugh. "Okay, so Richard must keep from, uhm, okay so he not only didn't know he was to become High Priest, but he is off in another shed having to masturbate so he can perform without reaching ecstasy moments before the Great Rite is finished. How awful. I guess it will be tough for both of us. Is he afraid too?"

I again stifled the giggling, thinking about this poor dude having to stroke off, so he didn't embarrass himself by being a two-pump chump in front of the Elders. It also occurred to me all I had to do was lay there. Richard was the one under pressure to perform. I was still unsure about submitting to this bullshit. I did want revenge on Mistress Circe but asking me to fuck some fellow in front of the High Priests and Priestesses, and the Queen herself, was a bit much. It seemed to me maybe I should just pass up the Triple Crown. I really didn't think I could go through with it.

"Mother, you said no one has been raised in twenty years. The Sisters and Brothers of the Coven said they have never seen anyone do the Great Rite. Mistress Circe was not raised in this Circle, but you were?" I waited patiently to see her response.

She nodded. "Yes daughter. I was raised in this Circle. Your next question will be, did I have to perform the Great Rite actual to get my black cord."

I nodded. Mother Delleh knew exactly why I wanted to know. She was indeed worthy of Fifth Level. The woman was simply amazing at reading a human heart.

I was shocked to see her begin to weep silently as she said, "Yes, Daughter. I was raised through the practice Richard, and you are asked to perform today. It was an honor, but I confess, I was afraid like you are right now. Every Third Level that will be there to witness the act today was raised like this, Psycho. Only Sister Circe was raised symbolically. Understand, each of us will be with you and Richard reliving our own Great Rite, the trauma, the terror, the pleasure. It is human to be afraid. We have been where you are. The reason the Elders must be there is to make sure the ritual is correctly performed, and that it is completed. Calling down the God and Goddess is serious business. We must have someone there who knows how to correct it if the two inexperienced initiates accidentally offend the sacred. The last reason we must be there is very basic. You do not know your partner. We will be there to make sure his lust doesn't become rape. If you want it to stop, it will. We will also make sure it doesn't become violent. Richard is very devout and that is why he was selected, but he is still a man. We are there to make sure you are safe. He is to copulate with you in a peaceful, pleasurable fashion bringing you to orgasm as he achieves his own. We will not allow him to become a foul pig as some males tend to be when it comes to sex. This is something that is supposed to be beautiful, pleasurable and it is what makes life worth living, Psycho. Your Priest is very handsome, enjoy his unit as he enjoys yours. It doesn't have to be an ugly experience."

I nodded at her wise words. "I understand, Mother. I agree having others there may be smart to protect me from rape. I understand why the ritual is to be actual. What I don't understand is that if the experience is beautiful and pleasurable, then why are you crying while you remember your own?"

Delleh looked at the ceiling and laughed while wiping her tears. "Ah, Psycho, you are going to make an incredible Priestess. So, perceptive. Daughter the man selected for me was not my husband. My husband was only at the first level when my raising came. He had to leave the room while I had sex with a man I did not know. It broke his heart and mine. However, we are both devout, so we tried to forget about it. Then the day came that I had to watch Kevin stag with another woman when he was raised. Understand it is balance in our tradition. I am crying because of the silly pain both myself and Kevin felt over our own black cord initiations. Kevin was killed five years after he took his place at my side. Do you know what I would give to see him again? I would even be happy to have to watch him staging that Priestess for the rest of my life. I had to lose my beloved to realize sex is just an act. It is love that brings souls together. If you can understand what I have just told you, you can overlook the physical and you will be a true High Priestess, Psycho. Let your unit be joined with Richard, but let your soul be loved by the Goddess." She patted my hand then stood up to leave me to meditate.

She instructed me that if I wanted to stop my initiation all I had to do was knock on the door. A Summoner was left to guard it while I took my one hour to decide. Somewhere in another shed just like mine, my betrothed Priest Richard was struggling with the same issues. He was further insulted by having to prepare his unit to function throughout the entire long-winded ritual. His door was also being guarded by a Summoner. Either of us could choose to stop the ceremony at any moment.

During my hour I struggled with the idea that I had never wanted to be a High Priestess. There was so much doubt that I would take this initiation only to punish my Mistress. I wondered if that was not an insult to the Gods. Mother Delleh had told me to only do this in perfect love and perfect trust. How could I justify revenge? I couldn't, plain and simple. I laid back on the ground trying to recall the blond Summoner who had led me from the van. I had not been paying attention, but I could recall he was indeed quite handsome. He had long dirty blond hair with a goatee and moustache. He was wearing a green robe, but I could see he was fit and young. Richard had appeared to me to be in his twenties, and at least six foot two. He and his partner had come to lead me to sit with the Mother and he had known he was to be raised by then. I realized he must have been satisfied with what he saw of my unit too, or he would have rejected me by now. Unless he just wanted to have his black cord. It was hard to justify that I was supposed to feel flattered he had agreed. What man wouldn't agree to have sex? Then again, Richard would have to gain and maintain an erection in front of the Elders. Sex like this surely would not be fun for him either.

I finally realized I was not there to enact revenge on Mistress Circe. I was there to cleanse the Circle of Gold. Mother Delleh had said so, as did all my own prophetic dreams. Revenge was in this case Karma. Mistress Circe had abused her privileged status among all the Coven members, not just with me. Mother Delleh would pass someday soon, and if I didn't stop this greedy soul, it would gobble up all these pure hearted people. It was my duty to do whatever was asked of me. To be a leader of others, I had to be willing to submit to the will of the Covens. Mother Delleh and all those before her had done the same.

In an epiphany, I suddenly understood why the Great Rite was a requirement to wear the Triple Crown. It was the way to prove to my circle that I had become a vessel and had given up my identity to be filled by the needs of another. That is what a true High Priestess, or any good leader, really does. It is not about having the power over others. It is about being capable of aiding your followers in finding themselves. I would need to be there for those who are lost without letting my own selfish needs get in the way. Mistress Circe had allowed her need for money to rip off her members and the community at large. She required members to buy her items or they were not true Wiccans. She charged a monthly fee and kept others from joining if she believed they may ask too many questions about her shady practices, such as Linda. This had to stop. Being a child of the Gods and Goddesses shouldn't cost money. I also don't believe any religion has the right to charge to receive the information required to practice it. Mother Delleh had told me in my healing of the Shattering I was chosen to end this abuse of her Coven. Everything finally made sense for a change.

I was now ready to become a true High Priestess of Wicca. The final hold on my spirit had been severed. I no longer sought revenge on Mistress Circe. My reason for taking the initiation was to facilitate the growth of the circle by ending the drought of greed. It was time to accept my fate by taking my place in the destiny of the Circles of the Green Rings.

The hour had passed, the door opened. A Summoner stood waiting to escort me to the panel examination before the Elders. I kept my eyes to the ground and followed steadying myself for one of the hardest things I would ever have to do to this very day.

The panel of Elders had been split into two groups. One was elsewhere to question my promised Priest Richard, and I was brought in front of the other. My group included Mother Delleh.

I was grilled mercilessly regarding my reasons for believing I could be a Third Level Priestess. Many questions were asked regarding my understanding of this ritual or that one. I was required to name the most important Gods and Goddesses and for what they stood. It was an awfully hard exam, but I passed without missing a correct answer or giving one that upset anyone. I was asked to kneel while the group got into a circle to discuss if I was worthy, ready, and able to take the Great Rite and black cord. The decision was unanimous, I was accepted with perfect love and perfect trust.

I admit my heart almost exploded with terror at those somber looking men and women dressed in black robes all grilling me like that. Every time I answered they seemed to look angry. I was sure I would piss myself and run away crying each time one opened their mouth. Somehow, I got through it. Mother Delleh never took her gentle loving eyes off my kneeling and trembling unit. She told me in my mind I would be okay. She wanted me to relax. I did my best to mind her requests, but it was a fail. I was scared.

Yet the real horror had only just begun. I was told to rise. Mother Delleh herself walked to me and told me to reach for the sky. I did as she told me. She removed my robe. I was now naked before the panel of Elders who nodded that I had passed examination as "Female." They didn't discriminate gender, but The Great Rite must have one female and one male participant. It was tradition to have the panel of Elders visually exam and verify the genders were correct to prevent any embarrassing scenes when the couple walked out to join the circle to begin the ritual.

Mother Delleh placed a crown of white flowers on my head. At least now I had something on. Just as Mistress Circe appeared, she had obviously been on Richard's panel, to announce my Priest had passed both examinations: the questions and he was viewed as male. The Summoners waiting outside the doors were told to announce the Great Rite was about to begin and all members were to join in the ritual room. I took a deep breath to calm myself while Mistress Circe told me to follow her.

She walked in somber silence with me following trying to clear my mind. I saw all the other members still wearing their robes, as I was the only one sky clad, heading to a door I had never noticed before. They went inside side by side with their consorts if they had one.

Each was stopped and asked by the two Summoners guarding the door, "How do you enter?"

The answer said by each member was, "Willingly. In perfect love and perfect trust."

Mistress Circe and I were joined by Richard's High Priest Solomon and Richard himself. He too was sky clad. I tried not to look but I was unsuccessful. I stole quick glances at the man I was about to have sex with as he stood next to me. He was doing the same. We were the final members in the lengthy line waiting to enter the sacred ritual room.

Richard was indeed the picture of perfection of the male frame. He was buff, well-formed, and covered in Celtic knotwork tattoos. He had a square powerful looking jaw and fierce green eyes. He was wearing a pair of stag horns on his blond locks. I looked down out of curiosity and to my fear he was also very well endowed. I know this because while he stole looks at my own naked unit, he apparently liked what he saw. His manhood was eager to perform this ritual. Oh well, at least he was good looking and apparently he thought I was too. Physically, this was doable. Now if only I could stop shaking.

High Priest Solomon and Mistress Circe went into the room after answering the Summoners. Richard and I were next, but the Summoners blocked us with their staffs not asking us the question they had just said over what seemed a hundred times.

I looked at Richard confused. He shrugged. Then the answer came. Mother Della and her current consort came to the door and asked the Summoners the questions. The males answered and were bid entry.

The Crone and Sage then looked at Richard and me as Mother Della said, "You both are here to perform the Great Rite today. Your partner selected is not your own. It is the will of the Gods and Goddesses that you will enter this place and engage in this sacred rite of your own freewill. Do you Richard accept initiate Psycho as your Priestess and if so, how do you enter?"

Richard stood straight and then said in maybe the most masculine voice I have ever heard, "I accept and worship my chosen Priestess with great joy. I enter this union, and rite, willingly, in perfect love and in perfect trust."

Mother Delleh looked at me and said the same thing with the same question.

I looked at her fiercely and said, "I accept and worship my chosen Priest with pure adoration. I enter this union, and rite, willingly, in perfect love and in perfect trust."

Mother Delleh and Father Orin smiled as Mother Delleh said, "Then enter this rite as Summoner Richard and Maiden Psycho but leave this place as High Priest Roary and High Priestess Arodia. Your names have been chosen by the God and Goddess. Enter and erect your ancient altar with our blessings. The circle is now yours." She took my left hand and Richard's right hand then joined them.

The King and Queen of Green stepped out of our path. Richard and I entered holding each other's hands. He and I looked forward as we slowly walked toward the center of the room where an altar that resembled a stone bed had been placed. We stopped at the center, and I took my place sitting upon it facing south as Richard took his place in front of me to begin the anointing of oil, kisses, scourging, binding, and incantations of this complex ritual to call down the God and Goddess into our units. Neither of us forgot our words as we took our turns saying our parts and playing our roles.

All the members of the Covens – old, young, and small – were there to watch us perform this early part of the Great Rite. Richard and I were the only members that were sky clad, and the only members allowed to speak. Mother Delleh and Sage Orin had caste the circle so no one could leave or come in until Mother Delleh opened a doorway.

With our scourging and binding completed, I laid down on the altar my head to the East, while Richard knelt beside me from the North. He kissed my stomach then began the incantation to erect the sacred altar (that is me beauties, I am the sacred altar). When he had finished his final words, he laid his unit on top of mine being very careful not to crush me under his weight.

He held still at this point, both of us looking into each other's eyes as the circle was opened and everyone was rushed from the room. Only Third Level and up could stay for the next part of the initiation. The entry of the word into the Chalice.

I could feel Richard's unit shaking. He was as nervous as I was. I smiled at him trying to let him know it was almost over, we had made it. He smiled back appearing grateful. I know it must have been just as nerve racking for this man to deal with all this craziness especially since he was never even warned to prepare for any of it.

He then whispered, "If I hurt you in any way, please say so. I want this to be passionate not painful." His eyes told me he meant that.

I nodded, doing my best to hold back my own tears. I was not happy about having to submit to sex with this man. He was beautiful, and apparently a kind and generous lover, but after my life of forced sexual congress it was hard to hold back the terror of yet another male I didn't chose having pleasure with my unit.

Richard saw my eyes begin to well with rain. He frowned and looked sad. He put his lips to my neck and gently kissed it, then petted the side of my face with his hand. Richard was trying to calm my terror, it worked. I understood he was there to adore my unit not just use it for his own interests. I forced myself to relax by closing my eyes and breathing slowly.

The last of the non-participating members had left. Mother Delleh rejoined the circle. It was time to finish the Great Rite.

Richard called out to the Gods the incantation:

"Make open the path of intelligence between us.
For these truly are the Five Points of Fellowship
Foot to foot,
knee to knee,
Lance to Grail,

Breast to breast,
Lips to lips.
By the great and holy name Cernunnos;
In the name of Aradia;
Encourage our hearts,
Let the light crystalize itself in our blood,
Fulfilling of us resurrection.
For there is no part of us that is not of the Gods."

He then merged with my unit putting his Sword into my Chalice. I was caught off guard by the sudden rush of pain from his entry. I gasped loudly and jerked upward. He stopped and looked at me with concern. I took a deep breath, steadied my nerves, and nodded for him to continue.

Richard was an amazing lover. As the initial pain of his entering me began to soften I felt my unit give into his lustful thrusting. I felt a sudden surge of carnal drives from the drops of his sweat as they fell onto my face. Before I could think better of it, I found myself thrusting back wantonly. This further excited Richard's pace. We became one as the room fell away, the Elder watchers forgotten. Only the sounds of our moans of pleasure and the rhythmic movements of two units in their sexual prime filled our senses. With great relief I felt the warmth of impending orgasm begin within. The spasm of ecstasy exploded sending my eyes back into my head as I let out a groan of pure hedonistic bliss. Richard felt my satisfaction gripping him. He immediately reached his own apex, also emitting feral sounds of gratification. His seed released into my vessel. Our spiritual marriage was now consummated before the Gods and the Elders.

He and I gasped for air for a few moments still locked together in our conjugal embrace. Richard smiled at me affectionately. I smiled back noticing we both were sweating like pigs.

He very gently rose up from my unit then went to the eastern side of our altar and said: "*Ye Lords of the Watchtowers of the East, South, West and North, the thrice consecrated High Priestess greets you and thanks you.*"

Our ritual was now complete. Richard and I had become High Priest and High Priestess of the Covens of the Green Rings. The Elders rushed forward to hug and welcome us using our chosen names. My consort High Priest Roary reached for me and aided me to stand. Mother Delleh came forward. She hugged us both. She asked us to remove our headdresses. She then placed a Triple Moon Crown on my head and an Oak and Horn crown on that of my High Priest. She handed us our black cords, along with the black and purple robe of the High Priest and Priestess. The Elders than allowed us time to dress in our robes. I tied on Roary's black cord as he did my own. From that day forward he was to be my Spiritual helper and consort.

We were never expected to have sex again unless we wanted to or performed the Great Rite ever again. He was to be my partner at all events and the absent but always present High Priest of my own Coven. Until, or when, we found working partners of our own, that is. However, neither of us ever took another. To this day, we are still viewed as a partnership in that Coven. Though neither of us are practicing High Priest and High Priestess of any Covens.

The honor we received that day was for life. We both still have the titles and the respect even if we both gave up our seats of power to the next generation a decade later. That story will be told in another chapter. He and I would indeed do what we were prophesized to do together and heal the hearts of the broken Green Rings. So, stick around. You won't want to miss those stories.

It was time for Roary and I to raise Mistress Circe and Roary's own High Priest and Priestess to that of Crones and Sage. Together he and I raised them and granted them their Elders' chalices, as they gave up their seats of power to myself and my Priest. Once the final incantation was said, Mother Delleh finally opened the circle. The horror of the initiation and takeover of Mistress Circe's Coven was complete. I was no longer Psycho. I was now High Priestess Arodia of the Coven of the Green Rings.

Mother Delleh had the Summoners called in to announce that the new leaders had achieved their cords. High Priest Roary came up next to me and again we walked hand and hand into the main hall to the sound of clapping, yells of joy, and sounds of celebration. He and I followed the Summoners to the head of the long table where the feast of Beltane began. Outside, the young girls were "jumping the fire," while the young boys danced the May pole. Inside the hall, Roary and I sat like a King and Queen accepting the gifts and hugs of our adoring Sister Coven members.

Everyone had lined up to greet us and show reverence for our new powerful positions.

NOTE: *I will now take a moment to tell you how I felt about all of this. It was one of the most terrifying experiences of my young life. Somehow, I was able to shut down, do what was expected and even found pleasure in the Great Rite as Mother Delleh had told me to do. To this day I can only thank the Goddess for the strength that it took to do what I did that day. It helped that the High Priest selected for me was a good and devout Wiccan. I can't say anything bad about him. He was and is a very handsome fellow.*

All that aside, you are all aware I am a child of schizophrenia with a history of extreme abuse and rape. Richard/Roary was able to overcome my terror in a situation that in my dark past had been very ugly. He accomplished this by being compassionate in those moments before he took me. He was empathetic and kind, which allowed me to let go my hang up and just enjoy the act of lovemaking. I was so focused on my consort I completely forgot about our audience.

Until Master Jon, I would never have another sexual encounter so satisfying and completely wonderful. I went into that room expecting it to be ugly, cruel, and torturous. I left feeling whole, beautiful, and full of hope for the future. Performing the Great Rite actually opened my heart, mind and eyes to the wonder that is creation itself. I no longer viewed carnal congress as a task that was to be endured but one that should be valued. It would be a long time before I found a partner who could raise my blood pressure like that again, but eventually I did with my beloved.

As the final members had come by to pay homage, Roary grabbed my hand and said, "Priestess, will you spend this glorious night with me in my bed? I would like to get to know you better. We could make love without the pressures of ritual."

I laughed as I pulled my hand from his. "Thank you but no, my dear Priest. I believe we know enough about each other. Thank you for your kind offer but I am presently trying to be monogamous to another. This was a special forgiveness but that is over now."

I was not lying. Mistress Circe still held my Key. She still held the right over my sexual behaviors too. She had ordered monogamy unless she deemed otherwise. Her allowing me to enter the ritual room even though she knew I would have to fuck Richard was her way of allowing this one-time exception. As for Master Peggy and Mistress Andrea, the same. She only agreed to the allowance of special services of the collar to each lady if she finished her probationary period of thirty days and then again it was only for the one time. I never betray my collar even if the owner of it is a jackass. My High Priest would have to attend to his own urges from there on out. I was not his real wife. I owed him nothing more and didn't feel the need to repeat the performance of the Great Rite, even if he was exceptional at lovemaking.

Are you surprised? You shouldn't be. I had no feelings about Roary other than gratitude that he was not a rapist or cruel person. I don't have lust, Simon has that one, and I was not smitten with him. So, it was as easy to turn him down as it had been to say goodbye to Master Peggy and Mistress Andrea.

Never forget experiencing sex as a function without emotions behind it is not only a curse, in my lifestyle it is a blessing. I would never be able to satisfy the needs of Masters/Mistresses of either gender I don't like/hate or find attractive otherwise. I also wouldn't have been able to enjoy the sex at this ritual. It is because I am schizophrenic that I can survive horrible things normals simply cannot without being psychically ripped to shreds.

Besides, Mistress Circe would never have granted permission to a night of carnal pleasures with my Priest when she was having to spend the night alone by herself. One quick note: I did revel in the fact that she had to watch me and Roary have sex. That was funny to say the least. I know it must have chapped her ass when she saw I enjoyed it. She was sitting at the Elders table looking sullen while Roary and I received the congratulations and adoration of the crowd. No one was congratulating her or the other two who just made Elder.

The reasons are varied but the main thing preventing anyone rushing to those three is their stations within the Covens. Elder status meant you were too high up to rub elbows with the lowly members. The position of Crone and Sage was one of complete respect. Once she had taken that step, she had cut herself off from the Coven. She was now expected to reflect, study, and become self-sufficient. The problems and activities of the circle were no longer her problem. Mistress Circe was supposed to be seeking the Gods, not adoration from her followers.

This lofty title was meant for the High Priest and High Priestess that had done years of heart wrenching service to his or her Coven. They could take the Fourth Level to basically "retire" from the rigors of dealing with constant drama of ritual life. The True Elders, including the Queen of Green herself, were always over fifty-five years old and had to have a lifetime of experience in the Third Level. Mistress Circe had been in such a big hurry to try to take Mother Delleh's place she forgot that being a Crone meant she had just lost all her power over the Coven. That now belonged to me. She was now a memory, a spirit, a has been. I was now the Mistress and she the powerless.

If she was unsuccessful in her bid to take the position of Queen, she was forever forced to watch the game but never again allowed to play it. The Queen of the Green was a position of popular vote of the Sister Coven members. Only a Crone of good standing could even apply, and the position had to be empty of course. Mother Delleh looked pretty damned healthy to me. I was aware that the longer Mother Delleh stayed on the throne the more time Mistress Circe had to spin her web to capture that throne the second the Mother was gone. It was my goal to turn the Coven against her and get Mistress Circe exiled from the Circle of the Green Rings. Once a Crone is exiled she, of course, cannot apply for the Queen's title.

I had to sleep with a man I didn't know in front of a bunch of old coots, but I had earned my spot as the only voice heard by the ears of the members of the Covens. Mistress Circe's telling her members that she had only done the Great Rite symbolically would come back to bite her. My standing tall and doing the unthinkable had earned both the respect and awe of her old Coven witches. I was now viewed by all of them as the Devout and she is seen as the Poser.

I glared across the hall at her till she noticed me. I shot a "gotcha" smile at her. She frowned at me then stood up. She stormed off to her room leaving her plate of food untouched at the almost empty Elders table. That made me chuckle.

My Priest Roary was immensely popular among the members of his own Coven. They all viewed me as their Priestess as much as my Coven viewed him as their Priest. We had married our two circles. Mother Delleh came over to point out our symbol would be that of Eternity since two circles intertwined meant forever. I watched as HP Roary burst with pride. His green eyes danced with joy at having obtained what he told me later he never thought he could, leadership. He didn't have a wife or even a girlfriend. Don't ask me why, beats the fuck out of me. The dude was incredibly good looking. Maybe too devout for non-wiccan girls, who knows. He told me they had come to him that morning and asked him to take the black cord.

"Bet you about died," I said laughing.

He smiled. "I have, and this is where all good Wiccans go. I was scared, sure. They told me they had a Priestess for me. I would have to perform the Great Rite with her. I said okay, can I at least get a look at my wife first? Then Orin said sure, you join Johnny and retrieve her when she gets here. Johnny and I waited for Sister Circe's van. So, I saw you get out and thought to myself, hell yeah."

I rolled my eyes. "Sure you did, Roary. Look you can pack up the bullshit. It is over, you are HP now. You already put your Sword in my Chalice, no need to continue useless flattery. It is done."

His smile melted. "I am not flattering. I am being truthful. This was the best day of my life. I am wearing a black cord, got to have amazing sex with a Goddess, and am sitting next to the most beautiful wife a man could ever dream to have. I woke up this morning expecting to be Summoning for a Third Level initiation, instead, it was mine that was Summoned. When I saw you get out of the van I was smitten, but when I saw you sky clad, I was in love. Then we made love, now I am your slave." He looked at the table appearing sincere.

I smiled at him. "You are truly kind, my Priest. I would like to say the same to you but that would not be truth. I will say I was pleased to see you are very handsome and everything a Priestess could dare to wish for in her consort. You're a wonderful lover. I was brought to ecstasy, and I thank you for the favor. It will be my pleasure to stand beside you as your Priestess until our jobs are complete and the Gods call us home."

He grabbed my hand and kiss my knuckles. "You are truly a blessing from the Gods. I am humbled that they love me so much as to send me a most desirable Priestess. May you have beautiful dreams, my love."

He got up and joined his male initiates as they left to drink ale and tell lies about their conquests of women and wine. I sat there on my throne chair wondering about a life I would never know. If I had been normal, I could have run off with my Priest. We could had made love under the moon, raised a family of Pagans, and caste circles calling on the universal elements together till we too became Sage and Crone.

Instead, I was bound to a Key and my wedding ring around my neck in a circle of silver. Despair washed over me as I retired to my own room – because I was High Priestess now, I had one of my own – to cry over a life that I could never have. My Priest, just like Kick Start, Zeppelin, Boyd, and Linda, before him was everything I could desire, if I could desire (Simon owns that too). I was cursed to see the paths that I could never travel fall one by one before me as I walked the lonely path of schizophrenia. I believed that along with the stress of the day I deserved a few tears at least. I was able to grant more than a few that night.

The next morning, we left the Springfields early. James of course was driving like a bat out of hell. Mistress Circe was still sullen and pouting at her loss of status. The girls and fellows of my Coven were curious as to what happened when they all left the ritual room. I told them

106

using euphemisms because children were present. They were all stunned and in awe. I was asked a thousand questions about how I was holding up. My ladies loudly announced they would have done it too if Roary was the one selected to be the stag. This was to the protests of their own consorts. Everyone had a good laugh at the fake indignation of the husbands.

Half-way home the Coven gave me their collective gift, a leather-bound Book of Shadows with a large brass Pentacle on the cover. It was an expensive item. I had seen it in Mistress Circe's shop priced at near seventy-five dollars. My Coven children were all factory workers. They were far too poor to afford such an elaborate item. I was touched they had given up their hard-earned income to honor me in such a beautiful way. It was time for me to give them my own gift in return.

I had been keeping a secret, even from you, the reader.

I had bought five acres of land in the forested area near a river. I had made a good deal with Ralph. I just paid it off the day before our Sabbat. I paid over seven thousand dollars for this little plot. I had gifted the title to Mother Delleh after the Feast of Beltane was ended the night before. It was now officially property of the Covens of the Green Rings. This land was bought for my members. I intended to erect a temple in the wild for them so we could remove our circle from Mistress Circe's shop. She had been soiling their circle of green with her greed long enough. It was time to end that practice.

Mother Delleh wept when I gave it to her. She told me no one, no matter how devout, had ever granted a title of land to the Covens before. I told her that I did it so that I could ask proper permission to move my Coven away from the evil of money. This way my Coven would never have to pay to pray again. Adoration of the Gods should be free for those hearts who seek it. She wept even harder, to my confusion, when I said that.

"How will you build your temple, Sister Arodia," she said through her tears.

I laughed. "With my bare hands Mother. I will make sure that all beasts of the land and air are welcome guests since we are borrowing from them, not them from us. I will make sure the floor is of Mother Earth and the roof only there to shelter the items of ritual from the tears of the Gods. I will re-plant all that I have to uproot, and the temple will become part of the wilderness, not apart from it. Our circle will be Green not gold, Mother."

She nodded still silently weeping, "You have my blessing, Sister Arodia. You seem to understand my displeasure that the Coven was in a shop designed to sell goods not to call the Gods."

I nodded. "Sister Circe misunderstood the hearts of the followers. I hear them Mother. It is time for a change. I heard from you too. You told me to cleanse and heal the circle. You have now raised me. The Wheel has turned from Winter to Spring. It is time to sow the seeds of our future harvest Mother."

She looked up with shock in her eyes. "I told you that? You heard me tell you to end Sister Circe's abuse of the Coven?"

I nodded smiling. "Yes. You came to me at Yule the day you approved I become Maiden. Don't you remember?"

She looked at the ground. "I dreamed of you that night. I dreamed of, never mind. You and Brother Roary will heal the Circle. May the Goddess be praised for her goodness." She hugged me tightly.

"So mote it be." I said as I hugged her back understanding, she would back my bid to exile Mistress Circe for good.

You could have heard a mouse fart in that van when the Coven realized what I had just done. They looked at each other in amazement and excitement.

"We get to have our very own temple. Our very own land," squealed out Lisa suddenly making everyone in that van almost jump out of their skin.

I nodded. "Yes. I just have to build it. That will take some time, but I hope to have it finished by the end of summer."

James snorted, "Alone? Come on Psycho. We will all help. Won't we guys."

Everyone began to chatter excitedly that they would all pitch in to build their temple, except Mistress Circe. She was glaring angrily.

"The shop has always been the temple. There is no reason to move the holy place to the woods. Ticks, mice, bears. You all need to think. What about when it gets too cold or too hot? You won't have any electricity that far out in the sticks. Humph. This is the dumbest idea I have ever heard," Mistress Circe growled.

Tracy looked at Mistress Circe appearing irritated. "No one has ever liked going to do rituals in your shop, Mother. We are children of Mother Nature. Tick bites, mice, hell they got to eat too. As for bears, there aren't any bears where Sister Arodia bought this land. Don't be silly. I vote we move to the land we own and leave the shop. Who is with me?"

Everyone in the van voted to move to the land. Mistress Circe and I are not allowed to vote due to our status as Elders. The Coven is the real power. Every HP must do what the Coven decides. We are helpless when they vote unanimously to change or implement something. This was something Mistress Circe never honored. Her Coven was now flexing its very atrophied muscles. I was happy to aid in the rehab of that ability of the Coven to rule itself and become stronger for it.

"I veto that vote. The circle stays in the shop," yelled out Mistress Circe.

I looked at her calmly. "I am sorry Sister, but the Coven has voted unanimously. You and I must do what the children request. We are honor bound to give in to their wishes. Please don't be angry at their eager hearts. The God and Goddess speak through them. Cannot you hear that?"

She glared with hate at me, "Psycho, you have twisted their minds. That is not the God and Goddess speaking. It is your foul tongue."

Tracy sucked in her breath as every other member gasped at Mistress Circe's lack of respect. "Mother. That is not Psycho. That is Mother Arodia you are talking to. She is not speaking through us. We want our temple on the land that the Coven owns. How dare you accuse us of being so easy to mislead. And how dare you disrespect Mother Arodia, after what she just went through to earn her black cord."

Mistress Circe realized too late that her impulsive verbal attack on her ward would anger the members at her. No one said another word the rest of the way home. The Coven was angry, and I was satisfied as I sat staring at the fuming Mistress Circe. She was finally feeling my wrath. She shouldn't have fucked with Simon or me.

When we got back everyone was in a hurry to get going. The work week would start the next day, plus everyone was feeling salty over Mistress Circe's insults. I had spoken to Mary about the planned move to my secret home as soon as my college semester ended in two weeks. She was very happy to hear I had finally acquired housing and would reunite with my family very soon. I asked her to keep my children until then. I needed them stable just a bit longer. I gave her a hug and kissed my children. I wanted to go with them, but I had business with the angry Mistress Circe first. It was best my family leave while I and my Mistress discussed the future of my collar. She was now Crone, and I had fulfilled my contract. It was time to select a new Keyholder. I walked into the house with Mistress Circe as Mary took the children to her house.

She turned around and backhanded the fuck out of me soon as we were alone in the living room. "How dare you embarrass me in from of my coven, Psycho," she screamed now getting red faced with her flowing anger.

I rubbed my cheek. "Be careful Mistress. You hit me again, I call Dennis. Remember he knows all about you, darling. I told you not to fool with me. I have done nothing wrong. You embarrassed yourself, Mistress. Now, sell my Key to Peggy or Andrea and I will go. You are Crone. I am High Priestess. The Coven is no longer your affair, it is mine."

She growled shaking all over with fury, "I will make you pay for this. You tricked me. I have been robbed."

I began laughing manically. "Oh? Have you? How? You wanted to be fucking Crone. You are Crone, Mistress. You are getting exactly what you deserve and what you asked for. I warned you not to force me to be your Maiden. You greedy bitch. You should have left Simon alone. Now you are trapped in my voodoo jar. Ain't karma a bitch, Mistress?"

Her mouth flew open as she looked startled, finally realizing she had brought her own house down on her head by forcing her will on me in the first place. Now she would have to deal with the repercussions of it. She looked up at the jar that had once held Simon.

"I will let Simon go. You leave town, and it will go back to the way it was," she trailed off trying to think of a way to get out of her own trap.

I shook my head. "Too late, Mistress. I am High Priestess now. You are the Crone. It is done. I did what you asked of me. Sell my fucking key and release me," I demanded, becoming angry myself.

She sat down with a thud in her bean bag chair, appearing to be in shock. "No, I will not. Not yet. I will put you back on auction. If I am going to lose my Coven, I will need the money. Nikki is the next Interim. It is time for you to start her probationary period. Her address is on the table. Get it and leave me now. I don't want to see your face. Now get out."

I shook my head. "No, I will not. Peggy or Andrea will work. Choose one of them."

She looked up angrily. "I still own the fucking Key, Psycho. I say I am not happy with the bids so far. Nikki had offered more. You go check the woman out and I have three more after her lined up. I will only sell to the highest bidder of the six. You will finish the probation of each one. I will not have you coming back to me later saying I was unfair in who gets that Key. The auction will happen on September the 2nd. The highest bidder of one of the Interims you have approved will be the one to gain the Key. You can do what I say or I will give your fucking Key to Linda. How would you like that, Psycho? Do you think I am stupid? I know that is one of your fears. Well, fuck with me any further and I will make it happen. That is my final word on this. Now get the fuck out you ungrateful slut before I forget myself and rip you apart."

I just about fainted. "What? You rotten bitch. Four more! That is fucking insane, Mistress."

She glared at me. "Want to try me Psycho? Go get that address and leave me. You can have the next name in thirty days and then the next till we are done. So, help me, I am going to call Linda."

I looked at the floor. "One of the four is not Linda, is it," I gulped feeling my unit begin to shake in terror at that idea.

Mistress Circe laughed bitterly. "No. Linda wouldn't have the money I am asking for that fucking Key. But if you try me, I would be willing to give up my income to pay you back. Now get out."

I realized she had me dead to rights. I walked to her kitchen table and retrieved the address. I remembered seeing this name before putting my foot down in March. I sighed deeply as I went to the bathroom to change from my robe to street clothing. It was apparent I was going to have to play Mistress Circe's game till the bitter end. At least I had the comfort of knowing the whole mess was over in four more months. I dared not test the old bat on how determined she may be to punish me by granting Linda my Key. Damn it.

I came back into the living room to grab my coat. Mistress Circe was still sitting in the bean bag chair. "I will need to borrow the fucking Honda until this bullshit is over, Mistress."

She nodded. "So be it. Now get out. Fucking ingrate."

I snorted. "You should know Crone Circe. See you on the flip side." I flipped her off as I left for the Honda.

My brother, the sun was blazing as I drove the fifteen miles to my next Interim Master's house. I pulled into the driveway of a large ranch style brick home that looked a lot like Julie's house. I sat there staring at it unwilling to get out to meet the latest in the line of potential suspects who may or may not hold my Key. My stomach was tightening with the stress of this latest news regarding my continued servitude to Mistress Circe. I had really believed Beltane would be the end of this nonstop march of Masters. Too bad reality isn't my strong suit, eh?

The fall of Mistress Circe was long in coming but no worries, it is still coming. You have just seen her first drop down that steep ladder. She will cling tightly, trying to keep her grip on the Coven and our Collar, but in this battle we will win. Her greed knew no bounds, but it blinded her to reality. She had just made herself disposable, and us Powerful. Now she will throw a temper tantrum like the child. She was making damned sure we pay dearly for giving her exactly what she asked.

Chapter 20: Master Nikki & the Green Temple
The Fall of Mistress Circe

The summer of 1994 is a time of great spiritual awakening. It is a time for healing and change. Many things that we have sought will finally be within our grasp, but just within it. Until our Keyholder is selected everything is in flux. We are now flexing our powers as the seeds of creation of the new have taken root. We watch as the sweat of brow water the saplings of a future beyond anyone's imagination. The Child of Schizophrenia has become a Mother of the Lost. She has opened the circle, and many will come to her summoning of the Goddess. The circle will expand with the nourishment of loving hearts after years of starvation and neglect. Everyone is pleased with this great harvest except one dark heart.

Crone Circe is bitter that she had ascended to her lofty spot among the stars. She watches the High Priestess she raised accomplish what she tried to prevent. Her anger will be deep as she plots to pay back the insolence of the one she once commanded. The Crone will sit and wait, refusing to assist, refusing to speak. This will be her fall. Without an apology, the last words she spoke will be her testimony. Those who heard them will never forgive her for her greed.

Mistress Nikki is quiet and intelligent. She desired the circle of silver. She wants to purchase it from the Queen of Gold, but will her attempts to obtain this coveted gift be successful? It is all up to the mighty force of a thwarted villain to decide. Three more are waiting in the wings for their chance to enjoy Psycho's favors.

So ready to meet our sixth Master? Great. Bring your thinking caps, a warm cup of tea, milk for the cat and your reading glasses beauties. Mistress Nikki enjoys a deep conversation, and she likes it quiet, so make sure to tip toe.

"Dean's list again. I knew you would excel, but Psycho, this is amazing. I just don't understand why the courts think you need a guardian. You are even smarter than me."
Mrs. Moore to Psycho at the announcement of 2nd Dean's list for straight A's – Spring Semester 1994.

I took a deep breath. I reminded myself that just like Beltane, the horrid situation of being passed from Master to Master would come and go. Time tends to heal all hurts. Steadying my nerves as best as I could I got out of the Honda and went to the door of what was to be my third Interim.

I knocked but backed away from the door this time. Master Peggy had pulled me inside by force. Mistress Andrea had almost blown my head off. I had learned to knock and get out of the way in case this one was nuts too. However, after several minutes, there was no answer.

I stood there unsure what to do. It seemed to me that Mistress Circe would have told this woman I was on my way. Perhaps I had the wrong house. I was looking at the address written on my piece of paper to make sure I had the right place when suddenly the door opened.

A woman of around fifty-five with medium length thinning brown hair and large glasses was standing there looking at me. I noticed she was wearing a shapeless blue dress with an oversized sweater of light blue. She wore soft soled white shoes and a black knee brace. She was around five foot four and frumpy being at least twenty pounds past perfect weight for her frame. Immediately, three cats appeared, one coming out onto the porch to sniff and rub on my legs.

I reached down and petted the curious calico cat. "I am Psycho. Mistress Circe told me to come to provide service to someone called Nikki French?"

The woman lowered her glasses then looked me from head to toe as Master Peggy had. "Yeah, I am Nikki. I have been expecting you. Grab Silkie there and follow me." She pointed at the cat.

I nodded while I picked up the purring feline. I went through the door as Nikki closed it behind me and Silkie.

She stood there appearing to be unhappy with what she saw. "A bit young aren't you? I expected you to be older. How old are you sixteen?"

I laughed out loud. "I am flattered you would think so Ma'am, but no I am twenty-two."

She snorted. "What the hell would a twenty-two-year-old know about anything. I think maybe Circe is deluded. You will never do."

I looked at the floor. "As you wish Ma'am. I am happy to leave. I do apologize for my shortcomings. Thank you very much for your time."

I started to head back for the door feeling relieved that at least one of these misguided women was smart enough to send me away quickly.

However, Nikki put out her arm to stop me. "Hey, wait a second. Did you just say you apologize for your shortcomings?"

I nodded. "Yes Ma'am. I did. If you don't agree that someone my age could warrant perfect service in return for your own attendance to my adaptive functioning needs, then I am not one to argue. If Mistress Circe has misled you, don't despair, she tends to spin the truth to suit her needs."

Nikki's face broke into a smile. "Ah, you are intelligent. I thought you were too young to be able to carry on a conversation much less clean a floor or cook a meal. I see I have been too rash in my assessment."

That confused me a tad. "I apologize for not providing my credentials first, Ma'am. I am only a first-year biology student in college, but I have over fourteen years of experience in service to Masters. I am well trained in all areas domestic, yard work, and other specialty areas. What I don't know I will learn when requested." I was grateful that this potential at least didn't get the wrong idea of what I do for a damned change.

Nikki asked me to sit down. "Okay I confess, I don't understand how this whole collar business works. Would you care to enlighten me?"

I sat down in her very overstuffed chair noting the presence of five cats in the room. The house smelled of dirty litter boxes. All the furniture was "marked up" with scars from felines sharpening claws. Tons of books and magazines lay everywhere throughout her living room, and stacks were piled on her kitchen table. Then I noticed the appearance of two more cats in the background making seven in all. I sighed realizing Nikki was a stereotypical "cat lady."

I began the process of mild submission in which an Interim is told of the duties expected for services rendered. The potential Keyholder is given a temporary title, and allowed to ask for specific services, but unlike a full submission they can change their minds if they do it within a few weeks. They are not allowed to override any directives held by the true Keyholder, and they cannot order monogamy, chastity or other. They also do not get leash rights. If they fail to meet their duties, I can walk away and so can they without any reason or notice granted.

Nikki understood and was ready to start her thirty-day Interim probationary period. She was more interested in my ability to converse than of any other service offered, though she would eventually try almost all of them. She chose the title Mistress Nikki. Then within moments of my ending the rules and regulations of her position, began to want to pontificate on the nature of humans to need to control each other. Sheesh, this was going to be a long thirty days.

Sixth Interim Master (Collar-No Key)
Interim Mistress Nikki: the Cat Lady
May 2nd to June 2nd, 1994

Mistress Nikki had been a high school teacher in her youth but had left the job due to rude teenagers. She then had married a man who like her was in the world of education as a professor at a small community college. Her husband and she enjoyed a happy fifteen-year union when he died quite suddenly of a heart attack at the young age of forty-three. Mistress Nikki was crushed by the loss. The heartbroken widow vowed to never love again. To comfort her in her loneliness, she had bought a kitten since she nor her husband ever had any children.

Over the last ten years she had found herself taking in more cats, finally ending up with fifteen in all. She thought that was a lucky number since it was the exact number of years in her lost marriage. Mistress Nikki was quiet, introverted, and intelligent. Her lost husband had been a smart man too. His life insurance policy had afforded Mistress Nikki the freedom to stay home with her family of felines in a beautiful house with no mortgage. She had enough money to do as she pleased, but what she pleased was six feet below.

She told me she had been seeing Mistress Circe for spiritual counseling for almost four years. Mistress Nikki reported to me that she had been complaining of loneliness when my Mistress had convinced her to try out her trained schizophrenic. I was advertised as useful, obedient, and able to converse. Mistress Circe had heeded my warning to stop passing me off as a prostitute. I told her about Dennis and Boyd; okay, I threatened her with Dennis and Boyd. Therefore, I thankfully did not have to clean up that misconception. Mistress Nikki was only looking for another voice in her big house that didn't meow or yeow in the late hours keeping her awake. Piece of cake, right?

Mistress Nikki wanted to talk all night. She went on for hours discussing philosophical topics such as reasons for socioeconomical inequalities to the meaning of life. While it was noticeably clear the woman was incredibly intelligent, I had class and work the next day. The stresses of the Beltane ritual, the fight with Mistress Circe, all lead to my extreme fatigue. I did my best to be a clever conversationalist until at last Mistress Nikki had her fill and was ready for bed. I was permitted the couch, I was still not fond of them, for the two hours I had left before my class.

Finals week was about to begin. This latest Mistress and her desires threatened my performance on the most difficult exams in Chemistry, Microbiology, and Anatomy. I decided there was just not enough time for real rest, so I went to the Honda, grabbed my books, and studied instead. At least I was finally able to let the intense focus shift from Wicca to more mundane topics.

I did not have to provide wake up service to Mistress Nikki. She tended to sleep during the days and was up at nights. My brother was only just rising above the belly of the sleeping giants when I got into Mistress Circe's car to rush to meet Cherie who I'd had no time to inform of my latest move.

I parked the vehicle in Mistress Circe's yard and waited for Cherie's Z28. My Mistress was up early. She saw me sitting outside waiting.

"What the hell are you doing here. I told you to beat it," she came outside yelling from her porch.

I nodded. "Happy to do just that, Mistress. As it is, my ride to class didn't know I moved. I will correct the problem today."

She glared at me. "You will correct it now. Get off my property you whore." She picked up a crystal from her collection in a basket next to her door and threw it at me.

I dodged the projectile. "Whoa. Damn. Okay, I will go to the fucking road," I said as I grabbed my backpack headed for the still quiet main road.

"Don't fucking ever come back. If you touch the Honda again, I will report it stolen," she yelled.

I nodded as I flipped her off. Now I was dicked. I couldn't get back to the Honda. I began to stress, wondering what I was going to do now that I had no ride. Shit.

Cherie showed up while I stood there looking back at the angry Mistress. She looked confused when I hand-signaled for her to follow me. I walked to the neighbor's drive then got into her car that had been slowly following.

"Go. Go. Now," I yelled looking back to see Mistress Circe hobbling to the end of her drive to hurl more crystals at Cherie's car.

Cherie panicked and put the pedal to the metal roaring down the road like a madwoman running from whatever unknown I was warning her about.

We were at least two miles away from my wild pick up when she felt safe enough to slow down. She didn't hesitate any longer to glean information from me about that strange scene.

"What the fuck was that about? Was that Witch trying to break out my windows, Psycho?" Her big eyes were even bigger than normal with fear.

I nodded. "Yeah, she is riding the cotton pony, Cherie. Don't worry. I am not staying there anymore. Here is the new address, though I am not sure how I am going to get back and forth to work from now on. That shit Honda belonged to Circe."

Cherie snorted. "Lover's quarrel?"

"Something like that smart ass. Does it matter to you that fucking much," I said irritated that we were going to argue about her homophobia yet again.

I was just too tired and stressed for another argument so damned early in the morning.

"Psycho, this address you gave me is that crazy cat lady from the next town. I am not driving that far to pick your dumb ass up. This is ridiculous. You fuck around with these old hags, and I am supposed to pick up the slack. Why don't you just learn how to eat pussy right so one will keep you for good," she said quite rudely.

I looked at the redneck princess. "You are quite the lady, Cherie. Where did you learn manners, at a truck stop? Geez. It is not like that."

Cherie laughed hatefully. "Sure it isn't. You know if you would start fucking the fellows and leave those old biddies alone you may finally have a real house. Hell, for a good blow job they may even loan you a car. Men appreciate a cheap piece of ass. You are playing for the wrong team, Psycho."

I don't know what got into me, but I spit at her.

"You are a fucking bitch. You just spit at me with that nasty mouth of yours. I have had it. Find your own fucking ride. After today we are finished," Cherie yelled beyond angry while she wiped away my saliva that had made a direct hit on the side of her face.

I sat back in my seat and covered my face. This was just not my day. I had managed to lose both rides in only thirty minutes. Ugg. I didn't bother to waste my breath apologizing. Truth is I wasn't sorry anyway. Cherie was a bitch to continue to insinuate I was nothing but a whore. Her small-minded vision of the world was nothing more than added stress to my already stressed to capacity life. I spent the rest of the very quiet ride trying to solve my travel difficulties. It was time to get the Motorpsycho I had been putting off. Finishing my yellow house would have to wait. As it was, I was stuck till September moving from house to house anyway. I would need to talk to Mary immediately to let her know my plans to bring the children to my home had been temporarily delayed.

I had been interested in a Shadow bike for sale just down from Master Peggy's house for several months. I had even test driven the metal God. I had the money for it long as I forwent my purchase of the final supplies needed to make my new home livable. It was not beyond my understanding that had I not purchased the land for the Coven, I would be in tall cotton despite the latest loss of transportation. I had sacrificed my own comfort for that of a greater good, or so I hoped. Though I still was not sorry, I did wince realizing that I had indeed fucked myself. I made a mental note to tell Simon to remind me that is why we have a guardian to manage our money. We do not always make proper decisions. Our lack of understanding of self would put us back in the cemetery outhouse if we were not careful. It turned out I was far too generous to be trusted when it came to my income. Not that it was much of a surprise. I had done without all my life. Tangibles and money didn't mean much unless you don't have them. With my lack of recalling I had needs too, I was a sitting duck for complete destitution if given reign over my own monies. This was going to require an honest guardian. Where the fuck was I going to get one of those. Well shit, I couldn't even get an honest Master.

I decided that when Cherie drove me back to town, she could drop me off at the home selling the bike. I would purchase it that very afternoon and solve at least one issue in my world. She could find someone else to pay her weekly gas fees. I was done with this closeminded bitch.

I had now been in the longest residual of my illness recorded since my onset. I could still hear Simon and the Looper. However, I could no longer make out the tapestry and the static had disappeared. My delusions of being the Prophet brought me to tears of laughter now that I realized how silly it all was. I was not sure if it was the fact that I was finally taking my medication as prescribed or just the cycle of the disease. If I made it to September without any significant symptoms of psychosis, I could claim remission for a full year.

The shock treatment side effects had started to wear off. I no longer was feeling incapable of anger as was just demonstrated by my spitting on Cherie. My tendency toward violent outbursts was starting to rear its ugly head once more. I noticed I had become preoccupied with ways to murder Mistress Circe. That along with the increased level of terror felt within my void worried me a bit. I wondered could it be a prodromal coming?

I didn't want to be sick again. The idea of going back to the nightmare world of hallucinations, confusion and insane behavior terrified me. I had been secretly increasing my dosages of medications. This would come back to bite me in the ass over that summer. I still had not learned that there is no stopping Schizophrenia. When the psychosis time comes, it comes. There is nothing on earth that can stop it. Overdosing on antipsychotics with a compromised GI system leads to pancreatitis and liver failure.

NOTE: *It was not that during the residuals I was "normal." Not even close. I still demonstrated color symbolism, and mild auditory hallucinations, and even spoke in schizophrenic speak more often than I like to admit.*

Within one hour of being around me, everyone would always ask the same question: "Mentally ill or drug addiction?"

The curse of my disease is that no matter what phase of the cycle I was a bitch to its expressions. No one ever raises an eyebrow in surprise when I tell them I have it.

They simply say, "Yeah that makes sense," or "Ah, of course you are. I wondered what the hell."

My Cognitive Behavioral Therapy, interactions at high school with the class of 1993, and ongoing bimonthly interactions with the Coven had improved my overall affective appearance. I could smile, laugh, and even frown at the right moments. Sometimes, okay often, I would miss my mark in demonstrating proper outward demonstrations of emotions. I was still considered cold and hard to approach, even intimidating. However, I had come a long way already. People were not openly shunning me as they once had been. In some circles, such as with my Wiccan sisters and brothers, I was viewed with profound respect despite the difficulty expressing my empathy.

I was still plagued by tactile hallucination of touch and tended to shy away from crying people, unable to provide proper behaviors designed to show concern. The pain of others was just not my area of specialty. It was not that I didn't care, I did a great deal. I had no idea what to do when other people cried. Hugs were out of the question unless absolutely necessary, and then only for a few seconds. Only a Master could break through my pain of touching by directive. As a High Priestess this was something I had decided needed to be dealt with immediately or I was going to miserably fail to win the hearts of my members.

That afternoon of May 3rd, 1994, I would purchase my third and final Motorpsycho. Final since to this date I have never bought another one. This one was exactly like the other two, only a few years newer. I drove the metal God back to Mistress Nikki's enjoying the wind in my face, letting go for a few moments all the heaviness of my crushing problems. Nothing like riding free to forget you are anything but.

I drove to Mary's house first. I visited my children and discussed with my most devout Coven member my latest problems with cash flow that had interrupted my ability to move my children in with me. She as always was understanding and helpful. Mary was a great person. I offered to pay her more per month since the kids were getting big enough to need more in resources. She happily took the pay increase and promised they would always have a place no matter what happened to their mother. I left Mary's wondering if I would not have been fairer to my little ones if I had signed them over to her. She loved them so much, and they loved her. I heard Simon roar in my ears that we would do nothing of the kind.

"Drop that shit right now. You never thought parenting with schizophrenia was going to be a picnic now did you fool," Simon said.

I started the bike shaking my head no. "You are right Simon. I just feel so awful not being able to give them a home."

He laughed which echoed around my head. "You will. Be patient. It takes time to raise up from the bottom. Keep pushing, you got this."

I nodded. Simon is not always right, but this time I knew he had a good point. There was no way I was going to let the likes of Mistress Circe or Cherie's bullshit stop me from my goal of family re-unification. I would have a stable Keyholder by September and the home would be finished by then. This was nothing more than an unexpected detour. I had setbacks before. I may be a lot of things. I may even be a loser, but I am never a quitter.

NOTE: *When others would give up, I take a breath, steady my nerves, roll up my sleeves, brush the dirt off my ass from the fall and try the fuck again. I even imagine that the day of my funeral I will be trying to kick the coffin lid off with my scuffed platforms. When it comes to calling it over, I am a total idiot. I never stop. Even when it is very apparent the battle is lost. Some would call me hardheaded. I agree with that and so does my neurologist.*

I have bashed my head into a ton of things and somehow my skull has held. So, I have proof that much is true. This fact (never giving up, not my headedness) is likely why I never succeeded in my bid for suicide. I am just too foolish to call the game lost.

I arrived back at my new Mistress's home to find an extensive list of chores left for me on the refrigerator. She had been heading off to a book club meeting when I pulled up on my bike. She told me she would be back in a few hours, but I should start my services right away. Mistress Nikki also told me she had left a turkey TV dinner on the kitchen table. She ordered me to eat it before I started my tasks. I nodded then went inside.

Well, the cats had eaten my dinner, so I just chuckled and threw away the empty tray. I took the list from the fridge and almost fell to my knees crying. Mistress Nikki wanted me to do everything but paint the fucking house. The list was three pages long. I had studying to do and work that night at the funeral home. I needed rest but there was no time with a list like this. I stood there thinking about running away for a good ten minutes before I pulled myself together. This was my job. I had to deal with it. If the Mistress wanted me to construct a new home, then I would have to do it. I took off my jacket and started on the duties assigned me by this very greedy woman.

Mistress Nikki was a terrible housekeeper. I started in her kitchen cleaning up dishes that were beyond disgusting. Food from eons had been dried on every plate, glasses, and utensils. When I finished scrubbing down that room, I began the foul job of cleaning the litter boxes. I heard Mistress Nikki come home a few hours later, but I didn't stop my attendance to her list. I kept right on with vacuuming, scrubbing the bathrooms, changing her sheets, laundry, and moping. I had begun the work in the late afternoon, I was almost done with the list by eleven when I needed to head off to the funeral home.

I stopped my endless scrubbing, marking off the finished tasks then headed for the door to grab my coat. Mistress Nikki was sitting on her couch reading a book. She looked up while I put my arms through the sleeves of my signature long black jacket.

"You really are gifted at service. The house is beautiful and hasn't smelled this nice since, well not in years. Tomorrow I would like to try your cooking skills. Make me something fancy. I like French cuisine. Think you can handle that?"

I nodded somewhat irritated that I had not even finished my first tasks and already she wanted more. I didn't even get fucking dinner.

"Anything in particular or just use my imagination," I grumbled.

She smiled. "Surprise me Psycho. Oh, and tomorrow I want to discuss this book I am reading too. Bring your thinking cap. I will eat and you can talk to me." She looked back at her book.

I rolled my eyes. "As you wish, Mistress." I stormed out to the bike and left cursing the day I was born, as usual.

I arrived at the funeral home to find Nikki Jaimes standing outside the door sitting on the receiving ramp. I killed the bike wondering what this little drama was about. Pat's car wasn't even there. Why was she?

"Can I help you, Nikki," I said as I hurried to unlock the funeral home doors.

She stood up, then began to cry very loudly. "Pat isn't here."

I looked around at the silent houses that were neighbors to this somber place of business. "Hey, hush. People are sleeping. Get in here. Lower your voice," I said while ushering the wailing Nikki inside the door.

Once inside I pushed her rapidly to the casket display room avoiding her seeing the possible customers who were waiting for my loving attendance.

After I had her in the room and the lights on. "What the hell, Nikki? What is going on?"

She shook her head, still wailing. "Pat hasn't been answering my calls, Psycho. I have lost him. I don't know why he ran away."

I looked at the floor angry that Pat had done what I expected him to. He had misled this poor simple girl with promises of love only to abandon her.

"How long since you last heard from him, Nikki," I inquired, still damning myself for not punching him out as soon as I discovered he was trifling with her.

She looked at me with a fresh onslaught of tears. "Two days, Psycho. He never has done this to me. I put his privates in my mouth and then he went away."

I almost hit the floor stunned when she yelled that out. "Well, uhm, okay, let's calm down, Nikki. I doubt that is why he hasn't called. Uhm, normally that keeps a fellow calling back."

She interrupted me. "I bit him on his wiener by accident. It was nasty, Psycho. It had this stuff come out. I was scared and he got so mad."

I looked at the ceiling. I was not having this conversation.

"Okay, look, Nikki, I am sure it will be alright. Let me see if I can talk to Pat and get this straightened out. He is reasonable. I will talk to him for you. I will get him to at least call you," I said trying not to run off into the night ripping out my eardrums so I would never hear this kind of shit ever again.

Her tears stopped flowing immediately. "You would do that for me. Oh, thank you so much, Psycho. You are a great friend. Tell him I won't ever bite him again. I will do it right next time." She came flying at me before I could stop her hugging me tightly.

"Get the fuck off me, Nikki. Damn, okay, I will talk to him." I pushed her overzealous unit back.

She smiled. "I know you can fix this, Psycho. You are a witch. You will cast a spell and make him love me forever. Can you please make that nasty stuff stop too?"

I'd had enough. "Get out, Nikki. Go home. I will make Pat call you. This shit is between you two. Please for the sake of the Gods, never tell me about it again."

She nodded now completely calm. "Okay, Psycho, see you later."

I opened the front door and let her out. I slammed it shut and pulled the shades quickly. The last thing I needed was Nikki and Pat drama. I hadn't slept enough hours in my whole fucking life to have that kind of strength. However, I went to the phone and called my work master immediately. That dog had some explaining to do. No hanky-panky, my ass.

"Uhm, yeah Psycho? Something wrong? Did you have trouble with the machine? Frizzy said it was acting up earlier today," Pat answered sounding like I had awakened him.

"No, the fucking machine is fine. I am calling because your girlfriend was just here raising holy hell, Pat. What the fuck man. She was talking about a botched blow job. I don't need this kind of shit," I growled into the phone.

He cleared his throat, "She, uhm, told you about that?"

"Yes, she did, thank you very much for the nightmares. I told you not to fool with her. You said you were honorable. Nikki is just a child. How could you? You know what? Not my fucking business. Call her Pat. Stop being an asshole. The girl is beside herself over your leaving her hanging. If your dick got chomped, serves you right screwing around with someone who couldn't tie her shoes without her mommy's help. You call her and tell her you are leaving. If she shows up here again telling me you never did call, so help me I will kick your ass myself. I don't give a flying fuck if you are my boss. Fire me if you want but I will not stand by and watch you fuck that girl over, Pat. She doesn't deserve than this," I was yelling feeling my heart race and skip as I unloaded all my pent-up aggression on this creep.

He cleared his throat. "Okay, calm down, Psycho. I will call her. I don't want to break it off with her. It was just, well, I was embarrassed when it all went so bad. I just assumed she knew how. I was avoiding her because I didn't know what to say. I mean what girl doesn't know anything about sex?"

I growled. "Nikki wouldn't. I told you she is retarded but now I think you are the one who is stupid. I don't want to have this conversation, Pat. Not my fucking business. You call that child and work it out. I suggest ending it. You are going to hurt her. Hell, you already have. She is not stable. If you don't hang up and call her right now my next call will be to Violet, you hear me? I bet she will love to hear what I have to say today."

137

He snorted as he interrupted. "Okay, I hear you loud and clear. I am calling her now. You have work to do. I will see you later." He hung up.

I slammed down the receiver. I couldn't believe this bullshit. It was as if I had fallen into another rabbit hole. Everyone around me was nuts but I was the one on medication. Go figure.

That night I had a full load with a couple of cool customers who needed to be prepped for their public debut. It took me the rest of the night to finish. I again would get no rest. It was time to head to my labs, and then I had to get to my children, followed by cooking for my Mistress, not including finishing my list of tasks.

The newness of driving the Motorpsycho was helpful in keeping me from sleeping while riding. My classes with monotone professor lectures were not so helpful. I fell asleep in my Computation class, had a nightmare, and awoke with a scream knocking all my books off the desk. Everyone in class had a good chuckle at the nutjobs little episode. The professor let the class out early citing "scaring the class to screams" as his reason for it. I rolled my eyes at his shitty attempt to be funny. I was a bit more than irritated.

I ran into a large girl in the hallway while I scurried to my bike to rush home. She was five six with her brown hair cut short into a crew cut. She had deep brown eyes with a square jaw and was dressed masculine. When I say ran into, I literally ran into her. I was half asleep and didn't move in time. I knocked all her books from her hands, and she sent my ass to the floor. It was like slamming into a brick wall. The girl was solid, full of muscles.

"Hey chick. You okay." She reached down to help me up.

I waved her off. "Yeah. I apologize. It has been a long night. I didn't see you. I hope I didn't cause you any harm."

The girl jumped back. "Wow, now that is a voice. Damn baby. Dude looks like a lady."

I sneered at her insult. "Excuse me? Looked in a mirror lately, darling?"

The girl looked stunned for a moment then began to laugh hard. "Hey, that is fucking funny. I like you. My name is CJ, and you are?"

I stood up grabbing a few of her books to hand back to her. "They call me Psycho. Pleased to meet you CJ."

She laughed even harder. "Get out of town. Psycho? Really? Is that like a nickname or something?" She took her books from me.

I snorted. "More like a character description. Now, if you will excuse me, I have shit to do. Again, I apologize for my clumsiness. You have a wonderful day."

CJ laughed even harder, "Character description? You are a fucking riot. Love the look. Very creepy. Hey, where are you headed? I was on my way to meet my live-in girlfriend Diane for coffee. Come with me. She will get a kick out of you, and I think you are someone I would love to get to know better. Just looking at you tells me you have one hell of a story to tell."

Brushing off the hall dust from my coat I looked at her rather irritated. "Uhm, no you don't want to know me better, trust me on this. The only story I have is that I am late. See you around CJ." I took off leaving the stunned girl standing there unsure how to counter my response.

I jumped on my bike and to my amazement sped by a very surprised looking CJ. She had followed me to the parking lot but didn't catch me before I had left. She just stood there smiling with admiration. It was a weird meeting that would mark the beginning of yet another strange new journey in my very complex past. CJ would in time help me to change many hearts and minds regarding those who live alternative lifestyles.

For now, however, I still had a Key that needed a new holder, an Interim to please, finals on the horizon, a temple to build, a circle to open and heal, revenge to plot, work to finish, and a home to prepare for my family. It seemed like a there simply was not enough time in the day that summer.

Thursday the 9th was the new moon that month. I had promised Linda she would receive her white cord initiation if she came to the Esbat. I knew I would have to move the Coven immediately now that Mistress Circe was angry at everyone over my gifted lands. I had decided despite my very overloaded schedule that this weekend I would begin to clear a spot for the temple. We would all meet there, and

I would build the temple around the circles we would caste through the summer. No more Esbats or Sabbats were to be held in that tainted shop. While I visited with Mary and my children that day, I told her to spread the word to the Coven members. We were meeting at the land and raising a new member. I also asked her to get a list of all names of persons who had applied for membership but were denied by Mistress Circe. I wanted everyone to vote on who could attend from that list. If their name appeared on the list but was denied I wanted to know why. Mary nodded. I had begun the open invites to grow our Coven.

Mary smiled when she realized I was doing what Mistress Circe had prevented. "Mother, it is about damned time. Our circle needs hearts. Some of the would-be initiates are really devout. Circe had no business denying them the white cord."

I smiled calmly. "No reason to rehash a past that cannot be changed daughter Mary. Just call the members, find out who qualifies, meet and vote. Then when I visit this Friday, I will have a list of the accepted for me. I will need phone numbers. I will personally invite the new ones for their year and one day try outs. If they survive until Beltane next year, we will grant them white cords. Also prepare everyone for the initiation of Linda. She has asked without fail for three years. She qualifies for the white cord now. I will encourage all the potential circle members to attend a full year of the Wheel, even at Springfields. It is only right they see what they are getting into before they take the cord of the initiate."

Mary's eyes went wide. "Oh Mother, you are our prayers answered. We all have wanted so much to grow but, well, you are right. The past is done. You said you will begin to clear this Saturday on the land?"

I laughed. "Yeah, but Daughter, it will take me months to finish that temple. I hope everyone is okay with casting circles out in the open. If it is raining, we will just have to work it out. Without a roof it is the way it goes. I am only one person, and I only had enough to buy the post for the frame of the temple to the Goddess. So, it will happen, but slowly."

She nodded. "We all understand, Mother. It will be amazing no doubt. I will make the calls, get your list, and prepare everyone for Linda's initiation."

I started to leave but stopped. "Daughter, I almost forgot. I need a Maiden for the circle. You are the best suited for the task. Will you honor me?"

Mary looked at the floor tears welling in her eyes. "Yes Mother. I never thought you'd ask. Thank you for allowing me the duties of Maiden."

I chuckled. "Oh Daughter Mary, I only facilitate what the Goddess asks. You are the best heart for the job. I will ask that James stand as Summoner for the circle unless you can see reason otherwise?"

She nodded. "He is the perfect choice, Mother. He will be honored, I am sure."

I smiled. "Make sure to ask him for me. So Mote It Be. Merry Part, Maiden Mary."

She smiled back. "So Mote It Be Mother. Merry Part."

I pulled into Mistress Nikki's drive to find the lady home. I went inside to start my prep work. I had left a grocery list that morning for her to pick up the items I would need to make her the French meal. That night I made her a full French meal from hors d'oeuvres to dessert as she had commanded. The meal is forever stuck in my Looper thanks to the complexities and amount of mess I had to clean up that night before I headed to work: Melon Frappe, Chilled Melon, Consommé celestine (clear soup garnished with strips of savory pancakes), Omlette aux champignons (mushroom omelet), Spaghetti Napolitan (spaghetti in a tomato and garlic flavored sauce), Sole cubat (fillet of sole poached, dressed on a mushrooms puree and coated with a cheese sauce) and for dessert, Crepe suzette (pancakes in a rich fresh orange juice and flamed with brandy). Mistress Nikki was thrilled and ate every single bit of it. Well she shared the fish with the cats.

I continued with the list from the day before while I was cooking and noticed with great irritation that new items had been added. I cleaned all the litter boxes again too without being told by the way and PU. Once again Mistress Nikki had made a TV turkey dinner and left it on the table. Once again the cats had eaten every bit of it. I had to sit the taskmaster down and warn her that continuing to leave me without food and too many services would result in my terminating of her probationary period. I was not resting, had forgotten my medication twice, had not eaten in two days, and was filthy. She was not doing her job.

She apologized and promised to try harder. While she ate her French meal, she held me hostage at the table while she bored the shit out of me with a discussion regarding the fictional book she was reading. I of course complied and offered well thought out responses to her analysis of the story. I did my best not to fall asleep while she droned on. I was beyond exhausted. I started to notice while she was speaking that the webs of the tapestry were more visible than they had been in many months. I chalked it up to fatigue. Again, I am not real reality based.

Finally, eleven o'clock had arrived. I left my Mistress well satisfied with a full belly and ultra clean house. My energy was spent. I prayed to the Goddess that no work was waiting for me at the funeral home that night.

I arrived to see Pat's car in the darkened drive. I sighed, realizing that there was sure to be more drama regarding last night's little scene. I seriously thought about driving back to Carter to use the pay phone so I could call in sick. However, I got off the bike, took a breath and went inside.

Pat was cleaning the embalming table. I looked around relieved to see no further patrons taking it easy while waiting for my attendance.

"You did my work for me, didn't you," I said realizing that it was very unlikely he came all that way to just scrub down the table.

He nodded. "Yeah, just finished the two stacked up waiting on you. You look tired, Psycho. I got this tonight. If you want to head home, I got this covered."

I sighed. "I am very tired, Pat. I will be happy to take you up on your offer. Have a good night boss." I turned to leave but I knew it wasn't going to be that easy.

"Psycho, about that business with Nikki yesterday, I am sorry she involved you," he said to my back as I headed to the door.

I waved. "Don't care, Pat. I don't want to know. Have a great night, thanks for the favor boss." I was not in the mood to deal with whatever bullshit he was selling.

I was getting on my Motorpsycho when Pat came running out of the funeral home and blocked my path to leave. "Psycho wait. Please, I need your help with something. Don't go just yet."

"What do you want, Pat? Look I am tired. Please leave me alone. Whatever this is about it can wait, right?" I already had a bad feeling it was something he didn't believe could wait.

"I need you to have a talk with Nikki about, uhm, sex. I want you to explain to her about how it works." He looked at the ground in genuine shame.

My jaw dropped. "Are you fucking serious. What the hell, Pat. She has a mother. She has you, and apparently you are more than happy to teach her hands on." I started the bike ready to run this idiot over if he didn't move.

He looked up startled that I didn't just agree to this weird request. "Violet refuses to talk to her and she keeps crying when I try to tell her that this stuff is normal. She has so much respect for you. You are her only friend, Psycho. She will listen to you. Please do this favor for me. I will lower the amount I charge you in the work guardianship arrangement. Please, I need your help."

Now he had my attention. My court order demanded that I have a work guardian that I had to pay out of my own pocket with any employment I acquired. Pat had been charging me a ton of money from my paycheck just to come by and make sure my work was not tainted by psychosis and I was not threatening the public. If he was willing to lower his take of my hard-earned cash, I was ready to listen. I killed the motor.

"How much and what do I have to do? I refuse to talk this simpleton into fucking you, Pat. That is immoral and downright disgusting. You should be ashamed of yourself subjecting her to oral sex as it is," I said very abruptly.

He snorted. "I am marrying the girl, Psycho. How are we supposed to have kids if she can't have intercourse with her husband."

I rolled my eyes. "I have two kids, Pat. How the fuck is she going to raise babies? Being a mother is hard as hell. She is just a kid herself and can never grow up. You have no business making children with her much less making her suck your nasty ass dick."

He stomped his foot. "Don't judge me. Look, do you want to work out a drop in my fee to do this thing for me or not?"

I looked at the bike handle bars. "Yeah, okay what are you offering and what do I have to do for it."

He smiled. "That's better. I want you to give her a full discussion about sex, what it is, what to expect and what she is supposed to do. For that I will cut the fee by one hundred a pay period."

I snorted. "For how long? What if she doesn't listen to me?"

Pat laughed. "She will listen to you, and for good. Come on, Psycho. It is a good deal, and you know it."

I glared at him through the darkness. "Like hell it is. I will take your deal. Bring her by tomorrow night and I want your agreement in writing Pat."

He laughed. "Don't trust me?"

I started the bike again. "You are bringing your girlfriend to me so I can have a talk about the birds and bees, Pat. You are offering to cut my court ordered employment fee. That is a challenging thing to justify in front of the court, it is so insane. I don't trust anyone. I have been fucked over enough to know all of you sons-of-bitches are looking for a way to get what you want without paying up. You put it in writing or no deal. See you tomorrow. I am going to bed." I left him standing there looking grateful. What an asshole.

I drove back to Mistress Nikki's house to find she was still up reading. When I walked in, she appeared surprised.

"Home so soon? Did they fire you? If they did, they would be idiots. You are a great worker." She narrowed her eyes.

I shook my head. "No. Sometimes I don't have a lot of work. It varies. Look Mistress, I am tired. Would you mind if I laid down on the couch to sleep? It has been a couple of days. I am beat to hell."

She gasped. "Oh I hadn't realized that you work the graveyard shift, then go to school all day, and serve me all afternoon. Wait, when do you sleep?"

I chuckled. "Good question Mistress."

She looked at the couch she was sitting on. "Well, I am not ready for bed, Psycho. Guess you will just have to sit and talk to me until I am ready."

My eyes went wide. "Uhm, Mistress, I don't mean to be insolent, but I just told you, I can't continue anymore. I am tired. If I don't rest, I could be injured getting to class tomorrow. I have finals coming up and other duties outside your home to attend this weekend. I need to sleep now."

She snorted. "You need a bath, and to eat. Didn't you tell me that earlier? Well, go into the kitchen and fix yourself something. Bring it here and eat while I talk with you. Then when that is done go take a shower. Then I will be ready for bed. You can rest on the couch when I am done with it."

I looked at the clock. "It is midnight Mistress. I must be ready for class and out the door by no later than seven. That is not even a full night's rest if I hit the sofa now."

She glared at me. "You want me to provide my end of the services. Then you do what I say. Go eat, then shower. No arguments, Psycho. Do it now. You will get a few hours. Seems to me you have been doing it this way for a while now. Don't try to shortchange me thinking I am ignorant. You had this schedule before me and a Master before me too."

I wanted to beat this woman to a bloody pulp, but she had me dead to rights. I grumbled but went into the kitchen and grabbed a can of chicken noodle soup. I returned and was bored to tears with Mistress Nikki's latest discussion of yet another fantasy sci-fi book. I don't like fantasy or sci-fi for obvious reasons. My whole fucking life is like a scene from the Matrix or the Twilight Zone. I don't need anything to add to my nightmarish existence.

When I had finished, I went and took the blasted shower. When I came out to dry off with my towel, I nearly had a heart attack. Mistress Nikki was there staring at me from the doorway.

"You scared the shit out of me, Mistress. Do you need something," I said while wrapping the towel around my naked unit.

She looked at the floor. "Yes. I want you to remove the towel and let me get a look at you."

I looked at the floor. "Excuse me? I don't understand." What the hell was this happy bullshit about?

Mistress Nikki stepped inside the bathroom then shut the door behind her. "I said I want to see you naked. Now drop the towel and come over here so I can see."

I shook my head. "Why? You are a girl. I don't have a damned thing you don't have."

She laughed. "That is not true. I don't have a twenty-two-year-old supple body. I see you have tattoos. I didn't know that. I want to see what else there is to this package deal. If I am going to purchase that Key, I want to know what I am getting."

"Mistress, the special services of the collar are reserved for a one time call out when the probationary period is over. You are asking for privileges that are not yours yet." I backed up just a bit in case this got ugly. Once again I was surprised by a straight woman looking to take a step on the other side of the fence.

Mistress Nikki looked hard at me. "I am not trying to sleep with you, yet. I want to see what I am going to have when I get that Key. I have decided to buy it. I love this service you provide and I am keeping you. I have even started to make arrangements for your children. They can move in as soon as this silly auction business is over. I am not asking to touch you or you to touch me. I just want a look. Now remove that towel so I can see what I want to see. I command it damn it."

I nodded then removed my towel feeling once again like livestock at some fucked up barn sale. She told me to turn around several times. She came closer and I backed away.

"Hold still I am trying to get a closer look," she said.

"No touching. I don't like to be touched," I said trying hard to hold still as she got too close for my comfort.

She reached out suddenly and snatched off my wig. "Ah, so Circe was telling the truth. You are indeed without locks. Interesting."

I grabbed my wig back angrily. "Are you done trying to humiliate me? Not going to work, Mistress. I am used to this bullshit. Now are we done here?"

She chuckled. "Well, even without hair you are indeed beautiful. I never thought of being with a woman before, but you have changed my mind. I could certainly learn to enjoy having you with me at night. It makes sense. That way I am not betraying my one and only. He wouldn't understand me taking another man to bed, but a girl, not the same thing."

I put my wig back on. "You are very strange Mistress. I should know. Now if you don't mind, I would like some privacy to dress now."

She reached out and grabbed my unit pulling me toward her and began forcing her mouth to mine.

I let out a yelp from the shock and pushed her back hard yelling, "Do not touch me. Get off me now."

She let me go and I fell to the floor from the force of my pulling away. "Psycho, please, I just wanted to have a kiss is all. It has been so long since anyone has kissed me." She turned around and left, closing the door behind her.

I sat on the floor panting in sheer terror. This lady was cracked in the head. I made a mental note that I would tell Mistress Circe not to include this one in the bidding. I wanted out already. She was overworking me, not allowing rest, not doing her job, and now tried to take services not earned yet. This was just not working out.

The next day, however, she had cleaned up her act. In the biggest rebound of bad behaviors I have ever witnessed, Mistress Nikki fixed her errors. Every day she left notes or called me at work to make sure I had eaten something and was taking my medications. She ordered bathing every night but never repeated her bad manners from that night. She began to decorate two rooms in her house and purchased beds for my children to stay with me when I was serving. She even told me that if she won the Key, she would put her cats in a separate part of the house so that the kids would be safe from the roaming felines.

More than that, she started demanding I get at least four hours of rest a night. I was ordered to sleep when I was not at the funeral home working. She also took me to every single appointment with Vocational Rehabilitation, the Probation Officer, and my Psychologist/Psychiatrist appointments. I still provided her services such as cooking and cleaning, but she lightened the load only asking for what I could finish in the time allotted me with my schedule.

By Saturday I had started to feel better about Mistress Nikki. I drove out to the land that I had purchased for the Coven. The Quikrete and foundation studs had been delivered by the local building supply store and dropped off on the ground along with a post hole digger and shovel. I had purchased all the items earlier in the week for this groundbreaking for the future Green Temple of the Coven.

I had just started a hole for the first post when I heard vehicles driving down the very remote dirt road that led to this place. To my amazement I saw the red van and ten other cars pull up. My coven and the twenty members I had called to invite to join the Esbat that Thursday, including my Goddess Linda, got out of those varied cars. Everyone walked up laughing at the shocked look on my face when trucks began to arrive loaded down with tin, nails, and more building studs. My members and future members had come with everything they could find, buy, borrow or salvage ready to build their temple in the wilderness.

My Summoner James took the post hole digger from my hands and said, "We told you we would all help, Mother. Now let us males do the heavy stuff. You ladies go unload the trucks. We brought food for lunch, and no one is leaving until this Temple is finished."

Everyone clapped and cheered at his words. I aided the true hearts that day as our Temple was built ground up by every hand that would embrace the creation of the circle birthed by the Priestess Arodia. Young and old pitched in. Stories were told, songs were sung as each member sweated in the early summer heat, smiling as they worked. These small-town people were used to hard labor, none had much money, but everyone donated something.

Everyone helped build that temple in one way or another. Even the smallest child aided, including my own, by collecting stones to mark a circle within. It was a sight that to this day brings tears of gratitude to my eyes. My gift of love had healed the broken hearts of the Coven. My copulation with my Priest during the Great Rite had conceived seventeen new children.

Twenty-five devout Pagan people and their children erected a Temple to the God and Goddess that day with their bare hands before my brother went to his rest behind the sleeping giants. As promised to Mother Delleh, the floor was Mother Earth and the roof and walls just enough to protect the circle items from the tears of the Gods. A large door that didn't touch the ground was fashioned to open and close easily. It was built with the idea of allowing for the beasts on the ground to easily find shelter if they needed during a storm. It was built of tin and wood. It was not meant to stand the test of the ever-powerful elements. We intended for it to be slowly overtaken by them if the day were to pass that our Coven was no more.

The final touches were the planting of trees, grass and brush the next day. Everyone came once more. This time bringing a tree or native shrub or even just a packet of grass seed. The ground was sown with the many types of vegetation, but the harvest would be of the spirits of those loving people.

James and Chuck had spent the entire night working on a wooden sign, Lisa and Tracy had burned the words, "*All are Welcome Here*" on it. Not a single person there, man, woman, even the children, had a dry eye as the sign was placed above the makeshift doorway. Our Temple of Green was complete. The Coven was healed and was now ready to embrace its destiny within the Sisterhood of the Green Rings. Everyone was excited and could not wait to hold the very first new moon Esbat that Thursday night. No one was more excited than Linda. She was finally going to get her white cord.

I had of course tested her first to be sure she knew the ways and manners of the circle well enough to be included in rituals. The rule of any Coven in Wicca is that for one year and one day a person was supposed to watch the rituals and learn the wheel. It is the time for the would be initiate to decide if this sort of thing is for them. They can walk away, not show up or stay without anyone saying a word. They also cannot be included within the circle during ritual. After that if they choose, they can be initiated as a first level Wiccan. They then are entitled to participate in rituals and rites.

The reason for these strict rules is not to keep people out. It is twofold. First the person needs to be sure they want to worship as a Wiccan. Some Christian religions believe that to become Polytheistic means you are forever damned. So, if you come, worship the God and Goddess circle, then change your mind, uh oh for you. By only watching but being kept out, you can still back out without endangering your future options if you believe otherwise. Now the second reason is that Wiccans do believe they are working with the sacred. To bring a novice within a sacred rite where deities are being invoked would be disaster. Bad manners or poor behaviors could insight anger from the Gods themselves. Therefore, only those who have studied proper procedure can be involved with such serious matters such as rituals and rites.

Linda had been a solo practicing Wiccan for over three years. She knew proper procedure, rituals and rites, and many invocations. Due to this, she was given special consideration as I myself had been given in my ascension to High Priestess. At the new moon Esbat Thursday night, we would embrace my Goddess as our Sister and Daughter to claim this devout Wiccan as our own within the Circle of the Green Rings. The other sixteen possible initiates were also excited. They would get to witness what they all hoped to achieve during Beltane in Springfields the following year. This was also to be my second raising of an initiate, remember Roary and I raised Circe and Roary's HPs, but my first for my own Coven. It was going to be an amazing night indeed.

Everything continued to go well with Mistress Nikki that week. The raising of the Green Temple had my spirits higher than normal when I suddenly began to see Simon again. At first just a glimpse of him walking behind trees, but by Wednesday night I could see him very clearly. There was no longer any doubt, prodromal had begun. My residual was over. I only had six months before the onset of acute psychosis would start again. I tried not to weep when Simon appeared. I didn't want him to think I didn't love him. However, he understood my despair at seeing him once more. The nightmare had begun again. Schizophrenia would try to rob me of all I had built, and believe me, it would do it without even breaking a sweat.

Chapter 21: Master Marie & Prodromal Paranoia
The Fall of Mistress Circe

Things are changing fast now. No more forgettable cemetery, homeless, schizophrenic banging her head into lockers. Now a mother of two children, oh wait, the mother of many children. Oh, my goth. How the hell did that happen? Well, there is no one better suited to help guide others out of the deepest nights in life than one who has adapted to seeing in the dark.

Mother Delleh was wise in her choice of Priest and Priestess. She has suffered through poor health but watches her children begin to grow strong, healthy, and tall. She is immensely proud the Goddess granted her time on this plane to witness her legacy fulfilled. Rain clouds fill her tired eyes as the storm of the void builds on the horizon. Her Wheel is turning, her Winter is coming. Every heart in the Green Rings beats for her, as hers slows. The greedy Crone of Gold watches with hopes that a reaping will be right around the corner. Roary and Arodia must hurry. Father time waits for no one, and the cup will soon be broken, but who's cup? The Crone may find she was not as clever as she thought. Those crows circling may not have been for the Mother, but for her. Karma never forgets a debt owed.

The time of Mistress Nikki is coming to an end. Her reign was marked by many wins and spiritual changes. One of them is dark. An old demon is stirring within Psycho once again. It is stretching its claws. It treats her mind like the Mistress's cats treat her furniture. The battle has begun for control of the shards. This time there is so much at stake, but there is no way out. Psycho will have to prepare for the loss by trusting those around her with all that has been built. To do this she will show the Coven her true self. The devout hearts will find beauty and wisdom in her scars. As the tapestry webs grow more evident, so does the resolve of the hearts to survive.

The beginning of a nightmare as soul destructive as the beast schizophrenia itself has engulfed Psycho. She will try to stop someone from taking the wrong road. The one that leads to a slow death. She will fight with all she has for this simple soul but will not be able to hold off the brutality of a neglectful world. Once again, it is proven to her that the broken like herself do not matter to normals. Unless they are willing to bend over and take it up the rear end.

A new Master is rising. Master Marie will put a song in Psycho's ears. She teaches her the proper way to dance around despair. As the God comes to his maturity, High Priestess Arodia will find her own. After all, no one knows how to Loop into a perfect circle like she does.

Ready for Master number seven? We knew you would be. Tonight, bring your dancing shoes, your favorite tunes, oh, and take some Ibuprofen just in case that bum knee of yours acts up. Don't worry if you only have a dad's wedding moves. No one will be watching except for us, and we never judge. We will be dancing the hours away because Master Marie loves the nightlife.

"Do all of you believe in magic? All of you should. Look around you. These walls, this roof, was created by the most powerful of spells. You wanted to honor the Gods. Now, from just a whispered prayer, out of nothing, there is such a place. We built this temple with our own hands, together. That my children is real magic.

However, it is not this temple of tin and wood that is the true honor to the Old Ones. Feel the pounding in your chest and the heartbeat next to you. Each of you has found the Priest or Priestess within. Any and every one of you could stand in my place should I ever fall. Each of you is a powerful leader in his or her own right. By your own actions you have all proven that you have learned the most important things about living life as a Wiccan.

You have found belief in yourself, fellowship without judgement and demonstrated the perseverance to do what it takes to make your world a better place in perfect love and in perfect trust. The God and Goddess surely celebrate tonight at the sight of so many of their children who have found their way home. All are welcome here. Blessed Be."

High Priestess Arodia's speech to the Green Temple Community during the New Moon Esbat/Temple consecration and initiation of Linda – May 9, 1994

The night of the New Moon Esbat that May was a deep and dark night. I drove the Motorpsycho down the desolate dirt road that led to the temple. We had planned the ritual for ten that night due to the work schedules of most of the members and hopefuls. I had the night off from the funeral home. I had known about this date for over three months. An initiation would take time, and as High Priestess I needed time to meditate, clear my mind, and purify first.

Linda would finally get her white cord this night. She had waited for so long, I wanted this to be special. A true gift for one who I adored. She had given me so much, it seemed so ridiculously small a token in return to grant her what was rightfully hers anyway. Despite my belief that a piece of white rope was never enough, I was going to do my absolute best to make it a memory worth reliving until the Gods called her home.

When I pulled up, I found my devout original members already there in the red van. I dreaded having to deal with our Crone, but regardless of mundane hurts I would overlook them. In the sacred space of the Temple, I would need to remember spiritually I only had to answer for my own behaviors. If anyone was going to act an ass, it certainly would not be me.

I walked into the Temple of Green. My Maiden Mary putting all the ritual items for the ceremony and circle casting in their proper spots. Summoner James was prepping by practicing his calling of the people to ritual. Lisa and Tracy were playing with Delilah and the children. Chuck was nailing up candle holders to the inner studs so there would be enough light to see. I strained my eyes through the darkened space, but my seeking did not yield the Crone.

"Has anyone seen Mother Circe," I asked, still looking to be sure I was not missing the slight woman in a corner somewhere.

Mary frowned. "Mother Circe said that the circle is not to be caste here tonight but in the shop. If we don't come, then she says we are all dead to her."

I looked at the ground. "Maiden are you certain she meant that? I understand it is hard for her to let go of her seat of power. Perhaps she is just having difficulty adapting to her new place as an Elder." Tracy interrupted me.

"I apologize Mother Arodia, but Crone Circe meant it. I was there. She spit at Sister Mary and I when we told her we built this temple. She said our Priestess is a whore and insane. She told us that you need an exorcism and hobbles for your ankles. She said you aren't worth pissing on if you caught fire." Tracy looked down, appearing ashamed to have repeated those words.

Every member looked sick as they listened. Finally, Chuck cleared his throat and said, "Well Mother Arodia is right. Crone Circe is having trouble adapting. I will say it if no one else will. It is not just her losing her seat of power. She is pissed she was stopped from robbing our pockets in the seat of our pants."

Delilah snickered at that till Mary shot her a warning look.

I sighed. "I apologize children for Crone Circe's foul words. I will not deny I have been cursed by schizophrenia.

All of you know that. All of you had to watch my incarceration last year for behaviors from symptoms of it. As for the other accusation, I suppose if I were a Christian, I could be such. I don't live with my husband. I don't take lovers based on gender or even desire. I am not Christian. I am Pagan. My husband was united with me in a legal way not in a spiritual one. Therefore, I am breaking no laws of the God or Goddess."

Lisa frowned. "Mother Arodia, forgive me, but I believe I speak for everyone here when I say Mother Circe has no right to say shit. No one here has lived a life of innocence when it comes to sex or relationships. No one here can say what they do now. Neither can she. She claims a husband that belongs to Maiden Mary's bed but then she takes you to her own. Then, she beats the terror out of you for being sick. We saw her abuse of you, Mother. You were so good to her, but she repaid you with a leash. She is disgusting. You have no need to apologize to any of us or anyone for being sick. We are the ones who should be sorry for standing around and letting it happen. I stand here ashamed to know I stood there and did nothing. Yet, you still love all of us so much you bought this land, slept with a man you never met in public, and come here tonight showing nothing but tolerance for someone who is evil to you." She looked at the ground tearing up as she said that.

I for the first time in my whole shitty life suddenly knew what to do when this kind of emotion was being heaped my way. I thank the Goddess for helping me to understand what they all needed that night. It was time to heal their broken hearts and forget the past.

I walked over to Lisa and took her hand in mine. "Don't cry, Daughter. This is my path to travel, just as you have your own. We all will have pain in this life, doubt, and fear. That is what we are here for. That is why we built this Temple. To comfort each other when the things that cannot be stopped come to break our hearts. I want you to smile, be happy, feel peace within these walls. No guilt or doubt is allowed. In this Temple we are one. If you are sad and weak, your brothers and sisters will loan you their smiles and strength. Our circle is never ending. Now everyone, come together we will hold each other's hands and unite our energies. Caste away all old hurts, forget what was and begin what will be. Let this night be the night we are reborn as true children of the God and Goddess."

Everyone came and we did as I instructed, holding hands in a circle focusing our hearts on our healing of all the hurts. Lots of tears were shed as they cast away their pains and doubts. Each member was given the right to take a new name. They all did happily. Most had already desired one for many years, but Mistress Circe would not allow it. Once this pre-ritual uniting of all the old Coven members was done. We were all strong, new, and ready to caste our circle and perform our New Moon rituals without any dust clinging from the Circle of Gold. Now we were truly a Circle of Green.

NOTE: *Taking a working Pagan/magical/Wiccan name is a way of allowing someone to be their true spiritual self by breaking away from the mundane trials of daily life. In the world of Wicca, it grants the practitioner a marker in life of achievement, honor, and respect. To* *not allow it is to hinder the spiritual growth of those who desire, are ready for and need it to feel more inner peace in a sacred place. Mistress Circe was beyond cruel to forbid the practice. From that day forward no one had to take one, but everyone can earn the right to have one.*

The hopefuls and Linda all arrived just as instructed twenty minutes before ten. I left the temple with Lisa and Mary while Tracy and James made sure all the watchers (want to be initiates) had comfortable places to sit. The elders of the seventeen were seated in chairs donated by various people. They young and middle aged sat on the ground. All were to keep out of the circle itself. They could watch but they could not enter until they were sure this was the path they were called to walk. Linda was taken to the inner part of the circle with Tracy, Deliliah, and Chuck.

Note: Their Wiccan names are private. Tradition dictates that if the name is not mine and they are not an elder I am not at liberty to share it. So, for this story they stay the name you already know them by.

I stood outside under the New Moon sky as my "Maidens" attended me while I meditated before casting the circle and drawing down the Moon. I heard the Mother's voice on the wind say to me: "Be truthful. Do not keep secrets in my sacred place."

I opened my eyes startled. This was not the voice of the Looper, not Simon, not any voice I had ever heard before. I was aware prodromal had started but what if, just what if?

Mary and Lisa noticed my sudden look of surprise. "What is it, Mother," asked Lisa.

I looked at her suddenly understanding the voice. "I must enter this place without hiding my truths. I must be who I really am, Daughter." I took off my robe and wig, throwing them to the ground standing naked and bald before my two very stunned Maidens.

They didn't know I couldn't grow hair because of the poisoning. They had seen me Sky Clad already. What they had never seen was the heavy scars on my head that told a tale of abuse, neglect, disease, and survival. Mary covered her face weeping.

Lisa tearing up also said, "Mother Arodia, we never knew you are so beautiful."

I smiled at her then took her hand. "I embrace my fate. Now each of you must do the same. No secrets, no lies. Here we are all one. Remember to draw strength when you have none but lend when you have much."

She nodded then removed her robe. Mary did the same. The three of us entered the Temple Sky Clad without fear of what the others would think or say. Tracy, Chuck, James, Delilah, and Linda stood there in the circle with their eyes wide. Not at our naked units but were staring at my bald scarred head. My Maidens took their places without a sound. I took up the salt and Athame to cast the circle. Behind me the remaining members took off their robes as if they just understood the meaning of this strange entrance. I began to trance but saw each watcher also begin to disrobe without shame or fear.

The entire Temple was Sky Clad before I had even closed the circle. Even my Goddess Linda herself. She stood in the center, her eyes wide in amazement. She knew I was bald. She had picked up my displaced wig a dozen times at the jail when I was in a psychotic fit. She told me later she was in awe of the aura that I seemed to emit from my unit as I walked in the door. I always chalked her vision of that night to the excitement and nervousness she must have felt being initiated. However, who am I to question what another person perceives they see?

Linda's initiation came at the end of the New Moon Ritual. She had waited while the watchtowers were called and the Moon Drawn down. The members lined up and birthed her through as they had done for me almost two years before. I was the last to grab her hands and pull her between my legs. Once she was through the line, so to speak, she stood up dancing excitedly telling me she couldn't take the pressure of being so close to her dream come true. Everyone laughed at her sexual innuendo as I took down the circle. We all re-dressed in our robes (or if a watcher, in their street clothes) still chuckling at Linda's randy comments about finally getting between my legs.

NOTE: *Beauties we are not Christians so such sexually charged or even humorous talk is allowed when we engage in rituals. Only during the most sacred rites do things have to be profoundly serious. Any other time, a good laugh is not only enjoyed but encouraged. People*

miss their lines, say silly things on accident or even make
sexual insinuations during early and late parts of circle
work. It is part of the freedom of being Pagan. You can be
human, not stuck in the mud of humorless reverence all
the time. After all, we are imperfect. That is what makes
us each uniquely beautiful.

Tracy had made Linda a robe of Maroon and I granted her the white cord of the first-year initiate. She squealed and hugged me tightly thanking me dozens of times for accepting her into the family. I caused further clamors of laughter throughout the Coven by stating that if she didn't stop squeezing me she would hurt the baby I had just conceived with her during the initiation.

I was asked at the meal about the deep scars on my head by a few of the non-members. I didn't lie. I told them they were caused by numerous incidents of self-abuse due to the symptoms of psychotic episode. No one got upset. Most were very empathetic, and some told stories of their own relatives struggles with the disease or other mental illness.

In that temple, that moonless night a real family was born. Each heart was beating in unison for the good of all. Only initiations would be sky clad in the future. Had you been there on May 9th you would have understood like those folks did the true meaning of the words in perfect love and in perfect trust. All seventeen watchers would become full Coven members before the year was up, most for life. The circle had just grown from eight to twenty-five with over twenty-five children under the age of fourteen.

We had just blown up into a strong Wiccan Community overnight. This my beauties, is something that to this day I still cannot believe.

NOTE: *In the middle of nowhere, southern, and backward, somehow the Goddess had seen fit to call that many open hearts to one place deep in the woods. They came to listen to the words of a well-known, allegedly violent, homeless, disabled, schizophrenic High Priestess. Amazing, incredible, mind blowing, beautiful, destiny for those of you who are wondering, Yes, that temple and that Circle is still there to this very day. Those twenty-five children grew up, including my own. Yes, my grandkids are in that Coven and had children who are now the next generation. New leaders are raised every decade. So, the problems of the Coven are always with the youth who can adapt to them. Another change implemented by Priest Roary and Priestess Arodia.*

PS: It makes me smile to think Mother Delleh would have been so proud to know her legacy of love still lives on. She is remembered through the stories I told of her in the Book of Shadows the coven gave me when I ascended. The gift given in the Van. It is the Circle's High Priestess's cannon now. Each new leader is given my book to study and add their own story. That book, and the land are my own legacy and gift to the Wiccans who became the family I never had. Mistress Circe's greed backlashed into something beyond incredible. Till the day she died she never forgave any of us for it. Stick with me, this amazing story will continue. We have only just begun.

The New Moon initiation and Green Temple complete, it was time for me to refocus on my final exams for the semester. I had also been waiting for a conversation with Nikki as per my written agreement with her fiancé Pat. I didn't agree with the contents of this so-called talk with the very intellectually disabled girl, but I have my way of spinning things just like the liar Pat did. Nikki had already missed four attempts to meet with her. I was ready to give up when that Friday night I heard a knock on the door at the funeral home. I had just finished up work on my customer and was cleaning up for the night. I didn't need to look to see who it was. Only Nikki would knock on a door meant for corpse delivery at two o'clock in the morning.

I opened the door and rushed her into the casket room. I sat her down on one of the fluffy couches, then sat next to her trying to think of what to say to someone in her IQ range that would help her to understand the nature of the act of sexual congress. This was something I found very wrong. The girl was not of a high enough intelligence to grant consent as far as I was concerned. I had already asked Linda to investigate the laws regarding consensual sex with someone with low intelligence. She had not gotten back to me. So, I decided to see how much damage had already been done, then go from there. I am a smart girl, I would figure this out, right?

"So, Nikki, how are you and Pat doing," I said looking at the floor trying to decide how to bring up this most private act with the child. Well, she had the mind of one even if she was twenty-three.

"Good, Psycho. Thank you for telling him to call me when I bit his wiener. I knew you could get him to stop being mad at me for that," she said smiling sweetly as she always did.

I winced at that. "Uhm yeah. I wanted to talk to you about that, Nikki. You said you put his private in your mouth?"

She nodded. "Yep. But it tasted yucky and spit stuff out. I won't do that anymore."

I sighed in relief. "Ah, that is good to hear. You don't have to do that stuff for Pat or anyone, do you understand? If you don't like that kind of thing, you say no. Tell them I said you could say it and if they want to be mad, have them come see Psycho, even if it is Pat, okay." I looked to see if she heard me.

She smiled happily. "Yes. I hear you, Psycho. You would tell Pat not to do that anymore and he would stop being angry like last time right?"

I nodded. "Damn right. He told me to tell you to send him to me if he ever does that again," I lied.

I no longer gave two shits about the money I had to pay Pat. I couldn't just sit there while this poor girl was forced to give a blow job she didn't want to give. That is rape, damn it.

I then looked at her hard. "Nikki, if Pat or anyone tries to put their privates into your privates, you can say no to that too. If they get mad, send them to talk to Psycho, but

171

first call Dennis and Boyd, okay? Don't take any baths or wash your privates until Dennis and Boyd say it is fine to do that. Do you understand?" I looked and felt my heart break as the smile melted from Nikki's face.

"It hurts, Psycho. Pat puts his privates into my butt. It hurt and I cried and cried. But he said I have to let him do that or he won't love me anymore." She started to tear up.

I looked at the ceiling feeling I may cry too.

I heard what she said but I didn't, I couldn't, I wouldn't accept the truth. "You mean he puts his part into your girl part. There is a place there for his part, but you don't have to do that if you don't want to Nikki. He is lying to you."

She screamed out. "No, Psycho. He puts it in my butt. Not my pee-pee. He says he cannot put it in my pee-pee until we are married. He makes me do it. I cry but he pushes my face in the bed and tells me to shut up. But it hurts so bad, Psycho. It hurts."

I held the girl as she wept, finally breaking down myself. Pat was anally raping Nikki to keep her virginity intact in some twisted attempt to say she was untouched on their wedding night or for a more diabolical reason than I wasn't ready to admit to just yet. This poor child was enduring humiliation, pain, and unnatural practice without any understanding of any of it. I cried with her because I felt responsible for not beating the shit out of this creep the second I realized he was dating her. She didn't have the

172

ability to consent, and he was like everyone else, when given the chance to take advantage, he did.

"Shh, there, there Nikki. It is going to be okay. Let's go talk to Violet. We can make him stop hurting you," I said while wiping tears from her pretty big eyes.

She grimaced. "No, Psycho. He will leave me if I don't. He said he would. I love him. I want it to stop but I want to marry Pat."

I couldn't believe this. "Nikki, he is hurting you. He doesn't love you if he is not listening when you say stop. Let me help you make him stop."

She shook her head violently, "No, no, no, no. I love Pat. He will leave me if I make him stop. He told me so."

"Okay, sweetie, okay. I won't tell Violet. Look, I will talk to Pat. I will tell him to stop, okay? Will you let me do that?" I looked into her eyes.

She nodded. "Yes, please Psycho? Tell him I love him, but it hurts so much. Tell him not to leave me. You will cast a spell, right?"

I nodded, smiling through my own tears. "You bet your baby blue eyes I will, Nikki. Now, calm down. How did you get here?"

She wiped her eyes. "Mommy brought me. She is in the car. Is Pat here? He said he and you are working so hard nowadays. He is never home at night because of all the work."

I frowned. "He said that did he? Well, I will see if he can get off work more often too. Alright, I am going to get you a coke. You stay here and wait for me? Promise?" I smiled as she nodded.

I walked out of the room right to the parking lot to confront the waiting Violet in her car. She was shocked to see my angry unit as I pounded on her window. She was asleep while waiting in the parking lot.

She rolled down her window. "Oh, Psycho. You and Nikki done talking already?"

I growled. "You God damned right I am, Violet. Pat is sodomizing Nikki. You need to call the cops. The girl is in tears. Where the fuck are you when this has been going on. Pat is a fucking pig."

Violet's eyes went wide. "What? Sodomizing? Are you sure? I mean he promised to wait until marriage."

I snorted. "To what, Violet, sodomize her? Damn you. The girl is a mental midget. Didn't you realize Pat was only there to fuck her. He is never going to marry her. He is only fucking her up the ass to keep from getting her pregnant, so he won't have a kid running around. Wake up. He is a fucking rapist of the worst kind. Call the fucking cops or I will."

Violet sneered at me. "You will mind your business, Psycho. Pat is a good man. I don't agree with what he and Nikki are doing but that is not my business either. He will marry her, and I can finally get on with my life. I have

174

waited for twenty-three years to be free of this manacle. They will get married soon. You need to butt out. Nikki is a grown woman."

My mouth flew open in shock at this so-called loving mother. "Are you fucking kidding me. You are going to sit back and call Nikki a grown woman. She is fucking retarded, Violet. She cannot care for herself."

"Psycho, what is going on? You don't mean that, do you?" I turned around to see Nikki standing there looking confused.

"Oh shit. Nikki, honey I am so sorry, I didn't mean, shit." I was stomping on the ground realizing she had just heard me yell she is retarded. Always look behind you when talking about someone even if it is in their best interest.

Violet looked at Nikki who was about to break up and cry again at what she heard me yell. "Get in the car, Nikki. Psycho is no friend of yours."

Nikki got into the car despite my fumbling apology that I didn't mean for her to hear me say it. I did mean it, and I refused to lie. To my discredit by the way, I maybe should have lied that one time.

Once in the car, Violet peeled out leaving me there cursing myself for not setting my foot down from the get-go. It was then I realized Violet didn't want to take care of Nikki. She didn't care if Nikki was anally raped if it got her out of guardianship for good. Violet viewed Nikki as a burden. Pat viewed her as a plaything. No one was going to step in to help this pitiful thing who was being raped. Not even her own fucking mother.

My chest was aching, and I didn't even know why I should care. She was not my friend; she was just an annoying girl I knew once. Oh no, Nikki was me. I fell to my knees in the parking lot in a full-on crying jag.

Nikki was just like me. She was chronically disabled, forever dependent on the honesty and kindness of others. Without help, she would die. Nikki was having to submit to sexual torture because it was her only hope of finding someone to look after her now that her mother was tired of it. No one cared because Nikki had nothing but that beautiful body and pretty face to offer. She didn't even have as much as I did. I too had been forced to submit to sexual acts fouler than most can even imagine. I couldn't just sit there and let this happen. I couldn't save myself, but I wanted to save her. She deserved better.

I pulled myself together and went to call Pat. He was first on my list. Maybe, just maybe his, house may burn down. Could happen, couldn't it?

"So, how'd she take it," Pat asked appearing excited to hear my voice.

"Apparently up the ass, Pat. That is how you give it to her isn't it," I roared into the phone.

There was silence.

"You motherfucking son of a whore. So, help me if I ever see you again I will bend you over one of these tables and shove the embalming hose up your ass. See how you like it, pig. Keep you fucking hands off Nikki. I am calling the police. Sodomy is a crime, Pat, you are fucking dead." I slammed down the phone, then picked it up and threw it on the floor.

I calmed down best as I could. My next call was to my Goddess. I woke her up. I didn't care.

"Psycho, hey babe it is like two in the morning," said a sleepy sounding, Linda.

"Couldn't sleep thinking about you Goddess," I lied.

"Oh?" She suddenly sounded very awake.

"Okay I will cut to the chase. That retarded girl I was asking about, Nikki. She told me tonight that Pat is sexually abusing her in the worse way, Linda. How can I help her," I said no longer willing to play bullshit games.

Linda cleared her throat. "Uhm, okay yeah, I could understand you being upset, being you and all, I mean. Okay uhm, I looked it up and if the guardian consents, then there is nothing you can do unless the girl comes forward. Must be the victim. Just like in your case, Psycho. We all wanted to help but you wouldn't admit it was Julie, remember?"

I sucked in my breath realizing I just got bit in the ass by the very law that protected me long enough to run years before. "Shit. Just shit. I can't just sit by and do nothing."

"You had better, Psycho. Stay out of this. Now you know how Dennis, Boyd, and I felt. You have your own kids and future to consider. If this girl isn't reporting, and neither is mom, well everyone's hands are tied. I am sorry, Psycho. I know this must be hard to watch but, well that is the law," Linda said sounding sincerely apologetic.

"Yeah, I hear you. Thank you, Goddess. I will see you at Full Moon Esbat." I sighed thinking of the amount of time in prison I was going to get for murdering Pat.

"Hey, Psycho," I heard Linda call out.

"Yeah? Still here," I said but really, I wasn't.

"I mean it. Something happens to this guy; they will know it was you. After Christine's place went up in smoke, I know you are very smart, but don't play the odds anymore."

I smiled, "Why, Linda, whatever are you talking about? What fire?"

She growled through the phone. "That is why I love you so much, Psycho. Go to bed. Dream of me. Good night." She hung up.

I stood there trying to decide my next move. Pat had to pay, and he was not going to hurt Nikki anymore. But how? I would have to think a bit. In the meantime, I called my boss and left a message on his machine. I was demanding Pat be taken off as my work Master. I would accept a position under the other Master embalmer June. I informed them Pat would be removed or I would walk. The next day, my new Master mortician was re-assigned. Pat and I were no longer partners. For now, it was all I could do.

However, that night I began to have vicious nightmares of my own. Memories that had plagued me for a lifetime gained strength causing me to behave again in sleep terror behaviors. Mistress Nikki was forced to restrain me any time I went to sleep after I wrecked her living room in one of my nightmare rages. Prodromal was no longer deniable. I was becoming psychotic.

I didn't hear another word about the Pat and Nikki situation till the day of my finals. Word came down that Pat had broken off the engagement. He was not going to marry Nikki. Big fucking surprise. He was no longer welcome in the Jaimes home. Pat had been screwing around town for months telling Nikki he was at work with me. She found out. It was, I heard, an epic blow out between him and the thwarted Violet. I say she was thwarted because she was the one who was pushing that union more than anyone. Served her right. Nikki was safe, for now.

I took my finals and despite all the trauma of the last few weeks before them, aced every one of them. I was again straight A's for the semester. I again was announced in the hometown weekly wipe as Dean's List, all A's. My first year of college is done. I was a four pointer, top of my class. Now, I was starting to get noticed by professors and students alike. My second year would end up being something more amazing than I ever dreamed even in my deepest psychotic episodes. That is of course, in the coming chapters.

At home, Mistress Nikki had been keeping the pace with my constant daily needs. She had become a stellar Mistress without failing since the night she had ripped off my wig. She still bored the shit out of me with constant droning about sci-fi books she was reading but I had decided if she got the Key, she would make a fine Master.

Despite my change of heart about Mistress Nikki the final day of my probation with her had arrived. I was not happy about that. Not because I had to leave the next day and meet yet another potential, but because I feared she may now call on the special services of the collar. She had made it clear that night in the bathroom I was to be a stand in for her lost love. I should have been used to the bullshit by now but damn it I am still a human being. Having to provide this service to someone you don't like, find attractive, or really feel anything for, well let's just say it is not easy. Not even for a pro such as myself.

I was not working that night, so I didn't even have that excuse when she did indeed come calling. She was neither polite about it nor did she mince words. I was sitting on the sofa reading an article she wanted to discuss later thinking maybe I had gotten out of it, silly Psycho. Get with reality will you.

She walked in, giving me that same strange look I recalled from that bathroom stunt. "Psycho, I have now earned the special services I believe. I am ready to be served."

I looked up at her surprised. "Now? I thought you wanted to discuss this article?" I was looking around trying to find something to distract her. You'd think I would stop trying that stupid shit, it never works, but I always hoped it would.

"Later. I have talked to my husband. He understands. Now come on with me. I have waited long enough. I want to see you, but I also want to believe it is him with me too. Is that okay," she said looking at the floor.

I nodded, took a deep breath, and said, "Yes, whatever you want. You are the Mistress." I got up and did my duty as commanded.

Like the others I was stuck the whole night. Just like Mistress Circe she was selfish. She refused my request to receive service back. I was again dissatisfied. Not that I was too surprised. Mistress Nikki was not really into females or anyone other than herself for that matter. She just wanted to be pleasured. The acts of sexual congress are always one sided when the Master is treating sex like a right to my service rather than a true interest in me as a person. Truth is she had earned her rights by contract. It is alright of course that she didn't see me as human. I didn't like her either.

I didn't have to pry her off me as I left like the first one. I didn't leave to sobs as I did the second. Instead in true Mistress Nikki fashion she arrogantly told me she would see me soon.

"Oh, and when that Key is mine, you will kiss me when I tell you to Psycho. So, you had better get used to that right now." She glared as I started my bike.

She was still pissed I continued to refuse her advances for such abomination. I just nodded and sped off. I would never see Mistress Nikki again. Her thirty days of probation and one-night special services were the only time she even got close to holding my collar. Turns out she wasn't smart enough to outfox old Mistress Circe when the bidding went down. While I would have been okay with it had she won, I won't say I would have been glad. The first two were still better than this very strange lady. I never kept up with her or heard about her again. I assume she spent the rest of her life with her cats, and the memory of a lost love to keep her warm at night. Oh well, next.

Seventh Interim Master (Collar-No Key)
Master Marie: the Dance Queen
June 2nd to July 2nd, 1994

I called Mistress Circe from the pay phone at the Nights Service Station. I refused to go see her in person after the whole crystal chucking incident. She growled out the address to me on the phone, then spewed obscenities regarding the Green Temple, my parentage, and some other crap about my relationship to the devil. I couldn't deny she had me on that last one. I hung up on her.

I got on the Motorpsycho and headed to the same town where my yellow house and funeral home job was located.

At least I would be closer to home. I hoped she didn't have a bunch of cats, or any dead husbands, or TV dinners.

I pulled into the driveway of a single level handsome home of a very modern look. It was white with a black roof, and a closed in garage. Outside I could see a small garden and a shed with a chain link fence. Her neighbors on both sides were closer to the main road. Her home was set back providing a bit more privacy than was common in her little housing area. I parked the bike then went to the door knocked and started to back away just in case.

The door opened to revel a very tall woman of almost five foot ten. She had short strawberry blond hair that was cut into a very modern "boy cut" for the time. Unlike the last three Masters this woman was thin, almost sinewy. Her skin was pulled tightly over high cheekbones with bright laughing eyes of green deeply sunk in their sockets. She was wearing a pair of dance leotards, with a sweat band around her forehead. I looked at her feet to she had on ballet slippers.

"Ah, Psycho. Come in. Come in. I am so excited to meet you." She stood up on her toes, literally, and walked away directing me to follow.

I just shrugged then went inside. I nearly lost it laughing as I saw this tall woman pirouetting around the very modern airy home. She was not doing it well, that is why I almost laughed. I love to watch a graceful ballet dancer as much as anyone. This lady was not one, trust me.

She continued to dance around the sparely furnished living room "So, Circe says you are gifted at dancing?"

I almost choked,. "Huh? Uhm, no Ma'am." I felt anger burn in my ears.

The evil Mistress was talking every damned one of these women into bidding for my key by advertising me as whatever the bitch was into. Shit. I hoped the next one was into exterminations. I felt like I could use some training in that area, just saying.

She stopped dancing or whatever that was she was doing could be called. "Oh? Well, that is no big deal. We can change all that. I have signed both of us up for belly dancing lessons. It will be great."

I stood there in shock. "You did what? Uhm, excuse me Ma'am, who are you? I don't know you, and that is kind of important if I am going to do my job." What the fuck. Just what the fuck.

The woman finally came and sat down on the leather-bound hard couch directing me to do the same. She was out of breath so I had to wait till she could speak without gasping. I sat in a recliner that matched the sofa, waiting for her to tell me what she was expecting. Then I was ready to correct that bullshit. I was now aware Mistress Circe was spinning more yarns than a good Viking's wife.

"Okay, whew. What a workout. I understand you are supposed to call me Master, cook, clean, take care of my yard, dress me, bath me, and whatever else I want. Then, if

I make it thirty days, I get to fuck you," she spewed like a busted water hose.

I stared at her, "Huh? Uh, okay? I guess? Master what?" She was not exactly polished here.

She laughed. "Wow you are braver than me. You don't even know my name do you. Now that is ballsy. Okay I am Marie, and you can go get me a bottle of water out of the fridge. I am going to rest a bit. Then I want to get a good look at you. After that, well I will find shit for you to do."

I did as she asked then went to return to my seat, but she grabbed my wrist holding tightly, "I said I wanted to get a look at you Psycho." She stood up towering over me like a giantess.

"Tiny thing, aren't you? How tall are you without those platforms? What size do you wear?" She was still holding my wrist.

I answered then almost vomited when she pulled me into a circle by my arm to see the back side of my unit. "Very nice. You must work out. Well enjoy it while you got it honey. I know I plan to." She slapped my ass hard making me yelp in surprise.

She laughed hard at my surprise. "Oh, you are going to be so much fun. I can already tell. You know what? I feel like shopping. Get to the car. I am going to buy us matching belly dancing outfits." She slapped my ass again.

I jerked out of her grip. "Yes, Master. Please stop hitting me. I am going."

She let out a roaring laughter. "Oh but you see I was told I couldn't get all your services until my time was up, but nothing was said about spanking, touching or grabbing."

I backed up very frightened. "That is not allowed. I will ask you nicely to keep your hands to yourself. That behavior is reserved for a Keyholder only."

She stopped laughing and smiled. "Good deal. You passed the test. Circe told me you were a whore. Apparently, the old bat was lying. I was going to throw you out if you turned out to be just a damned trollop. Okay, now we can go shopping. Sorry about that but you can never be too sure about the bullshit someone will spin when it comes to money of this amount. I am looking for a personal assistant, housekeeper, attendant, conversationalist, best friend, and lover. Not a fucking mindless whore. You are the real deal. Now, I better not tell you again to get to the car. I do have the right to correct injurious behavior, and I am willing to do that too. I have researched my role as a Dominant over the last two months awaiting my turn. I get this lifestyle of yours. Don't try any funny business. I am not as dumb as I look. Do I make myself clear?"

I nodded as I started headed for the door taking my place behind her three paces. "Yes, Master."

Master Marie was a fifty-seven years young, a no nonsense lady with a wicked sense of humor. She was intelligent, thrill seeking, and impulsive. In her youth she had done everything from construction worker, to failed ballet dancer. She married young, divorced then married again. Her second husband had been the one she truly had loved. Then on her forty-seventh birthday he gave her a special gift. The news that she was being thrown aside for the secretary at his very lucrative law firm. She was crushed, then so was he when she won a large chunk of his assets. Since that time Master Marie had engaged in many hobbies, distractions, and thrills. Her passion was dancing above all other things. She loved all kinds and had indeed signed us both up for lessons in the secret art, at the time, of belly dancing.

After being on her own for over a decade she had decided she didn't like the ball and chain marriage offered. She also didn't like the men her age reminding her of how old she was. Master Marie hated being alone but couldn't stand the idea of a Master lording over her again whether it be boyfriend or husband. She had been seeing Mistress Circe for spiritual counseling for the last year. Master Marie had told Mistress Circe that the only true way to be free but have company was to hire a personal assistant or have a live-in roomie.

It was then she found out Mistress Circe had something that could promise real magic hidden in a Jar on a shelf. A Key that held a genie who could grant all your wishes and would be unable to refuse your commands. The genie would even take care of your most personal needs for not much more than three squares and reminders to take medication. All you had to do was pay the right price and it could be yours forever.

Master Marie couldn't resist such a rare and extraordinary prize. She had thrown her hat into the bidding ring immediately. Then done her research on how to wield the power of the Key to its full potential. She was the first Master since Debbie and Julie to have any idea what this lifestyle is all about. She was not a thudder or into bondage, just D/s lifestyle. Her test in the beginning was not just to see if I had any morals, but also to see if I would know my role. I, of course, am the real deal, so Master Marie was in heaven. She had indeed been offered the chance to own her very own submissive, for lack of a better definition. For now, let's just call it what she thought she got.

Her reign would be marked by strict schedule adherence. Master Marie was amazing at making sure that I knew where I was supposed to be and what I was to be doing at any given time. She of course, made provisions for my outside activities such as work, my children, and Priestess business. She was enamored with the idea that I was indeed a religious leader with a Coven. She had decided after she won the auction for my Key, she would want to become an initiate watcher. I told her to wait and see how she felt after she had done more research on the subject and lent her several books from the Temple library. Several members had donated such objects for all to enjoy when they wished.

She also enjoyed watching the new budding symptom of my trance dancing. As my prodromal signs grew in strength, Simon would often take me outside. We would dance off the anxiety that was threatening to destroy me from the rising terror within. She laughed one night telling me I was a liar.

"Pardon, Master? I lied to you. I don't recall such an insolent act but if you say so it must be true," I said waiting to see if she was truly angry and what I had possibly told a lie about.

"You are a beautiful dancer, Psycho. You said you can't dance, but that was a lie." She laughed.

I shook my head. "Master, there is no excuse for lying but I will tell you I didn't lie on purpose. I have never seen myself dance. I only do it." That was an honest response.

"Well trust me, it is amazing to see." She got up and left the room.

She had been taking us to belly dancing classes for two weeks three times a week. I had found some interest in the art and decided to take it up even if Master Marie didn't win Simon's Key. It was good for stretching muscles, keeping down pain from my arthritis. Yep already had it. Remember I had a rough childhood. Shit catches up with you and dancing was a beautiful art that resembled worship of the elementals, or so I thought anyway.

June 18th of the year was the celebration of Litha or Mid-summer Solstice. The entire Coven and watchers were thrilled to be going to their very first of the big Sabbats at Springfields as a community where no non-initiate was forbidden entry. Under Mistress Circe's crown only members could attend. Under Arodia, everyone was welcome. The non-initiates knew they couldn't join in ritual, but they could join the festivities and the feasting. They could even enjoy watching the young male stags show off their skills and talents at weapon making, mock battles and of course, the grounds were open to all amorous couples hoping to conceive a child from the Gods.

I had accustomed both initiate and non-initiate to the sight of Sky Clad. This was to be a real blessing. Mother Delleh had requested that my Priest and I do all Sister Sabbat rituals Sky Clad from that day forward. That was fine with me. The whole group had seen HP Roary and I near copulation during our Great Rite. Neither he nor I refused her request. We no longer had secrets to hide from our children, Mothers and Fathers nor the God and Goddess. Since he and I were now the new leaders, we also were the ones who would perform all rites and rituals for the Covens from that day until otherwise told so. It was a great honor and a great responsibility.

I was more than worried as that sacred day approached. My Master had to keep me restrained when sleeping, and the trance dancing was getting more common. Worse still, I was suddenly not sleeping. Even with the threat of punishment, I was refusing to eat. My weight was dropping fast. Prodromal always causes paranoia that I am being poisoned or dying of chemicals in the food. I will refuse food no matter what anyone does. Don't forget they had to use ECT treatment more than once to end my so called hunger strikes.

Master Marie had called Mistress Circe to ask how to handle my refusal of her commands after soft punishments such as restraints, standing in a painfully compromised position for hours (bare knees on rice for example), and threats of thudding didn't work.

Mistress Circe had said, "Let the slut die. We'd all be better off."

Master Marie instead took me to my psychiatrist meeting. Doctor Commisso gave me a lecture and increased my medications. It was too late. I had already been overdosing on the stuff for almost a month by then. Nothing was stopping the steady march of madness. If you listened hard, you could even hear the drummer boy announcing the coming insanity.

That Saturday Morning of Litha, I arrived at Maiden Mary's home before my brother had even awakened from his slumber. I was feeling anxious. I had walked a rut in the wood floor of Master Marie's hallway pacing and wringing my hands all night. I told myself it was the pressures of holding a ritual with all the Covens present causing it. That was bullshit and I knew it. I had already performed the Great Rite in front of them. You can't get any more intimate than that. If I were going to stumble it would have been then.

I must have been a sight riding the Motorpsycho to Mary's house early that morning in my black and purple robe with the triple crown on my head. I made sure to avoid driving by the Freewill Baptist Church I had hijacked last year just in case anyone was there that early. I was sure they would have PTSD seeing my black robed Priestess ass coming back through so near the anniversary of our little tiff.

The red van with James at the wheel showed up right on time. I was worried that the Crone Circe would join us. We had to stop to offer her the ride, though everyone confessed they didn't want her to come with us. She had refused to show at either Esbat. She also was denying she would show at our own Litha celebration on the real date June 21st the next Tuesday. The community and Coven didn't take kindly to her snubbing them over what they all had not only voted on but built themselves. They viewed her anger at me as petty, and misguided. I just kept my mouth shut. As long as I was quiet never offering insult, then it made it much easier for the Family to hear Mistress Circe's foul cursing as well as her deafening silence.

To everyone's relief she was feigning illness. She told Mary when she knocked on her door, she was having tummy trouble.

Tracy brashly said, "Yeah, because she is full of shit."

Everyone started laughing as we began the long drive to Springfields. This time, James had to behave and drive with caution. We had a caravan of over fifteen cars behind us carrying every single non-initiate future Coven member. There were now twenty-eight of us all together. I couldn't accept another soul.

After the number twenty-eight we would have to "hive off." A HP and HPS (High Priest and High Priestess) can't attend more spirits than that without neglecting some. Without enough proper leadership to begin with, we would have no choice but to close the circle to any new possible initiates unless someone dropped out. We now actually had a waiting list.

The Summoners at Springfields saw our caravan of cars pulling in. They went and got the Queen of Green herself to witness what every single Pagan heart there never thought they'd live to see, a circle of the Green Rings filled to bursting. I got out of the van aided by my handsome Priest Roary who had practically knocked over half the crowd to be at my side.

He took my hand, kissed my knuckles, and said, "I have missed you, my Lady. Many a sleepless night I have spent in your arms enjoying the softness of your embrace."

I smiled at Roary. "Thank you, my Lord. I too have seen you in the land of dreams. May we caste a fruitful circle this glorious day together."

His mouth almost broke with the size of his smile as he looked at all the people who had followed our red van. "These our children? All of them?"

I laughed. "Yes, my Lord. You were quite virile. I was quite fertile. The God and Goddess have blessed our union with many sons and daughters."

He laughed as did my entire Coven who was listening gripping their chests at our romantic banter. "Only in a month? I was amazingly virile and you are truly fertile, my Lady. Got to love that ritual sex. It can even cut back the natural law of nine months."

Even the Queen of Green laughed at that one. I saw the Mother. She looked tired and worn. She motioned me to join her for a chat. I allowed my Priest to honor me with a bow and left him to attend our many children.

"Daughter, my heart sings today. You have filled the coffers to exploding. We are rich." She looked at all the future members who were following my Priest with looks of wonder upon their faces.

I chuckled. "Much more wealth than you can know, Mother. They built the Temple with their own hands and sweat. Maiden Mary has a photo of them with their honor to the Gods the day it was completed. Just as you prophesied to me at my Maiden Yule."

Mother Delleh nodded then looked sad. "My time is growing short, Daughter. They say the cancer has returned. Where is your Crone Circe? I did not see her face among yours."

I looked at the ground. "Mother, I cannot speak for another. You will have to ask her where she is. Illness is what she claimed to the Coven."

Mother Delleh looked at me hard. "You don't believe her, Daughter Arodia?"

I chuckled bitterly. "No, I believe her Mother. She is sick. But it is in her spirit not her unit."

Mother Delleh nodded. "I knew you would make a wonderful and perceptive Priestess. She will try to take the Green crown. It worries me what will happen to the Green Rings when she takes my spot on the throne."

I glared fiercely at that statement. "Mother, I promise you with all that I have, or ever will, that will not happen. The Gods have said the crown will stay Green, never Gold. The Coven is already angry at her lack of attendance, refusal to submit to them, and look at all these children she kept in the cold. That is not going to be forgotten or forgiven."

Mother Delleh nodded. "And you, Daughter Arodia. You have lost weight, a lot of weight. Is the burden of the crown too heavy?"

I shook my head. "No, but Mother I do fear that I am getting sick with psychosis again. I know that I am. Soon, I will be too ill to attend the Temple. I will recover, but until then I seek your wise advice. How do I keep the Temple strong when my mind shatters?"

She looked sad then brushed my face with her hand lightly sending strange shocking sensations like needles throughout my unit. "You listen to your heart. You answered the panel correctly at Beltane. Every man and woman in your Coven are a Priest and Priestess. Choose one to stand when you are forced to kneel. We all have our weaknesses. Your children will understand. Don't be afraid to ask for their help. They love you for loving them so much. A true Priestess knows that a time comes when her children may have to support her as once she supported them."

I nodded. "I understand, Mother. I would ask that you try to stay with us for a while longer. I know it is a favor I have no right to request. You have given me so much already."

She smiled. "Ah, but we are all in balance, Daughter. You gave back. I will do what I can to give you time to stop Crone Circe from taking my throne. In return remember to fight to stay with us too. Promise for a promise. All is in balance again. So Mote It Be."

I smiled as we hugged. "So Mote It Be."

I found my High Priest with the other males telling lies and flexing his testosterone. He was teasing all the unwed maidens. He did so love his admirers. I smiled as I stood back watching him flirt, puff up in pride, and preen his pretty feathers.

"Husband, my Priest. I leave for one moment and you are off chasing the young girls. You are no better than Pan. Girls run for your life. Cover your maidenheads. High Priest Roary will only love you until the Moon is pregnant with souls. Then he will go out hunting for new fields to sow," I yelled out laughingly.

Roary looked up to see me calling him out. His green eyes danced as he stood tall before the swooning girls now behaving as if insulted. I had called him out on his player reputation,

"Wife, my Priestess. You should be home attending to the children. I would be home and expect my venison to be cooked and on the long table. You misunderstand my intentions with these lovely young ladies. I would never seek to defile their innocence in such an unforgivable way." He was laughing so hard that by the time he finished he ruined the fake acting job.

He was indeed the picture of the perfect Pagan man. As if someone had pulled him from an old etching, then breathed life into the lines. The girls all loved him, and why shouldn't they? He was handsome, friendly, masculine, courteous, kind, and generous. He was also very devout and very, very clever. I accused him on more than one occasion of being a polished womanizer, with a poet's tongue. Though to the last time I saw him he continually denied it. Sure Roary, I still don't believe you.

He came with me to our place at the long table so we could discuss Temple Circle business. He agreed with me that our circles needed new blood and true hearts. He decided to take my advice and buy and build a sister Green Temple on his side of the state. We lived across the state from each other. I showed him our pictures, told him of the amazing raising of the Green. He ate it up like a ravenous dog. That very day my Priest, a construction worker in the mundane world, put the fire under his own Coven's ass, and by Sowen (Halloween, Samhain) they too had a Green Temple of their very own.

He and I cast the circle and lead the rituals of the Summer Solstice that day without missing a single word even though we were both Sky Clad once again. This time, everyone else was too. Outside our ritual room the children played, also Sky Clad, as the young uninitiated girls danced and the young uninitiated boys tried to woe them. Roary played the young God who vanquished the old dying Father in the mock battle, then pretended to kidnap and run away with me to ravish the Goddess deep in the woods. She was his prize, his mother, his lover too. It was all fake this time. Just a play for the participants of the celebration. Once Roary had me away from ears and eyes near the woods he begged to make it real.

I again turned him down. This time it was much harder. I was in the mood for this kind of adoration. He had already proven his prowess as an amazing lover. However, I was still a slave to Crone Circe's collar. I knew she would never find out, but I would know. Simon would know and so would Looper. I never betray my collar.

The sad look on my Priest face when I turned him away was enough to send me to my room immediately to take care of, meditate, errrr, invoke, uh, okay you know what. Okay that is a lie. It was the fact that the man was fucking Sky Clad still and he was playing his part of rutting stag a bit too realistically if you catch my drift. He was very interested in me, and my unit was interested in replaying that amazing Great Rite with him too. I left before I did something I would regret. That day I attended myself by myself, thank you very much. You would have done the same damned thing. Don't judge me.

Oh, and for the record Mistress Circe is a fucking dirty bitch. Grr.

After I meditated...*clearing throat*...several times, I rejoined my Coven family feeling a bit more relaxed. However, I noticed that the tapestry had gotten very thick while the day had grown long. In my ears the Looper had been joined by a loud hissing sound. The static was just in the corner of my visual field. To my absolute horror, I was about to have a psychotic episode, right in the middle of the summer Solstice event with everyone there to see it. Fuck me.

High Priestess Arodia is about to turn back into Psycho.

Chapter 22: The Family Exile
The Fall of Mistress Circe

We are really getting ever closer to the end of the Wicked Witch of the South. Yet, we still have two interim Masters to go. Then a choice will finally be made. Who will wield the Key? Still hopelessly trapped in the purgatory of temporary visitor Masters, Psycho is entering the murky world of psychosis. Will this have any bearing on who will win the bid?

Priest Roary and Priestess Arodia are young, beautiful, strong, gifted, charismatic, and above all, loved. No one holds more affection for the new leaders than the Queen of Green herself. Mother Delleh secretly revels in the blessings she has been granted by the Goddess. It has been a most welcome end to her long hard journey of sowing the fields of the human heart.

The Queen final wish now granted. She rests from her life of labor on her darkening throne. She is smiling as she watches her seedlings break the once barren ground. Mother Delleh is bursting with pride to have raised the ones meant for greatness within the Green Rings. The Queen knows that the popular Priest and Priestess are proof the Goddess does adore her. The Mother is amazed how in particular her Daughter understands the truth of balance unlike any she has known before.

However, the wise Queen understands that with great power comes unimaginable pain. After all, no one so short in years could have such deeply rooted wisdom without it extracting a horrific cost. Her beloved Priestess is fated to pay the price for her otherworldly enlightenment throughout a lifetime. Mother Delleh holds her Daughter tightly, crying tears of empathy while Priestess Arodia suffers the curse of insight. The Queen will call in her country to protect her defender of the Green throne.

Master Marie danced with gentle sternness around her most coveted genie. She has fallen in love. The idea of giving up the thing she has sought for a decade will break her heart. Yet, she must let it go. It was never meant to be hers. She will shed bitter tears but never forget the magical song of her schizophrenic that will now forever play in her soul.

Mistress Circe has a secret. She holds a key in a jar, or does she? She is tired of her ward getting all the attention. The Crone is angry that no one comes to buy her goods anymore. It is time for her to unburden herself of the all the things she knows about the High Priestess Arodia's true nature. She is calling a meeting of those who will be sympathetic to her attempts to save them from the insanity they are following blindly. The Crone thought herself clever but remember what you put out there comes back to you, three-fold.

Ready to finally see the fall of a Mistress whose reign will not actually end for two more months, but she fell before she sold the Key. How does that work? Read on and find out. You will need to keep on those dancing shoes but wear the ones with hard soles. We are going to do some stomp dancing, beauties. Let's play some heavy bass and make sure you bring all your pent-up aggressions too. This is a good night for exacting revenge. Let's start crushing our enemies under our feet.

"She didn't even want to be a Wiccan. I ordered her to do it. When she gave me shit about it, I just captured her imaginary friend Simon in a voodoo jar. Then the stupid slut had no choice but to do what I said. I convinced the mindless twit that I would kill Simon if she disobeyed me anymore. So, see she is not even real. She doesn't believe any of it. Psycho only does what she is told. She is too insane to even know you can't capture people who don't exist in a fucking jar. She has fooled all of you."

– Mistress Circe's words to the Coven of the Green Rings council members meeting at her house on June 23, 1994.

I looked about the crowded hall with terror rising rapidly throughout my unit. My brain was already shifting, about to fall too far to the left. I had to hurry. The sensory melt-down was moving swiftly. I didn't excuse myself from the circle discussion being held by Mother Delleh with the Elders. I decided my manners would just have to be excused. It would have been more impolite to interrupt the ailing Queens words, then to just get up to leave.

Around me the hundreds of units of initiates and non-initiates moved like blurs of color. I could no longer make out any faces or specific details. I staggered through them trying to push them out of my way in my wild bid to make it to the privacy of my assigned room. There were too many of them. Dancing, talking, laughing, noise, noise, noise. I became too confused to recall which direction to go. I was lost within an open hall. The world below my feet lurched, almost sending me to the ground. I held still trying to balance just as my mind shattered. It was too late. The episode had arrived.

My unit began to quiver as my head rolled toward the sky, my eyes rolling back into my sockets. My arms went out into the position of a cross, my legs were spread wide to steady as the transmissions smashed into my face sending me arching backward into an almost impossible contorted stance.

My ears filled with the voices of a thousand speaking in every language, pitch, and gender, all at once. I could see the whirl of the electrical grids above and below. Everything became the same while I felt the color of my robe become my skin, the taste of the sun filled my mouth. My muscles were frozen, held to the Earth by roots of the tapestry. I was now trapped within the webs that held the universe together right there in the center of the Springfields feast hall.

My beloved Priest had been at my side. He was surprised by my sudden departure. Roary watched unsure what to think of my unsteady gait, until in sheer horror he saw my receiving of transmissions pose. He realized I was having an episode.

Roary had been told of my affliction. This was not an issue for him. He is a devout follower of the old religion. In the Wiccan tradition, having mental illness makes one special. We are blessed and cursed but not shunned. To my new family, schizophrenia is the price I pay to have a deeper understanding that those without the disease could ever hope to have. However, even with this complete acceptance, they are aware that expression of psychosis can be deadly, and there is no doubt in their mind it is amazingly painful.

Roary interrupted Mother Delleh. "My Queen. Forgive my rudeness but my Priestess is having a spiritual attack. Help me," he yelled at the old Priests around him while he left his chair to rush to my side.

The old males looked and immediately rushed from their chairs following Priest Roary to aid him to get my struggling unit to safety. Those celebrating around me had started to notice this very spectacular but odd pose. They were moving back unsure what to make of the scene of their High Priestess standing in a backward C stance with her arms outstretched and groaning in agony from the force.

He reached me and wrapped his arms around my waist whispering in my ear, "I have you, my Priestess. It will be okay. I will get you out of here."

His touch sent the feeling of electricity throughout my straining unit. The pain was unbearable. I began to scream, guttural and desperate, "Ah, help me, help me, please help me."

This loud and sudden sound frightened my Priest so that he briefly let go. It was too late, the partial complex seizure from the stress began. My unit began to quake violently as my knees gave way. I fell to the ground landing on my back quivering and releasing my bladder while yelling for help in a repeating loop. I was no longer conscious, but this was not a full Grand Mal. I would come to in only a few more minutes

The crowd, now very frightened, had backed away to grant room for my fit to finish. My Priest, the other Elders and my Queen could do nothing but wait for the seizure to abate. Suddenly, a non-initiate came out of the crowd. She threw herself over my unit. She had a rolled-up shirt in her hands as she forced my mouth open and tied it around my head as if trying to gag me to keep me quiet.

My Priest rushed up to grab this woman. "What are you doing. Get off Arodia." He pulled her back as she tried to finish tying her knot holding my head off the ground so I could no longer reverse head bang it as I had been doing.

The woman yelled out, "Stop, I am trying to keep her from biting off her tongue, idiot. She is having a seizure."

Roary let her go realizing she knew what was going on more than he did. The woman glared for a moment then finished her job restraining my jaw from biting down with great force. My mouth was already bleeding from biting my tongue several times during the initial onset of the fit.

The quaking was beginning to settle. I could hear and see again but was confused. I began to scream in terror unsure what was happening. Voices were chanting, taunting, threatening. The room was pulsating and moving fast. I couldn't recall who I was or why I couldn't move. My mouth seemed to have been gripped by one of the many shadows around me. I couldn't bite down or use my words. This didn't make sense. What was going on? There was someone standing over me trying to rip my head off. I began to claw at her in a desperate bid to survive. I thought she was trying to hurt me, and maybe it was her fault I was confused.

The woman took my claws for a moment then grabbed my wrists screaming for someone to bring her rope. I would need to be restrained, she yelled frantically. Everyone stood around not sure what to do.

"Go get what she wants. Grab the ritual cording in the circle. Go now," said the Queen of Green, now realizing I was in big trouble.

"Grab her feet. Hold her down damn it. She is going to hurt herself or someone else. Help me," yelled the woman to my Priest.

He dropped to his knees holding my legs still from trying to kick and struggle to get my arms free from this strange woman I thought was trying to injury me. I was screaming and crying, completely gone into a full-on psychotic fit.

The cords were brought, and the woman took them quickly tying my wrists together she threw some to Roary instructing him to do the same to my legs. Within only a few moments I was completely restrained.

"We need to take her somewhere dark and quiet. Is there somewhere that is so," asked the woman who was watching my writhing crying unit as I tried without success to free myself of the restraints.

Mother Delleh nodded. "There are rooms in the back. Priest Roary. Help her take Arodia to my room. Be gentle. Everyone, get out of the way. Back up. Let them through," said the Queen to the curious watchers of this drama.

My priest gently scooped up my terrified unit carrying me like a husband would a wife over the threshold on a honeymoon. The woman followed him as he rushed past the crowd headed for Mother Delleh's room in the back of the hall.

Once inside the woman instructed my Priest, he needed to find someone to strip off the flat sheet from the bed.

"Have someone drench it in cold water. We need to wrap her in the wet sheets. It will calm this attack," she said as I continued to scream and cry wriggling on the floor where Roary had placed me carefully once the door had been closed.

The woman turned off all the lights making the room dark. The lack of bright lights and noise of the crowd helped the visions of colors, blurs, and sounds of too many voices at once. However, I was still gripped by painful terror within. My mind was shattered in complete confusion as every part of my unit seemed to have its own mind. It tried to strain against the cords, pulling, flexing, stretching. It was horrid, and I was very aware of it. I just couldn't seem to understand what or why this was happening.

My Priest had done as instructed. Within only fifteen minutes the flat sheet from the Queens bed was brought into the room dripping wet with chilly water. At the woman's direction I was rolled by her and Roary tight into the sheet like a human enchilada. Only my head was left free.

The sudden drop in temperature and tightness stopped the muscle spasms. It also started to knock me back into understanding. I still couldn't completely figure out what was going on, but I did recognize my priest. The woman was unknown to me, but I had seen her at the Green Temple during the New and Full Moon Esbats. She was one of my watchers.

I had stopped screaming but was still openly weeping. The pain was blowing my mind, and the understanding I was in episode was soul crushing. I struggled to get free of the tight wet sheet, but it was useless. I wasn't going anywhere. I finally rolled on my side and just cried while closing my eyes. I didn't want to see anymore. I just wanted to die right there. Anything to make the Looper shut up, and to end the pain, even death.

The Queen entered the room. "How is she?"

The woman who was knelt next to my despairing unit said, "She is calm now. She needs rest, and quiet. I will sit with her till she recovers. Not a problem."

The Queen came closer. "I will join you. Priest Roary, attend the celebration. Tell the Summoners to announce the Priestess Arodia is fine, just a seizure. It is the price she pays for her special connection to the Goddess. Tell them she will recover."

Roary looked at the woman. "She will be okay now?"

The woman nodded. "It is just a psychotic fit. She is okay. The blood is just from biting her tongue. She didn't bite it off. It will be sore, but no actual harm done. She could have another one, so we need to give her a few hours of observation. The Priestess is going to be fine, so stop worrying."

He nodded to her and left to do his duty as commanded by Mother Delleh.

The Queen sat down cross legged next to my "sheeted" unit. She asked the woman if she could touch me or if such a thing would cause stress.

"I don't think she could get more stressed. I am going to get a rag to clean up her face. That blood is drying. It is the least we can do while we wait." She got up and left the room.

Mother Della reached out and pulled me. She laid my head in her lap petting my shoulder and began to sing very softly a song in some language I had never heard. I wept even harder. I was so afraid. I didn't know what would happen. I was so sure the cops were coming. They would lock me up again. I wondered if I hurt anyone. I couldn't remember how I got there.

More than anything else, I wept because I heard the love in Mother Delleh's voice. She genuinely cared. I finally had found a real mother, and she was going to die soon. I would not have enough time to learn what she had to teach. I was too late, as usual. The despair was filling me taking me straight to the level of hell I had only experienced once before. The day Scruffy was burned alive!

When Mother Delleh showed me her true love that day it was both beautiful and tragic. The real cruelty of life is not the terrible abuse, pain, and loss I had suffered. It was that moment. I had found something wonderful and pure. Yet, I knew it would not last.

In all the brutality I had ever known. This was the most heinous of them all. It was my knowledge of experiencing what would soon be gone forever. To never know it existed would have been more merciful than living with the memory of what could have been but would never be.

In those moments, I could no longer deny why I was so cold and unfeeling. It was because I didn't want to admit I needed to be loved just like everyone else. That kind of weakness could threaten my survival in a world that had not ever cared. I also could no longer deny the things those people were doing and had done to me. They hurt me beyond just the scars on the unit. It hurt my soul, my heart, my spirit, my everything. I was not so tough. Turned out I really am a human being.

The grief of my horrible past gripped me in a flood of terror. Sights, memories, feelings, pain, all filled my mind. Everything forbidden my consciousness stood in line waiting for my attention. I wailed feeling my heart breaking with every single blow, slap, cruel word, whip, burn, rape, and so much more. Mother Delleh took my shoulders and held me tightly to her as I struggled against the horror dogpile of a lifetime of diabolical experiences.

She never stopped her soft song. I felt the drops of her own tears falling onto my face mingling with my own. I felt a healing of the Shattering begin within. This time, everything went into the ground below, never to reach my now healed heart again. I had finally become a human being, as I once had been before Debbie robbed me of my dignity when I was just a child. Mother Delleh had led me out of the Darkness. The light of life was more beautiful than I remembered. I stopped crying, finally falling into a deep peaceful slumber. She continued to rock me and sing of maidens, warriors, and lost loves, in a language from long ago.

NOTE: *I never told Mother Delleh what she did for me that day. I never felt I needed to. She was a woman of incredible insight, understanding, compassion and love. I* know she knew what she was doing. Her tears fell with my own while I psychically fell apart, releasing the torment of twenty-two years. The pain is not something I can describe in words. The result is the person you know today. Her holding me in my moments of greatest weakness, even against my wishes, healed my broken heart. She gave me a place to belong. She granted me a family. Then she rose me to lead her children out of the darkness. Now as the final act she would ever do for me personally, she had helped me find myself. All she had to do was show me true love.

I was able to find the strength to let go of my pain, bitterness, hate, need for revenge, and lack of empathy. The dark journey to redemption of my spirit was too frightening for me to travel alone. Thank the Goddess she had sent Mother Delleh to hold my hand so I could finally face my fears once and for all.

I am not a loser. I am not a monster. I am just a person who like everyone else bleeds when you cut me, cries when you hurt me, is humiliated when you rape me, is angry when you mistreat me, and more than anything else, deserves to be loved. Especially, when I still manage to love you after all I have been through. From that day forward, I found inner peace. My road was still fraught with terrors untold (yes, we will get to them all), but I was now able to deal with trauma in a much healthier, understanding way. I would no longer blame myself when it really was not my fault and take the credit when it was. I no longer hated everyone, I learned to give people a *chance, and to always have faith tomorrow will be a better day.*

Mother Delleh's unit has been long since gone now. However, I never miss a day where I don't tell her how much I love her for what she did. Her spirit lives in me and you too know that you know once a long time ago this beautiful soul walked the Earth. Blessed Be Mother Delleh. May you always know the peace you earned.

I awoke to the woman who had aided me during my fit rubbing the wet rag on my mouth cleaning up the dried blood.

I was wrapped in a wet sheet, in a dark room, bound and gagged. Mother Delleh had left but I had not awakened when she laid my head gently on a pillow leaving me to sleep off my seizure/psychotic fit.

I looked at this woman with curiosity. She appeared to be in her early thirties and about five foot seven with long flame red hair. Her eyes were a fierce looking light green, and her face pleasant to look at. She didn't have the freckles so common with a ginger but had the white pallor of one from a deeply Irish decent. Her unit was also very pleasant to look at with a well portioned breast, curvy waist, and heavy hips. In a sentence this woman was very pretty. I remembered seeing her during the Green Temple consecration as I had opened the circle. Her unit caught my eye with its very handsome lines. It is not proper to look at another like that when they are Sky Clad, but I am human. The girl was hot.

I was still gagged so all I could do was stare at her as she gently cleaned off the blood. I wondered who she was. Finally, I decided to attempt to let her know I was back from Mars.

I struggled a bit as I tried to mouth the words, "I am okay now."

At first the woman was trying to hold me down thinking I was having another fit, but then realized I was calm.

She smiled then removed the gag. "Feeling better now, Priestess?"

I nodded. "How long have I been out? Did I hurt anyone? Are the cops coming? Where is everyone," I droned out excitedly wanting to know everything at once, with both fear and hope in my voice.

She chuckled. "Okay, you are back with us. Great. You were out five hours. You only hurt yourself. Why would anyone call the cops? Everyone is still partying though some have retired for the night."

I looked around the room. "Where am I?"

The woman smiled. "Queen Delleh's room. We moved you in here for privacy while you dealt with your symptoms."

I sighed. "And last who are you?"

The girl giggled. "Ah, I am one of your Temple children. I am Ginger. It is a pleasure to meet you, but I hoped to meet you personally in better circumstances."

I snorted. "Yeah, this is embarrassing. I would shake your hand but seems my hands are restrained at the moment."

She laughed hard. "You are so funny. I love that about you. Always a laugh. I have never been a religious person but in your Temple, I believe I could learn to have faith. You're not like any holy person I have ever known. You don't take yourself too seriously. It is not every day the preacher shows up to church naked."

That made me laugh. "Well, first I am not holy. Holy terror maybe, but not holy in the pure sense. Second can you please untie me now? I can't feel my fingers."

She nodded. "Oops. Okay sure."

Ginger then unrolled my unit and untied my wrists and ankles. I stood up working the blood back into my limbs while she picked up the sheet and cords. "I will go see if I can return these to their rightful owners. Are you going to be okay now?" She looked at me, seeming concerned.

"Yes, it is over for now. Thank you, Sister Ginger. You were most kind. I will not forget the favor. See you at Litha on Tuesday at the temple." I reached out and shook her hand.

She smiled as she shook my hand back. "It has been a pleasure to help. I hope you don't mind me saying let's not do it again?"

I laughed out loud. "I agree Sister Ginger." I watched her leave.

I went to the bathroom and cleaned up the mess I had made of myself as best as I could. I had not expected to seize and have an episode. I told Simon to make sure next time we brought extra clothes.

I was walking down the hallway back toward the hall to find Mother Delleh to thank her for aiding me in my darkest hours when my Priest suddenly came rushing toward me.

"My Lady, are you alright? Anything broken? Anything I can get you?" He grabbed my hands, appearing sincerely worried.

I smiled at him. "Thank you, my most handsome Lord. I am fine. It is my disease. No need to worry. It happens all the time. Pay no mind. I always recover. I hope it didn't disrupt the celebration."

He smiled, appearing relieved. "Everyone has been worried, but that is because they love you, my Lady. It is so good to see you are fine. I was scared, but I understand you have schizophrenia. It makes me sad to know you must suffer like that. Does this really happen all the time?"

I nodded. "Yes, unfortunately, my Lord, what you saw is part of my normal existence. Try to remember I have been sick an exceedingly long time now. I am used to it. If ever I do that again, do what you must to protect everyone from me. I am not aware of what I am doing."

He looked at the floor. "There isn't a cure, is there?"

I shook my head no. "It is okay, my Lord. Now let's go let everyone know their Priestess is alive and well. I am sorry to frighten everyone like that."

Roary frowned. "It seemed to me, no matter how frightened everyone else was, you were the one truly scared. I will beg the Gods to find a way to heal you, my Lady." He kissed my knuckles.

I chuckled. "I would rather you not remind them I am around, my Lord. They may decide I am due a good ass kicking."

He seemed startled by that. "You, my Lady? What could you have done to fear wrath from the Gods?"

I kissed his knuckles this time. "For denying the favors of my most gifted Priest, of course." I winked at him.

He grabbed his chest as if wounded. "You're a cruel Mistress, my Priestess. You break my heart with those blue eyes. I would beg your favor just once more. I would worship your temple more lovingly than the first time."

I took his hand and began to walk back to the hall. "Oh, of that there is no doubt, but I can't Roary. One day I will be free. Today is not that day, my Lord. Till then I will just have to dream of your eyes."

He laughed. "I am already haunted by yours. I am indeed your slave."

I snickered. "You are the most beautiful liar I have ever known. Maybe even better than your Lady, my Lord."

We entered the hall to a throng of rushing Coven members who all came to see that I was unharmed. I had more than a few psychotic breaks in my day. Never in all my days before that or after were so many concerned about my insane welfare. I just smiled and told everyone it was just a nasty seizure and I was fine.

Mother Delleh arrived and we hugged. She told me she had been meditating while begging the Goddess to allow me the time to secure my Temple before the madness took me for my ride into the abyss. I calmed her fears by informing her I would not go acute for many months yet. I was expected to break by Yule. She seemed mildly comforted by that. I gave her information regarding the nature of my illness, its cycles, and usual timelines. She listened intently as did my Priest and the other Elders. They all got a crash course in how to handle a schizophrenic.

Before we left Springfields the next morning I had one more meeting with Mother Delleh. I requested a special exception for all non-initiates to be raised to the first level if they were sure before Lughnasa Sabbat in August. Many had been asking to join for more than a year already, but Mistress Circe had denied them. I was careful to ask for Ginger in particular. She had earned her right to a white cord by coming to the aid of her Priestess during a time of crisis. Mother Delleh of course was not only happy to grant her blessing, but grateful I had the wisdom to grant cords quickly. It was very smart to strengthen the Family before she took her journey across the Summerlands. I would need many honest votes to stop Mistress Circe in her attempt to steal the Green throne. If you didn't wear a cord of white, you would have no vote.

On the ride home, my Coven family was overly concerned with my welfare. My spill had upset everyone. They, more than anyone else, knew what they saw meant big trouble. They had been there when I had lost it the year before. No one was denying I was slowly going psychotic. They were anxious to know how I was going to stop a repeat of the long incarceration that nearly lost my chance of obtaining the Triple Goddess Crown.

I looked at Mary recalling Mother Delleh's wise words. "Maiden. I believe you would have worn my own crown had it not been for the taint of Crone Circe. Your heart is pure, your love is honest. When I am forced to my knees before my disease, I want you to take up the seat of power in my absence. Sister Lisa, I ask you to take her side and be her Maiden. Sister Tracy, I ask you to handle all duties of the Temple that are secular. Brother Chuck, I would request you to do all the maintenance. Brother James, you are Summoner until you choose to leave that position. Delilah, I will make you Maiden in training. One day you will wear the black cord. I have seen that in my visions. A powerful Priestess in your own Coven." She was, by the way, but again that will be another story.

Everyone in that van lowered their heads in reverence for their new positions within this growing Coven. I would grant Linda the title of "feast keeper" in which she was responsible for making sure all Sabbat feasts were well stocked with food for the hungry bellies of members, initiates, and anyone who came that needed a meal. Anyone could come to break bread; homeless, hungry, poor, non-Wiccan, even the beast and foul of the fields. Our Sabbats are for all, not just for the followers of the old religion. The original members were all worth their salt and had proven repeatedly they could handle power without abusing it. I had now given instructions that would keep my Coven safe through my entire reign no matter how many times I went Psycho, or worse, and it did.

The time of Sabbat was the final awakening I required to help create a dual existence. I was both leader and follower. As High Priestess Arodia, I commanded the hearts and futures of many. As Psycho I was on my knees before a Key and Collar. That June, I put a wall between my mundane and spiritual self, careful to never allow them to bleed into the other again. I determined that once the auction for my Key was over and a new holder chosen, I would only submit under new conditions.

First, no Master would be allowed more than three leashes in a reign no matter how long it lasted. This unlimited leashing ability was to never happen again. Leashes are important due to the possibility of a Master becoming ill or needing to travel without me. So, ending the practice was out of the question. However, I could limit such a thing. If the Master used the same leash repeatedly it would not count against the original number of three only.

Second, when I was to behave as High Priestess Arodia, I was to have my collar removed for the ceremony, Esbat or Sabbat. I would never wear the circle of silver within my seat of power as head of the circle of Green. I also would forbid a Master from joining my Coven. I couldn't be both submissive and Dominant to the same person. There is no ability to switch my role since I am not a true submissive. If I ever got power over my Keyholder even for a moment, they would lose the ability to control my psychotic self. This was something that would become a Rule of the Key as did the first change. Simon had worked on the problems of Mistress Circe's reign. His solutions made sense. There would never be another horrible auctioning of the Key again. However, we still had to finish our contract with the greedy Mistress before the new holder could be put on notice.

As I drove back to Master Marie's house, I tried to find a way to talk Mistress Circe into holding the auction right away. I was getting sicker by the day. More symptoms were appearing with prolonged periods of confusion evident. I feared my Key would be worthless if she waited too much longer. I stopped by the pay phone in Carter at Night's to see if she could be reasoned with. My Coven was now secure, my children safe with Mary. If only I could close this final gaping hole of weakness in the face of my oncoming illness, I could stop stressing.

Mistress Circe answered on the second ring. "What the fuck do you want? Did they finally figure out you are a fraud and toss you on your useless ass at Springfields," she said with a bit of hope in her tone.

I held back my urge to return her insult. Being nasty would not get me what I desired. At that moment, the old Crone was in the cat bird seat over me.

"Not yet, Mistress. The Springfields and Coven business is not why I am calling. I wonder, could you please just offer the Key to the six potentials looking to bid?"

She snorted into the phone. "You still have two more to try your so-called services out on, Psycho. I will not have you coming back on me saying I wasn't fair."

I took a deep breath. "I won't, I swear it, Mistress. I would request you just sell it to the lady or gentleman who is the highest bidder and be done with this please. I beg your mercy."

Mistress Circe cackled at that. "Mercy? Never, you ungrateful bitch. You think you are so high and mighty. I wonder what your so-called Temple would think of you if they knew you are a whore that can be bought? Just put a collar on you and you become a dog. You can rot, Psycho. You know what? I think your Coven should know about you. I will be there on the New Moon. If I were you, I would stay home that night. I plan to share information with everyone there about you. See you at the Temple, Psycho." She hung up.

I stood there listening to the ring tone in shock. I finally hung up the receiver and got on my bike. Mistress Circe was going to tell the entire family about my delusion. I would not be able to stop her unless I murdered the Crone. She had the right to address the Coven as their Elder. Truth is, I also knew everyone there had the right to know who they were following. I would have to endure whatever judgement the members would call on me if she decided to go through with it. I now understood why the Goddess had warned me.

I had heard her words, "Be truthful. Do not keep secrets in my sacred place."

Mistress Circe could tell them. I wouldn't even attempt to stop her. I had to trust in my members and my destiny that they could fully accept me, all of me, as I am. They had handled my truths so far. The final secret would be revealed then I would either lead or fall. It was in the hands of the Gods. It always had been all along.

I took off headed back to finish my probation trial with Master Marie feeling peaceful that soon I would never have to deny my nature again. There is freedom in just being honest. It tends to glean the false from the truth, and it allows one to live completely in the light.

Master Marie was great. I have to say I really liked her a lot. She was firm but fair. She never punished too much, nor not enough. She also didn't punish me unless I really was wrong. In my time with her my oncoming prodromal had tried her more than the hopefuls before. I was irritable, insolent, and even violent at times when she asked me to do something.

My Master knew it really wasn't me acting that way, but punishment was necessary, or I would have gotten further out of hand. She never struck me with anything other than a belt across my backside when I refused to kneel for her punishment. I had destroyed her favorite tape in retaliation for her telling me to clean her bathtub. I don't know why I did it, but my anger at having been ordered around got the best of me. I am not a natural submissive, so taking orders is hard. However, it is how I pay my debt and I owed Master Marie. She was more than good to me. Not too many folks would have put up with my prodromal self. I am mean, mouthy, paranoid, and sometimes have very cruel emotional outbursts. Master Marie never took it personally.

She would say, "I really hate to have to punish you for this, but I understand if you think me a softy, next time it will be my neck instead of just my broken tape deck."

She sadly was right. My prodromal is the most dangerous time for others. The acute phase is dangerous for me, but I lose the irritability in that cycle. Think of Prodromal as the homicidal stage and Acute as the suicidal stage. After all anger and depression cannot reside in the same unit at the same time. Prodromal is full of rage, and periodic episodes with seizures. It always lasts for six months then breaks down into full blown acute madness. During this early stage of psychosis, I cannot be reasoned with using words. I can, however, still be afraid of pain.

Unlike when I am acute, I still feel it when I am hurting. So, the Keyholder must take control of a sinking boat with force. If I am not afraid of the Master, I will destroy them if given the chance. The anger will well up unchecked from within. Why am I angry and wanting to take it out on the Master? They are just doing their job, right? Well, I am pissed that I must live this way. There it is the truth. It is not the Master's fault I am like this, but when I start to go crazy, I cannot control my deep-seated resentment over my forced life of submission.

NOTE: *I will always blame the one holding the Key in my misguided, unreasonable, paranoid, fury, no matter how fair, loving or kind they have been to me. It is my unconscious anger at being schizophrenic that causes this backlash, not the behaviors of the one to whom I am collared. So, even Master Jon or Master Marie before him wasn't safe from my Anger Demon when I started to go psychotic. They must be able, willing, and strong enough to keep this bullshit under control by use of punishment, restraint, or even calling the cops when I get like this, or they will be in great danger. I have always turned down people who went for my collar who were too squeamish about this hard part of holding my key.*

Do you know how many times I have heard this line: "I could never hit you or tie you up. That is cruel. No one should ever be treated like that."

Oh yeah? I would remember that they said that while I did my time in the mental hospital while going psychotic during prodromal. To not protect me from myself, and them from me, is not showing compassion or love. It is showing neglect. I sometimes require a heavy hand. It is my burden to bear. It is better to have someone whom I trust, the holder of Simon's Key, than the assholes at a mental hospital dishing out what needs to be done. Do you really think they are just letting me run around being an asshole there? Uhm no. I misbehave I get restrained, brutally. There is no stopping my demons. It is just the way it is. A true and fair Master will do this for me at home to keep me out of the hospital if humanly possible. Eventually, even the best, Master Jon), must lock me up. However, he managed to keep me home longer than ever seen before during the worst psychotic break recorded since I first onset. Now that is a Master. He knows when to restrain, punish, and when to give it up to the experts when he can no longer handle my psychotic ass. So, on with the story now that we have that explained. Geez, rant much, Psycho?

She and I had gotten along very well. She was fun, loving, funny and I was hopeful she would win the bid. Master Marie told me that she would mortgage her house to make it so. I begged her not to do something so rash, but she reminded me she was the Dominant. I was never allowed to tell her what to do or not do. Therefore, I stopped voicing my misgivings. She continued to plot ways to get more cash so that she would be the hands down winner of the auction.

Truth was, Master Marie was falling in love with me. I didn't realize it at the time since it was my understanding she was straight. However, as seen with Mistress Andrea, true love doesn't recognize gender. Sexual preference is not so strictly set in some. Master Marie, who never believed she could adore another woman, found what she believed was a soul mate in me.

Had she told me of her feelings I would have corrected them. What she viewed as a perfect match was only my expression of my situation. I agreed with her on all things, was ready to do what she wanted, took loving care of her bathing/dressing/hygiene needs, and domestic duties, because that is my job. She misunderstood my behaviors as the Ying to her Yang.

I liked Master Marie as a person. She was awesome as a potential Keyholder candidate, but as a love interest, I felt nothing. She was just another damned asshole there to tell me what to do because I was compromised. If she loved me, she wouldn't have wanted to control me but would have done all the things a Master does without asking me to submit at her feet. She would ask me if I wanted to belly dance, cook that night, or wash her ass. Instead, I was ordered and expected to do as told or be punished.

Now how the hell am I supposed to love you when you don't even care enough to grant the freedom of saying "no, I do not feel like doing that." I may be crazy, but I am not stupid. This kind of situation set up by my Collar and Key is not a love match. It is a business deal. Too bad Master Marie, like her ex-husband, was falling for the fucking help.

Mistress Circe decided she didn't want to ever set foot in the Temple of Green. So, the night before the Full Moon Esbat she called the original Coven members, including myself, to meet with her at her place. She wanted to "out me" to them. Since she never came to any of our Esbats or the Litha Sabbat she thankfully didn't know Linda was one of us. So, Linda was never called to this most infamous meeting of the Coven of Green Rings.

The red van was parking in her driveway with everyone else inside as I drove up on the Motorpsycho. They all got out as Lisa asked me what this meeting was all about. I just shrugged like I was lost to the meaning like everyone else. I knew what Mistress Circe's game was, but I would be damned if I would start this terrible situation off with my own words. If she wanted to destroy me, she would have to do it on her own.

We all walked in together to find Mistress Circe sitting in her bean bag chair holding the Simon jar in her lap. She told everyone to grab a seat. She was ready to get the meeting started. I took a deep breath and attempted to sit down.

"Oh, not you Psycho. You will come over here and kneel next to me at my feet. Now," she growled before my ass even hit the bean bag chair I had selected.

I looked around at the Coven members. They were all looking from me to Mistress Circe in shock that she would dare to speak to their Priestess like that.

Tracy spoke up. She always did, fierce one she was. "Mother, you can't disrespect Mother Arodia like that. It is not right."

Mistress Circe shot Tracy a look of anger. "You will be still. All of you. It is time you all learn some truths your so-called Priestess is hiding from you. Psycho, I told you to come kneel at my feet. Do it now. I mean it. Do you want me to carry out my threat and give what is in this jar to a certain person? Hmm?"

I glared at her feeling my ears burn at her threat. "No Mistress. As you wish." I walked over and did as she commanded, cursing her with every nasty word I could think of in my mind.

I kept my gaze to the floor, but I could still see everyone in the room looking at each other with confusion at my having minded this most inappropriate demand made by my Mistress.

Mistress Circe reached out and patted me on the head. "That is more like it. Now, children gather in close. I would like to tell you all a fantastic tale. You will all understand what is really going on very soon."

Mistress Circe began to spew the secrets of the Collar and Key. She told of her capturing Simon in the jar. She still didn't know I got him out months before and of her selling my Key. She also unleashed the story of special services of the collar granted to each bidder once in the thirty-day trial period. In fact, if she thought it would be humiliating for my Coven members to know she spewed it.

The old Crone left nothing to the imagination even making personal references to my very gifted abilities in the bedroom, the benefit of years of sexual training.

No one in that room said a word or made a sound while Mistress Circe attempted to discredit me in every way possible. I kept my eyes to the floor knelt by her feet wishing I could just fall into a pile of dust with each new secret she threw into the open air. I quietly thanked the God and Goddess for having granted me at least a moment to be in their family.

I thank them for having allowed me to see what it was like to be loved, adored, and truly valued for something other than what they could rape from my unit. I knew it was all over now, but I did have it. I was ready to face the cruelty of life alone once more, stronger to know that one day I could find this kind of reason for being once again a family member now that I knew it existed. I wasn't angry or bitter that this beautiful part of my life was over. I have never been greedy (Simon owns that emotion), my time was up. That is the way it goes. Everything comes to an end, good and even the bad. I am used to failing, but then again, sometimes I win.

Once Mistress Circe was sure she had completely laid my reputation to waste she stopped talking. She sat there quietly. I am sure she had a big old smile on her face too. The members sat there in stunned silence. They looked at each other. Then they began to speak. I will never forget what they said till the day I die.

Tracy appearing still in shock at what Mistress Circe said, "So you took this Key and Collar from a woman who abused Psycho, made her Maiden so you could be Crone, even though she didn't want to be your Maiden. You then forced her into your bed, used her sexually, forced her to do the necromancy, and when she stood up against you, you answered by capturing her only friend in a jar. Or at least that is what you led her to believe. You put her on a leash when she refused to put up with you in bed by breaking up your shit. Then she lost her mind because you didn't give her medication. To top this all off, when she finally stood up to you, your answer is to sell her like a piece of property to the highest bidder, but only after you allow them to rape her first."

Mistress Circe interrupted, "They aren't raping her, Tracy. You are being overly dramatic. Psycho is just a whore. She is crazy. She thinks an imaginary person is in this jar." She shook the jar at Tracy.

James growled. "She is not crazy. She is mentally ill, Mother. You are cruel. How could you?"

Chuck joined James. "You are the whore, Circe. You bought the fucking Key, Mother. You bought it to force someone who was sick to fuck you. You did this by force. She sure was not willing. If she were you would still be fucking her now, wouldn't you?"

Lisa put her arm on her raging consort. "Easy Chuck, your blood pressure baby. Mother, he is right. You are disgusting. You are selling Psycho like a piece of beef. You have no right to do so. I am sick just sitting in the same room with you."

Mistress Circe didn't expect this kind of response from her "children." To be honest, neither did I. Circe said, "Wait. I think you have all misunderstood. Psycho believes this shit. Not me. I am just doing the job."

Her once devout Mary interrupted this time. "Shut up, you bitch. You are not worthy of my spit," she screamed. Everyone including myself jumped.

She continued, "Mother Arodia has more love and compassion in her hair than you have in your entire soul, and she is bald, Circe. You abused a mentally ill person hoping to get something for yourself, you greedy bitch. Now, by accident, you have created the most devout, loving, beautiful heart I have ever known. You called us here to try to bring her down, but you only have shamed yourself. Now I can see you. We all can see you. Don't bother to come to the Green Temple Circe. You are not welcome. I vote Circe out of the coven."

Everyone in the room raised a hand saying, "So mote it be," in unison.

I looked up stunned. They had just exiled the Crone from the Coven. Then Lisa stood up next to Mary. "Give us your cup, Circe. You earned it through lies. Mother Arodia honestly answered the Panel of Elders and took the Great Rite actual. She is our true spiritual leader, but you are a nothing. We are taking you before the Queen of Green to see your cup smashed and your broom broken. You are dead to us."

Mistress Circe sat there not moving a muscle in pure shock. I didn't dare move wondering if she would kill me now that she had just lost everything.

Instead, I saw Chuck get up and go to the shelf behind her. He came back holding her Crone chalice. "Never mind. You don't want to give it to us, we will take it. We gave it, after all. Well, you are finished Circe. We have heard enough from you. Come on everyone. Oh, and Circe, Psycho will be at ritual tomorrow night Sky Clad. If I see a single bruise on her anywhere, I will call the cops, to have me arrested when I beat you to death."

With that everyone got up and left me and Mistress Circe alone. They slammed the door behind them causing both myself and my Mistress to jump. I looked at the floor unsure what to say or do now. This was most unexpected. My Family didn't leave me, they stood up for me. I felt the rain clouds in my eyes as my vison fogged with pure gratitude. I had not been abandoned. I was loved.

Mistress Circe threw the Simon jar. It smashed into the door, glass and honey going everywhere. "Now your Simon is dead, Psycho. I hate you. Get out, get out now."

I stood up and looked at her with tears running down my face, but I smiled. "I got Simon out months ago, Mistress. I also saved my Key. You finish your auction however you like. Betray me further and I will make sure karma does worse than exile your status. Don't fuck with me anymore. Remove my collar now. It is time to pass it on. We are done here. Release me."

She stood up slowly then told me to kneel. She took out her collar key for the lock and opened my collar removing it from my unit. "I will keep your collar and pass it when the auction is done on September the 2nd. The addresses of the final two are on the table. Get them, leave and I never want to see your face again. I will call Mother Delleh and explain what you have done. You haven't won this yet Psycho." She was looking at the floor appearing in shock more than anger.

I laughed. "Mother Delleh sent me to destroy you, Mistress. You are not so clever. She chose me because she read my hate for you in my eyes that Yule. Go call her, she will not back your bid. Tell her what you like. You see that went very well, telling my secrets to others. Try Mother Delleh. How will she feel that you are a peddler of Priestess flesh? Hmm, you will be black balled from all covens if you piss off the Queen. As it is, you can find another circle, even start your own. But the Green Rings is now a memory. You are no longer welcome. I will have you removed if you ever try to enter our Temple. It is my duty. My Coven has spoken, they are the real power, and I am their slave. That is what you never learned. You never run a Coven, it runs you. No one knows how to submit to the authority of another like I do. That is why I am the true Priestess, Mistress. I never want to see you again. Thank you for all you have done for me, even though you never meant to. For that, I respect you for all time. Goodbye

Circe, may life rise up and always grant you all you deserve."

I stood up, went to her kitchen for the last time and grabbed the addresses. Then walked out her door forever. Buh bye, Mistress Circe.

She would technically reign another two months, but I didn't see her again until 2013, but that is for another story. Since she does appear again in my long life, you must wait to see what eventually happens to her, and why I was visited by her in the first place.

I went to the Motorpsycho and to my shock Mistress Circe's chalice was sitting on the seat. I understood what that meant. The Coven wanted me to take the cup to Mother Delleh to be smashed and her cords cut during the Samhain ritual before the Dumb Supper. Mistress Circe was now exiled from my Coven to be officially removed from all the Green Rings during the Pagan New Year. This was a true death for a Wiccan. You must do some evil shit to have your cup busted and cords cut. I called Mother Delleh as soon as I got back to Master Marie's place.

Mother Delleh answered her sweet voice called out, "Yes Daughter Arodia, something wrong?"

I cleared my throat. "Yes, I mean no. I mean, Mother, the Coven has voted to exile Crone Circe. They repossessed her cup. I have it in my hands right now. They banned her from the Green Temple. The vote was unanimous."

There was a moment of silence. "Did you sway them, Daughter? Be honest."

I took a deep breath. "Yes, I did Mother. It was because of me they voted her out. They were angered over my personal relationship with Mother Circe, and the disrespect she showed me. However, I did not ask for, mention, or otherwise get involved in the conversation that led to this unexpected vote of exile." There I said it.

She breathed sounding as if weeping. "This is a blessed day. You kept your promise to me, Daughter. I approve the exile if this is what the Coven commands. We will break the chalice and cut her cords before the breaking of bread during Sowen. Thank you for giving me this glorious news, Daughter. My prayers are answered. Circe can never take the throne and use the Covens for her pleasure again. Blessed Be."

I smiled still feeling I may cry from the suddenness of my realizations that I was never going to be alone again. Like a real family they had stood by me, didn't judge me, and protected me for all times from the continued abuses of Mistress Circe. Well, as best as anyone could anyway. I had accomplished what I was raised to do, I had cleansed the circle of corruption by my very nature. Mistress Circe had tried to use it to beat me down but instead she had destroyed herself. Amazing, mind blowing, incredible, destiny.

"Blessed be Mother. See you at Lughnasa." I hung up the phone, still smiling and crying at the same time.

Master Marie came into the living room to find me weeping. "Oh no. You okay, kiddo? What happened?"

I looked up laughing through my tears. "Oh, I just found out I am not really an orphan. I had family I had never met all along. And Master, they are wonderful people."

She smiled at me. "That is wonderful, Psycho. You deserved to be happy. Tell you what. Let's go practice our belly dance moves in celebration."

I laughed. "Sure Master. Whatever you want." I got up and joined her as we danced the night away.

The next night I attended the Full Moon Esbat. All the council members who had been called to the meeting the night before caught me before I could enter the Green Temple. They had left the children with Delilah and Linda who had not been there. They intended to keep that discussion between us to my relief.

I followed Mary, Lisa, Tracy, Chuck, and James as they led me away from the Green Temple to a distance, they felt they could speak without uninvited ears. I was nervous about this ambush. I wondered if I had been too rash in thinking they had accepted my secret without judgment. Maybe they were going to demand my crown as they had Mistress Circe's cup.

Instead, they all started by hugging my unit tightly then asked that I join hands with them. Mary spoke, voted to be the one to say, what they all had decided in their hearts:

"Mother Arodia, you are our spiritual High Priestess by the will of the God and Goddess. We apologize for turning a blind eye to the abuses of the Poser Circe when she was tormenting you for being so loved by those above. The council has voted to never speak of the things we heard come out of that vile woman's mouth last night to anyone outside this group of hearts. Your burdens are heavy, and any one of us are happy to help to lighten your load if we can. You need only ask. We honor your path, your rights, your privacy. If ever anyone of these Keyholders tries to abuse you again, we will come to your aid. If you have nowhere to run, we will give you shelter. If you are hungry, we will feed you. We love you because you love us. We are here. You never forget you have us because we will never forget we have you. You told us this circle is never ending. Yes, it is, even for our High Priestess. You told us every person must be held up when in trouble or the circle is broken. We are here to hold you when you are tired, sick, or lost as you have been for all of us. The God and Goddess will be done. So mote it be."

I looked at those beautiful faces in the deepening darkness. I laughed through my new tears of gratitude. "I am going to have to stop wearing makeup."

Tracy looked at everyone then at me. "Why is that mother?" She was quite confused with my strange short comment to their well thought out speech to me.

I laughed harder. "Because it is getting too damned expensive. I keep crying it all off, damn it. I love all of you, now come on and shock the shit out of me by giving the bear hugs you all seem to adore so much."

Everyone started laughing as each took their turn hugging me till I almost barfed from shock and squeezing. I was truly safe now. No more useless, exponentiable, forgettable, on the verge of homelessness, cemetery dweller. I no longer was just a representative of death. I know also represented the guardian out of the darkness. I knew it so well and found my way out. I am trusted because I know my way. Just follow me, the path is hard, but it does exist.

That night I happily announced to all the watchers that if they wished to initiate, we would provide a full initiation for those who were approved, they had to answer a few questions first, during the Springfields Lughnasadh Sabbat. The walls rocked that night with the sounds of cheers of joy as every single watcher signed Linda's petition to be considered. I moved Ginger to the top of the list. That night I stayed late and tested ten of the twenty who applied. They all passed, including my Lithia savior, the red-haired beauty.

I told Mary, that the Lughnasadh Sabbat on August 1st was going to be fucking huge that year due to all the initiations. The girls jabbed me telling me that I needed to not miss that feast since I had gotten too skinny. That made me think again about my budding insanity. I worried the last few days were a hallucination.

That night I asked Master Marie to prove to me that I was not just hallucinating everything. She slapped my ass laughing. "Real enough for you, Psycho baby? Or do I need to smack your ass again. I don't mind." She winked at me.

I was shocked but laughed. "Yeah Master, you got me. That seemed fucking real. I think I am good." I immediately sat on the other side of the room eyeing her suspiciously.

My coy behavior made her laugh so hard she almost choked on her own spit. "Oh my God. You are killing me. After I get your Key, I will have to chase you around the house every time I want a little?"

I smiled bitterly at that. "No, Master. You will have to chase me through the yards. I am pretty fast, so better start working out. Or call Dennis. He seems able to outrun me every time."

My response sent my Master into spasms of heavy laughter that lasted for hours.

However, when her final day of the trial period arrived, I didn't run away as I had threatened. I was unhappy to provide the special services of the collar, but I never betray the collar or its contract.

She, like the ones before her, didn't mess around. She woke me up that morning by throwing me over her shoulder like I was a sack of potatoes. This Master was incredibly strong for a woman her age, hell of any age. I was frightened by her behavior and began to struggle.

She slapped my backside telling me that she was only calling in her right to the special services. I was told to stop struggling and play along or else. I immediately stopped, realizing that Master Marie meant that. No need to get punished over something that she had indeed earned.

She was a beautiful and energetic lover. Like Master Peggy, I had no complaints. She not only offered return in her service, but she would also not hear of it being otherwise. She wanted a full partner in her bedroom. When she was finally done with me, she even ordered me to her bathroom and told me she wanted to provide me with bath service. I tried to escape that strange behavior until I realized it was a sexual thing she was after, not just a straight up return for service. If I must explain what that last sentence meant to you, then you need to experiment in your own sexuality more. Just saying.

I was sorry to have to leave the next morning. It was time to get to the next address on the list. I knew Mistress Circe was not going to sell my Key until I had been humiliated to the hilt, or at least she thought that is what she was doing. I would need to just get it over with. My right upper side and diaphragm had been killing me since Master Marie had finally fell asleep still demanding special services the night before. I felt very sick as I got on the Motorpsycho. Master Marie came running up to the bike to say a teary goodbye.

"I will miss you until we are together again, Psycho. I will get that Key. I promise you." She reached out and petted the side of my face.

I smiled. "I hope so, Master. If not, then let me say thank you for not abusing the collar. You have been very fair. I will always appreciate you for that. You were a real pleasure to serve."

She looked hurt. "You mean it was just service? I thought, I thought you loved me. I know I love you, Psycho. I don't want to live without you anymore. Couldn't you just give me the Key? Or if I don't get it for some reason, run away, and I will take care of you?"

I looked at the ground. "You are most kind to offer that Master. It is tempting but love wanes. I have children to attend, and I hope for a future of some kind. You win the Key; I will come to serve you. If not, then this is goodbye forever. You never get a second chance. That is the rule."

She nodded. "Then I will get that fucking Key if I have to kill that old bat to get it. Psycho, did you change the color of your makeup baby?"

I shook my head as I started my bike. "No, Master. Why?"

She looked scared as she leaned down right into my face. "Because your skin is as yellow as a banana, sweetheart. Oh shit. So are your eyes. This looks like jaundice, Psycho. Your liver has failed."

Looks like trouble. Well, no worries, who needs a liver, huh? Someone should have followed those prescription doses a bit closer. We still have two Interims to go till we get to our next Full Master submission. The next two are real different sorts of cats and both have huge surprises in store for Psycho.

Chapter 23: The Final Interims
The Revenge of Mistress Circe

Master Tammy is full of wishes for things forbidden. She has come hoping to enjoy the collar. This circle of silver is a temptation too strong for the lonely one. However, she is unwilling to serve in return for service. She will never accept her role. Despite this Master's failure to do her duty, lust for those things she doesn't deserve will fill her mind to insanity. Psycho becomes her obsession. She will watch quietly behind doors, plotting, planning. She believes she deserve to get that Key.

Master Tammy doesn't have a chance. She has lied about her abilities all the way around. She is without the funds to obtain what she had wanted the entire time. She attempts to force her way in. She is hell bound to have her dark desires. She must have Psycho even if she can't pay the price.

The Goddess Linda adores her Priestess and her new Green family. She is ready to follow the God and Goddess for life. She is still distracted by the old demons of desire. She knows that her beloved schizophrenic is now unobtainable to her. In Psycho's role as her Priestess, Linda is finally close enough to see what can never be. She will fill up with the green-eyed devil of jealousy. Her anger will threaten the relationship by breaking the heart of the one she loves.

Ready to meet Masters number eight and nine? Yikes. Not us. These two are nightmares for real. Too bad for us this must be done. If only we had known then what we know now. For these Masters bring a friend to watch your back. If you see them sneaking around get into an open crowded place. She is coming for us. Run, run, run. Pray that those who love you will notice you are missing and remember rope burns heal. Unfortunately, when it comes to the soul, wounds that make it that deep never congeal.

"Psycho, I told you this was a dangerous game you play, damn it. You got really lucky this time. Now, I have to worry that one day I will be called to identify your remains left in a field for crows to pick clean."

Dennis to Psycho during rescue from three-day kidnapping – August 5, 1994

"Don't be so dramatic, Master. I am sure I will be fine. I need to be on my way. Excuse me, but you must move so I can get to my next appointment," I said trying to wave Master Marie out of my path.

She stood in front of the bike defiantly ignoring my request. "No, you are going to the emergency room right now. Get off the bike, Psycho. I mean it. I may have officially ended my probation period, but if you try to leave, I will call the cops and report you as dangerous."

My eyes went wide. "You would call the cops. Why? I didn't do a thing to you. Get out of the way, Marie."

I was pissed now. I couldn't believe this stupid woman thought she still had control. Her time was up.

She reached out and jerked me forward over my handlebars. "Get off the bike, Psycho. I will break that pretty face if I must, but you are going to the emergency room. Kill the motor now," she growled pulling me to her face.

I fumbled but killed the motor. "Okay, okay. Let me go damn it," I said frightened at her aggression over this silly idea I had a failing liver. I didn't look yellow to me.

She didn't let me go but dragged me by my coat collar off the bike. She grabbed my wrist pulling me to her car. "I will take you myself. You cannot be trusted."

I tried not to trip from her rapid stride. "But I have another Master, what will I do? They are expecting me."

She turned suddenly her eyes full of rage. "Give me the fucking address. I will go tell the bitch you are in the hospital near death. I think at this point you had better start thinking about survival Psycho and stop worrying about this crazy fucking delusion of yours. You could be dying for all we know. Jesus, you should see yourself. You look like a school bus."

I looked at my reflection in her car door window as she unlocked it to stuff me into the passenger's seat. I thought I was a bit more yellow than I should be, but dying? That seemed an exaggeration. Master Marie pushed me into her car then took off driving like a bat out of hell headed for the local hospital. I argued with her about it the whole way, but she ignored me. I was going and that was final.

Once there the admissions nurse freaked out over my odd pallor. I was rushed into the back. Blood testing indicated I was at toxic level of my prescription antipsychotics. My flooding system had tried to cleanse the overage by sending it to the garbage can of the unit, the liver. These immensely powerful drugs had irritated my liver so foully it shut down in retaliation. It was refusing to accept any more abuse. The doctors assumed I had overdosed in a bid for suicide. It took quite a bit of work to convince them I was only trying to hold off the oncoming acute stage of my disease.

Thankfully Master Marie was there to finally get them to hear what I was saying. I was still admitted and hauled off to a room, after they began the process of flushing my system of the poison I had accidentally, okay I really didn't know it was a dreadful thing I swear it, ingested over the last month and a half.

Doctor Commisso was called in. He gave me a stern lecture about following all labels. I was warned to never increase or decrease my dosages again or else. "Or else" is code for Inpatient in a mental hospital. I heard that threat loud and clear. The physician told me I was in for at least three days. There was no way I could be completely flushed faster. Luckily, no permanent damage had been done. Within twenty-four hours my skin began to lose its fancy yellow color. I really hate yellow and white.

Master Marie was true to her word, as always. She went to my next Interim and told her I would be there as soon as I was released. Master Marie even said she would come pick me up when that happened. I took her up on the offer since my bike was still at her house. I called my Coven and everyone was notified I would be okay, but I had taken a bit of a spill.

Unlike any other inpatient treatment I had ever had before, there were so many visitors and flowers I wondered when I would get to sleep. Master Marie never left my side. She even slept in the uncomfortable chair in my room. It is truly too bad she would not win the Key. It has always been my belief that had she won, my life may have been better sooner than 2013. However, it sadly was to never be. Mistress Circe made sure of that. She had one last horrible surprise in store for me. Well three more to be exact.

The first one began on July 5th. I was finally released from the hospital. Master Marie took me back to her house to pick up my bike. She had spent the last three days begging me to move in with her and give up my chase of the Key and Collar. It had started to get on my nerves. I even explained it wasn't my delusion but Simon's. She would have to take it up with him.

When she asked where she could find this dude I smiled and said, "You can't, that is the problem, darling."

I was glad to be leaving. While I appreciated and really liked Master Marie (I really did), I was not in love. She most unfortunately was. This made my departure more than uncomfortable. Master Marie broke into tears, promising money, adoration, and worse of all, fell to her knees begging me. I told her to get up and stop humiliating herself in front of one she hoped to submit in two months. She eventually moved out of my way and I took off. Had I known what was coming, I would have reconsidered my behavior that day.

NOTE: *However, I don't have the gift of seeing the future. Had I taken the path she offered, I would not be here now. She is still alive today at eighty-three. She developed dementia around age seventy-three. There is no doubt in my mind I would still be serving her right this moment. I never betray my collar. Even when her mind went, I would have stayed by her side. I never abandon my Keyholders when they need me the most. If they always kept their ends of the bargain, I stay. I got sick, she didn't dump me. It would have been the same when she got sick. It is likely Master Marie would have been a stellar Dominant until her mind went south. So, there it is. As it was, I left and followed my Key, just as Simon says I must.*

However, I kept in touch with Master Marie until she could no longer recall our relationship in 2012. My letters came back undeliverable due to her move to a nursing home facility. I was in deep shit myself by then, that story is in future chapters, so I never made it out to see her. I will be honest, she stopped writing back coherently before then. She may still be alive, but Master Marie is not here anymore. It breaks my heart this was her fate. She was a good hearted, independent, fun loving, strong woman.

Master Marie deserved better. For the record, she never took another to her home or heart if I am to believe her correspondence. She was always honest with me, so I will believe her until someone can prove otherwise. Normally when I leave a Keyholder I try to avoid keeping in touch for obvious reasons. Master Marie was an exception. She had saved my life and it was not over my liver incident to which I refer. If I had not met Master Marie, if I not gotten sick. I would not be alive today, believe it or not.

Eight Interim Master (No collar no key)
Interim Master Tammy: the Deceiver
July 5th to August 2nd, 1994, also August 3rd to the 5th

I drove almost twenty miles into the sticks to the next address on my list. This second to the last Interim lived in the middle of nowhere. The towns of course were all nowhere. I pulled down a long, near washed out, rutted driveway to find an unpainted, ugly house that was older than Master Anita had been. The porch was falling in on one end with an old-fashioned tin roof. This house was a shack more than a true dwelling. I sat there looking at it wondering if this Master was one of those people who had a lot of money but lived like paupers. I just shook my head thinking that I would be glad to submit to a real Key holder this time, almost. This constant moving around was starting to get to me. I needed stability especially with the winter coming and with-it acute psychosis.

I went to the door sending several rats running for their holes deep in the walls of this ancient place. That caused me to raise my eyebrows. Just what the fuck. I knocked and then got off the porch this time. No way I was sticking around to see what this crazy bitch was going to do.

The door opened and out popped a woman much younger than any Interim before her. She was only forty, with long black wavy hair. She wore a pair of big black glasses like Master Peggy and Mistress Nikki did. Her eyes were pale blue with a pouty mouth. She was neither heavy nor thin. I noted right away her clothing was as poor in quality as my own. If this lady was able to afford my Key, then she sure as shit was hiding it well.

"You finally came. It is about time," the woman growled.

I looked down at the ground. "Uhm Yeah. I was told Master Marie met with you, told you about my situation. Anyway, I am here now. I apologize. I get sick like everyone else sometimes."

She glared at me. "A woman came and told me you were in the hospital. She was a bitch. I want to know what you plan to do about my lost days. You owe me three." Her voice was high pitched and cut into my brain.

I shook my head. "Sorry Ma'am but I can't help you there. I must depart for my next appointment on the second of next month. It was only three days. I doubt it should matter much in the great scheme of things. You still have plenty of time to decide if the Key is something you want to obtain even with the loss."

She grabbed her glasses taking them off appearing quite angry. "Well get in the house then. You are wasting even more of my precious time standing there with your excuses and bullshit."

I nodded wondering what was up this woman's ass but followed her inside. The inside of the house was no better than the outside. The furniture was threadbare, worn, and sparse. Her kitchen was not well stocked and cleaning supplies were nonexistent.

I looked around this "slum" and then to the woman narrowing my eyes. "You are living a bit rough, aren't you Ma'am?"

She frowned. "With what Circe wants for that Key, looks like that won't change anytime soon. You would think your ass was made of gold. You had better be fucking awesome. I almost choked when she told me what that damned thing will cost me."

I backed toward the door realizing something was wrong here. "I had better be awesome. Ma'am, I don't even know your name. I also don't know what you think I am here to do. So, I think you had better tell me what it is that you think Mistress Circe is charging for."

She snorted. "She said you do whatever I want you to do. My name is Tammy. You will call me Master Tammy. I think we can get started now. As I said you have already screwed me out of three days." She began to move toward me.

I backed toward the door ready to run. "Whoa, Master Tammy, back off. I am not your whore. I am not here to satisfy some weird ass sexual fantasy. This is a service for service contract. If Mistress Circe gave you the wrong impression, I am sorry, but you can take that up with her. You step one inch closer, I will leave. I mean it." I was not going to fool with this weirdo.

She stopped in her tracks appearing confused. "Oh? Service for service? I don't understand."

I growled. "It means I take care of you when you take care of me, Master Tammy. You are not bidding on a sexual plaything. That is a service like everything else that must be earned. I don't just jump in your bed because you say so. Now you and I can sit down and discuss this, or I can leave. Up to you."

She looked at the floor then her ripped couch. "Okay, let's sit down and discuss this. I suppose Circe pulled a fast one on me. Damn woman. Have a seat, Psycho. Let's come to an arrangement."

I snorted. "Uhm, that is exactly what I am here to do, Master Tammy." I took a seat in her ratty recliner as she sat on her couch.

Over the next couple of hours, I cleared up her misunderstandings of the services of the Key. She seemed to understand and, unlike in the beginning, seemed to soften her hateful stance. Finally, she asked about my reported sexual services. I started to lie to her and say I didn't provide that service, but I knew that if this woman won my Key or spoke to any of the other Interims she would find out.

"The special services of the collar are offered once at the end of your trial period. This service is earned only by perfect return for the services I provide to you. If you don't do your job, I am not obligated to provide this service even the one time."

I sighed angered that once again this Master was going to insist on trying this out. Just once I wanted to find someone like Master Anita who was not interested in making me fuck them.

NOTE: *Let me just take one moment here to say something I have always wanted to say. If I were to meet someone who came to my house to provide services, I wouldn't force them to sleep with me, nor would I ever think about wanting to sleep with them. Do you know why? Because even though Simon owns Pride, I still don't want to be with anyone who doesn't willingly want to be with me. I am not talking about rape here, that is an obvious no, but if that person told me they offered this kind of service, I would say: hey great. If you find that you are interested, I am game. Otherwise, I am good as is. It is maybe just me but forcing someone to provide a service when they are clearly only paying back, and I was clearly making them do it is just not a fucking turn on.*

I would have found any of these women worth sleeping with had they allowed me to grow to want to. These idiots had no respect for me or themselves by forcing special services of the collar knowing that they may never hold my Key. I think of all six of them as Date Rapists. There I said it. If you think about it, you may see my point. A date rapist takes more than you were really expecting to give. It is hard to prosecute this type of rape because the law wonders how you didn't have knowledge that could happen. Well same thing here. It was wrong for these women to take advantage of my situation.

Can I sleep with a Keyholder? Uhm, yes. You will read about that in time. However, if they are only holding my collar for thirty days then there is not enough time to learn to like them, much less adore them. Anyway, so I am saying this whole situation set up by Mistress Circe was more than cruel and it was total bullshit. There I feel better now. On with the story.

Master Tammy nodded at the end of our discussion, appearing willing to continue this trial period. She asked me to cook her something for dinner. I did as commanded but noted that she sat at her shoddy kitchen table watching me while looking at my unit up and down as if I were the one she was eating for dinner. It gave me the skivvies to say the least.

The story she gave me, see I have reason to doubt anything she told me, about her situation was one of woe. She told me she had been married to a man at eighteen and had a daughter. Master Tammy had always known she was gay but was afraid to admit to it due to the likelihood of shunning. She secretly took a female lover. Her husband came home early one day and caught her in the act with her beloved Mistress. Master Tammy was immediately thrown out and her daughter's custody awarded to her husband due to her status of sleeping around with women. Her ex-husband had refused to let her see her daughter all her life. When the child had grown, she too refused to accept Master Tammy who now was open about her sexuality.

This loss of her child's love caused a deep depression that Master Tammy still grappled with to that very day. She had moved out to the sticks and bought this run-down home to fix up far from the society that she believed would never accept her. She had been seeing Mistress Circe for over two years for spiritual counseling due to her extreme sadness and crushing loneliness. It was then she was told of a Key that would bring Master Tammy an answer to all her problems. A hard worker, which would fulfill all her pleasure needs, and could never judge or leave her. It was a temptation too hard for Master Tammy to turn down. She had thrown her hat into the run for the silver ring at once.

I accepted her answers to why this home was in such bad disrepair and began to aid her by fixing it up wherever I could. However, she did not provide me with any materials, money or even tools. I brought some of my own from my yellow house and scavenged what I could from pieces that had been dropped off over the years. I killed the rats with poison and her BB gun she kept for scaring off raccoons and other vermin from her porch when they came making racket at night.

Master Tammy was very lazy. She didn't do any housework and only rarely went to the grocery store. Worse yet, she did nothing in return for my hard labor around her house. She never once offered me a meal, much less reminded me to eat. She didn't seem to care if I bathed, and never bothered to learn even the names of my medications. All that Master Tammy did was sneak around the house watching me while I worked. It was just fucking creepy. I would be nailing on a fallen board turn around and catch her sitting in a lawn chair just watching. I would even wake up at night to her sitting in a chair watching me sleep in the dark. I was beginning to think this woman was more insane than me.

I warned her several times of her neglect of duties. She would always promise to try harder, but Master Tammy never pulled her weight. As the month progressed rapidly, it was very clear, she was not capable of being a Keyholder. I would have called Mistress Circe to tell her to remove Master Tammy from the auction, but I knew better. If Mistress Circe knew I didn't approve of Master Tammy I was certain she would select her just to pay my ass back for her perceived injuries. If I left before my expected date, Master Tammy surely would call my Mistress and warn her. I couldn't risk that this idiot would win by being the worst thing Mistress Circe could still do to me. Therefore, I kept my mouth shut and counted down the days till I was free of this nutjob.

I was missing my medications constantly, but that didn't matter anymore I thought. I was already getting sick. The pills had not helped, or so I thought, so I quit bothering with them. Hell, the way I saw it they had already sent me to the hospital. Good riddance. As for eating, Simon was clearly visible now. About every three days he would insist I eat. I did but only after boiling the shit out of everything. Now, if you don't know, boiling will knock out valuable calories and vitamins when the food was never meant to be boiled. I was eating baby food. Boiling it was the worst thing I could do. It not only made it taste strange, further setting off my delusions I was being poisoned, it also killed any chance the food would help keep me from plummeting in my weight.

The Coven members noted my severe drop in weight, as well as my confused and agitated behaviors during the New and Full Moon Esbats that month. They called me for a meeting just after our full moon ritual was over when the circle was open.

"Mother, you are extremely ill. We want you to go into the hospital now. Please do this for us. We are afraid. You are thin, paranoid, and sometimes you are babbling. We love you, so understand this is not to get rid of you. We will be here when you are well. We will even come see you," said my Maiden Mary.

Tracy nodded. "Sister Mary is right. You look tired. Everyone is scared you are going to be hurt. Please listen to us."

I nodded at my members' sound advice. I assumed they may be right. It was unusual to have to go in-patient during this early stage of my psychosis but without a stable Master, it seemed the right thing to do. I needed help. Master Tammy wasn't giving it. I no longer could be trusted, and I still had enough sanity to understand that. The girls shed tears as I removed my Triple Goddess Crown and my Priestess robe then handed them to Maiden Mary.

I looked at the ground. "Take these, Daughter. It is time for you to do your duty and take up the seat of power in the circle. I will step down until I have paid my price to the God and Goddess without argument. From this day forward, keep these items here in the Green Temple. I will never take them with me again. That way if ever I am taken to the Summerlands by my struggles with the disease, the Green Temple can continue. Maiden, these items are only important in that they remind you of your burdens. Remember, you are not above anyone here, you are on your knees to their will. They grant you the power of leadership. They can take back the gift just as easily. Never forget you are not a Goddess so you cannot know everything. When your Sons and Daughters look at you, lead by pointing them the way but never force them to follow. This is their journey, not yours. If they choose to go another way, that is their right. Freedom of choice is the lesson you must teach. Never step in unless it threatens to harm the circle. Allow your children to make their own errors. If you do everything for them, they will become dependent. You clip their wings then they can never fly. It is a challenging thing to know when to let them fail and when to catch their fall, but if you stay true to your function as Mother instead of Ruler, you will know when which is necessary. Failure is a wonderful teacher of wisdom, my beloved Maiden. Just make sure you are there to kiss their wounds and help them stand again when things do go wrong. Remind them that a mistake is only a mistake if you never attempt to fix it nor learn from your errors."

Maiden Mary teared up as she took my words, robe, and crown. "I haven't earned the right to wear these, but I will do as you ask me. Mother, please return soon. I will be counting the days."

I smiled bitterly. "Me too, Daughter. Tell Mother Delleh and my handsome Priest, I love them."

Lisa, Tracy, and Mary gave me tight hugs as I got on the Motorpsycho headed back to Master Tammy's house. I assumed I would be gone for many months. I would even miss the Samhain Sabbat at Springfields. I had suffered much to make sure that Mistress Circe was thwarted in her attempts to steal the Green throne. It pained me to know I may never see it with my eyes, but I knew my Sons and Daughters would allow me a memory of it with their own reports of what happened. For now, I needed help. If I didn't get it soon, I would not have ears to hear their excited retelling of the day that evil witch's cup was shattered. I left that night feeling confident I had made the right decision for once in my life.

The next day I left Master Tammy's telling her I was going to the store. Instead, I went to the local hospital ER ready to turn myself in. They took me to the back to do reality testing. I failed but just barely. I was now officially in the early stage of psychosis. To my complete surprise they gave me a new prescription of antipsychotics and sent me home. I had told them I was feeling urges to hurt myself and even others, but I didn't lie when they asked if I felt compelled to do anything dangerous.

"Well no. I know it is wrong to hurt myself and other people. I am just sort of thinking about it a lot. I can't stop thinking about it. The voices keep telling me to do it too," I said honestly to the attending ER physician.

"But you know they are voices and are not right, correct," he asked, never bothering to even look up from my chart.

"Uhm yeah, for now. Sometimes, I think maybe they are right, or real but I recall I have schizophrenia. I keep telling myself not to listen to them." I looked at my shoes.

"Ah, good. Keep telling yourself that. Take this new medication that just came out, it will help. Don't forget to follow up with you psychiatrist in a month." He handed me a prescription.

I looked at him in shock. "Sir, I just told you I have schizophrenia. You read that in my records. I am almost sure it is mentioned often. I can't be sure I can tell myself anything. Do you even know what psychosis is?"

He frowned then looked over his glasses. "Young lady, I am aware of what psychosis is. You obviously are mentally ill, but you are rational. I think you just need to start taking your medications properly. If you would try harder, you could avoid these chronic hospitalizations you seem to have had in the past."

I glared as I interrupted him. "Seriously, you are going to try to blame me for being sick. I was taking the fucking pills. They are not working. Okay, you know what? Fuck you, asshole. I am out of here. Make sure to leave your address on your discharge sheet. I will see you real soon." I got up and stormed out of the hospital, not even bothering to get his prescription.

I drove home faster than I should have hoping the bike would veer off the road and end my cycling disorder once and for all. I was not truly suicidal, yet. I was, however, not against my dying. I truly didn't want to go mad again. The idea of a long, dark, quiet nap for all eternity sounded inviting. My attitude was already shifting from that of being a blessed peaceful Priestess to chaotic shards of rapidly shifting but shallow emotionality. If you want to know what that is like, think of my past descriptions of my thoughts and behaviors. I was erratic, agitated, paranoid, and becoming mean as a snake. I could just as likely hit you as hug you. The psychosis was slowly growing into a driving force of terror within. I was still lucid often, but the episodes of insanity were growing more numerous by the day, sometimes by the hour.

At my funeral home job, I had been adjusting well despite my growing problem. My new work Master June was a bit more involved in checking my work than was my previous, the rat bastard Pat. I would see Pat from time to time and just glare at the fucktard. I really hated him, and he knew it. I would spend hours imagining bowing him over tables and filling him ass first with embalming fluid. I knew Nikki was safe now, but I couldn't help wondering if

262

Pat would not just hurt some other poor girl. It was becoming a dangerous obsession constructing ways to end his days above the grass line.

It was becoming more and more common for June to come in to work to find me daydreaming of the evil things I wanted to do to Pat rather than finishing my job. She was very calm but a true task master.

"Psycho, I don't want to be a bitch, but you must start working dear. These folks are not able to do this for themselves," she would say when I was still attending my workload as she came in at sunrise.

I would smile bitterly. "Yes Ma'am. Sorry about that. I am having some trouble with focus."

June was a spinster of the mature age of fifty-five. She had medium length blond hair and was a bit on the short and fluffy size. Her smile was often contagious, but she tended to have a bit of a mean streak. Whenever someone she had not liked in life came through our door, she would say ugly things about them while we prepped them for their journey. I know they couldn't hear her, at least I hoped the couldn't, but it seemed disrespectful. When I pointed that out, she would laugh and tell me she hoped they heard her because she hated them.

Despite this most heinous practice of hers, she was fair in the price she charged, and she was a hard worker, unlike Pat. Overall, I had no complaints. I was glad I had asked for the re-assignment. June, unlike Pat, was all business when it came to work ethic. I seriously appreciated her.

I finally told her, after being turned down at the emergency room, that I was going septic psychotic. She raised her eyebrow and asked if I was taking my medications. I sighed and said not anymore because they didn't work. June became angry and demanded I start taking them again or she would call the boss and have me laid off.

She told me she refused to work with an unmedicated schizophrenic. I informed her that I often couldn't recall taking them. June didn't let that excuse fly. From that moment forward, she made sure I took them by reminding me when I was on shift. However, it only worked while I was at work with her. My pills required all day maintenance. To her credit she tried but it just wasn't enough.

NOTE: *The sad truth was the pills only slow down the cycles and knock off the deepest of psychosis. They never did manage to keep me from becoming psychotic at very regular intervals. So, why take them? When I quit taking the meds, the cycles speed up, increase in intensity, and last a lot longer. You are all aware there is no cure. There is no effective treatment either. Without the pills my psychotic breaks can last for two to five years at a time. With meds they are cut down to six to nine months. Either way I was doomed to suffer lifetime periodic trips to inpatient treatment, self-injury, idiotic and memorable public blowouts, and lost years while my unit rails and my mind is on Mars. Oh well, sucks to be me.*

As the month of trial Master status finally ended, I was more than frustrated and angry. I had tried to get help and been denied. My Interim was a useless bag of crap. My Coven was off limits till I could get my shit together. I also worried about losing my job when I finally blew my last gasket. I was not sure the boss would be okay with another seven-month incarceration in the Snake Pit. I wondered if a full Master submission would offer the stability required to at least keep me from going mad dog unchecked. I started to look forward to September 2nd more than I should have. I was getting desperate for assistance. I no longer knew what else could be done.

I called my Maiden and told her they had refused to hospitalize me. She was shocked. She and I decided I would come to the new Moon Esbat, and if I was lucid, I could work the circle, but if not, I would allow the members to send me away. They would check my mental health from that day forward before every circle casting. I eventually would have my Priest do this at all Sabbats too. It was for everyone's safety, including my own. I don't always know when I am off my rocker. Thankfully, I now had many around me willing to keep me from pissing in my own bed by acting a fool in my most important roles.

It was with great delight that I saw August begin. The next day I was due to leave the useless, creeper Master Tammy. She came to me that night demanding the special services of the collar. I have to say I was a bit more than incensed by her shamelessness.

"No Ma'am, I will not provide this service to you Master Tammy." I was sitting on the recliner reading a book on chakra cleansing when she came in demanding this service.

She stood there with her hands on her hips and a look of shock on her face. "You can't tell me no. It is the end of the probation period. I was told I got this service at the end. It is time."

I snorted. "I told you that a Master earns that service. You have done nothing but take too much already. You will never get that service from me Master. Now get out of my face."

She picked up a small glass ashtray next to her on a table and threw it at me. "You little bitch. I have waited to have what I paid for long enough. You will do what I say or else."

I was rubbing my now very smarting shoulder where her ashtray had made a connection. "No, you got what you paid for, idiot. I am out of here. Good riddance to you." I got up and left one day early.

This Master Tammy was a fool and lazy. I had figured out she didn't even have the funds to attempt to purchase my Key. She was either lying to Mistress Circe about being able to pay to get sex, she thought I couldn't say no remember, or she was Mistress Circe's attempt to punish me. The answer didn't matter. I was not sleeping with this idiot. She was disgusting in her entire person and just plain creepy to boot. I spent that night at my Maiden Mary's house. I was going to be damned if I would start my final Interim early just because the last one was an asshole.

The next morning was August 2nd. I was now only thirty days away from finally having a stable Master. I just had to make it a bit longer. I hugged and kissed my children goodbye and hugged my Maiden telling her I was off to my final Interim trial.

I need not tell you what Mary had to say about that. It was foul, trust me. She cursed Mistress Circe for putting me through this humiliation. I assured her that Mistress Circe had gotten hers, now I would have to finish my own punishment for not seeing the weakness in my Key rules in the first place. An agreement is an agreement. She accepted my explanation and told me she refused to judge me for it.

"One thing I can say about you Mother is that you always keep a promise. Your honor is amazing. I can't say I could be trusted in the same position." Mary hugged me as she said it.

I nodded as I started the bike. "You would if you were me, Maiden. I know it. Just take care of the children for one more month for me. Once I have a new Keyholder and it stabilizes we are moving home. I have it done. These dark days are almost over. Have some faith." I smiled as she smiled back nodding.

I drove back to the town where my yellow house was located realizing this new address was remarkably close to my funeral home job. That was very lucky I thought. I could walk to work from this Interim's house. There was no name as had been in the last three addresses. I hoped this last person was as good as the Masters before the last. I was in no mood for another Master Tammy.

I pulled into the driveway of a two-story handsome brick home with black shutters and a grey roof. It smelled of upper middle class with a huge yard in a fine neighborhood. I sighed realizing this final Interim had access to much more wealth than any before. This was at least a hundred-thousand-dollar home. In 1994, that made this Interim nearly rich. I wondered if I would have to wear a fucking maid or butler uniform for the rest of my days when this one won the auction. I no longer had any doubt this was the winner based on cash alone.

I sighed as I got off the bike. I was walking to the door when it opened. My work Master June stood there smiling at me.

My eyes went wide. "Uhm June? I think I have the wrong house. I will see you later tonight." I turned to head back to the bike thinking I needed to learn to read Mistress Circe's writing.

"Psycho, stop right there. You didn't make a mistake. Circe told me to expect you," I heard June yell behind me.

I stopped feeling the anger start to rise within as I turned around. "You bitch! You knew this the whole time and said nothing. How could you? Why? Just why?"

I yelled, realizing that this Interim had signed up three months ago. She had been working with me side by side knowing I would have to serve her in August. She never said a fucking word.

June started laughing. "Psycho, where is the fun in telling you? Now calling your Master a bitch isn't very smart now, is it? Get in here and let's get you started on your services. I am starving and I hear you can cook. Let's go. It will be fun. Oh, and bring those medications, we don't want you going nuts now do we?" She smiled as she stood there waiting for me to follow her.

I groaned but realized this was my life. I just had to get over myself. June had tricked me by never telling me she could afford my Key and was planning to buy it. All that time she had been watching, working with me, ordering me around with the full knowledge of my delusion. She had been also planning on how to use her probation period to full capacity. If she won the Key, she would be my guardian, work Master and full Master.

At least all my court ordered shit would then be in one household. She had been capable of reminding me to take my medications. So, it could have been worse I thought. I walked into her very snazzy home still grumbling over this most surprising turn of events. As Mistress Circe had promised, Linda was not one of the Interims. I could finally breathe easier in that fear. However, I was upset that like Nikki, I had been lured like a lamb to slaughter, never realizing the one I trusted was the one there to take advantage. I was already aware that June was a well-known lesbian and known for her won't take no for an answer attitude towards love interests. She had told me more than one horrid story of her forced conquests. I apparently was next.

Ninth Interim Master-final one of Mistress Circe's Interims (No Collar, No Key)
Interim Mistress June: the Work Master
August 5th to September 1st, 1994, and again September 28th

She made it clear immediately that I would call her Mistress. Mistress June already had a meal in mind she wanted cooked without even giving me a chance to settle in. She went on about how long she had waited to get her hands on me and how hard it was to work next to something that would soon be hers but couldn't touch it yet.

I began the process of making her dinner but sternly reminded her that special services of the collar were a one-time deal at the end of her probationary period.

She snorted then said, "I know that Psycho. I will have what I want in time, so if I were you, I would shut that pretty mouth and get to work. I will buy your Key, so it doesn't bother me a bit to wait this out. Soon enough I can do whatever I want when I want."

I slammed down the bowl I was retrieving from her shelf. "Uhm, no. I have the right to say fuck off, Mistress. I am not your fucking slave." I glared at this stupid woman sorry I ever met her.

She snickered. "Okay, sure Psycho. Whatever. You just cook that meal. I am going to relax. When you are done bring it to me on that waiting tray over in the left cabinet. We can work out your duties. I can't wait to try out this bath service I heard so much about from Circe."

I rolled my eyes. "I need eggs, Mistress. Do you have any? If not, can you get some? I can't finish this meal without them."

She narrowed her eyes. "No, I don't. You can go get them. I believe that is your job, isn't it? While you are at the store grab some of that food you can eat. You will eat tonight with me." She reached into her pocket giving me several twenty-dollar bills to do the shopping.

I nodded. "Yes, Mistress. As you wish." I sighed as I headed back out the door to the grocery store.

"Hurry back. I am starving," yelled Mistress June.

"Yes, Mistress." I was truly pissed off, but this is my job, so I got on the bike heading off to do her grocery shopping.

I parked the bike, went inside, and gathered up the items I was told to bring back. The whole trip didn't take more than fifteen minutes. Mistress June was just down the street from the local grocery. I walked back to the bike and tied the two bags to one of the handlebars thinking they would be fine there for such a short trip.

"Hey, Psycho. What are you doing?" I heard a voice behind me.

I turned around to see who called my name but was struck in the head by something hard, a piece of wood or pipe maybe. My mind whirled in confusion. My vision narrowed into a tunnel as stars blasted in my eyes. The world was spinning with the oncoming unconsciousness. I thought I felt myself being pulled, then stuffed into the backseat of a car.

I tried to get up, but my block was knocked off. My unit wouldn't respond to me, all of it feeling numb and paralyzed. I could feel the wetness of the blood as it poured down my forehead. I just moaned unable to do anything but lay there as I finally passed out from the blow. Just before the darkness of the void came, I realized I was being kidnapped. I was helpless to stop it.

I awoke but I was unsure how long I was unconscious. My stomach was rolling. I realized I was in a bed, but I didn't recognize the place. I tried to get up but with great horror I found I was bound to the bedposts by my wrists and ankles. I was completely naked. I turned my head and began to helplessly vomit. My head was pounding. There was no doubt I had a concussion from the kidnapper's whack to my noggin. Once I had emptied my pathetic contents from my rolling tummy. I tried wildly to get free of my restraints. I began to cry as I struggled desperately. I was terrified that Debbie had gotten the drop on me. I couldn't for the life of me recall who I saw when I turned around. This was beyond horror.

I heard someone in the next room hear my attempts to get free. Their footsteps were approaching. I went insane with terror trying to break free, willing to break my arms if need be, to get away before Debbie came to finish what she had started so long ago.

My writhing was useless. I was bound up tight. The person was at the door. I whined like a little bitch while I watched the doorknob turn. The door opened, but the figure was not that of Debbie. It was Master Tammy.

She stood there looking at me with a creepy smile. "Your awake. Wonderful. I thought I hit you a bit too hard. Oh, you have made a mess. I will get something to clean that up. No reason to get upset, Psycho. You will live here with me now. Until I am tired of you that is. So, if I were you, I would keep me happy. I am sorry it must be like this, but you just wouldn't listen. You belong to me. I am going to make sure no one else ever has you." The crazy bitch disappeared off to get something to clean up the vomit.

I laid my head back on the pillow. It was not Debbie, but it was just as bad. This woman was insane. She was planning on keeping me hostage for good. I felt the terror inside. No one would know where I had been taken, or maybe that I had been taken at all. She never aided me in attendance of my needs, and I seriously doubted she would now. I would starve to death slowly, while going mad in that bed. Worse still it was noticeably clear she intended to have her way with me. I would die a victim of kidnapping, rape, and murder after all I had done to avoid this very likely scenario.

I began to weep heavily when she returned with a wet cloth to clean up my sickness. "Please Master Tammy, let me go. I will give you what you want if you untie me. You don't have to do this. I am sorry I didn't realize you would be so upset that I denied you the special services." I was desperate.

I was willing to say whatever it took to get out of those ropes. If she would just unbind me, I could escape and report this nutjob. I prayed she would fall for it. She of course didn't.

She chuckled while finishing up her shitty clean up job. "Oh no you don't, Psycho. I would untie you, but you will just run away. I know better than that. Besides, I can't afford your Key. I want more than just a single night. I also don't want to be arrested. If I let you go you will tell on me. I have taken you by force. So, now that I have committed a crime. If I get caught, I can only be arrested once. I plan to make this count while I can."

I closed my eyes realizing she was going to kill me when she had her fill. This was a hard thing to deal with, but I would need to keep her happy. If I could buy enough time, maybe someone could find me before it was too late. I knew that with my history of luck that was unlikely, but it was my only hope. If I didn't comply, she would just end my life right away. I did my absolute best to steady my nerves. The sounds of her removing her own clothing told me that the rape of the unit was about to begin. I reached deep inside to find the strength to get through the nightmare unfolding.

For the next three days, I was tied to that bed. I was not even released to relieve my natural calls. Tammy would just laugh and pull the sheet and put another under the unit. She raped me constantly, in every way possible. I was not treated with any kindness or respect. She was often quite violent. I was battered, bruised and bleeding from every orifice. Tammy didn't care if she broke all my parts. She intended to murder my unit when she was finally tired of horribly abusing me. Only someone who never intends to use something for long would have been so careless. I was nearly insane with pain, fear, and humiliation before finally I heard a knock at the door late on the third day. Tammy had just finished hurting me again. She was sitting in a chair next to my bed talking about her lost daughter when the visitor came calling.

The suddenness of this sound caused her to rush from the room slamming the door, but she made the mistake of not gagging me. I heard her answering the door. I began to yell with all I had.

"Please, someone help me. I have been kidnapped. Call the police. Please help. Help me please," I yelled in a loop wailing like the loon I am.

The door swung open and there stood my hero Dennis. He had heard my yelling and busted into the house. He looked at me with horror in his eyes and then at once cut me loose from my bounds. He grabbed at sheet to cover my bloody unit while I shivered and wailed in gratitude. I had survived though terrified Tammy would come get me again. Dennis gently picked me up and carried me out to the squad car. I held his neck weeping like a little girl.

I saw Boyd. He had Tammy on the floor with his knee in her back pushing her down yelling at her viciously as he cuffed her hands behind her back. The ambulance was called. Dennis never let me go while we waited for them to arrive. He just held me while I cried full of thanks to the man who always saved me from my life of stupidity. Dennis was a great man, beauties. I spent my entire life trying to let him know, when I wasn't off my nut, how much I appreciated him. I would have died had it not been for his vigilant investigation abilities and Master Marie's having come to tell Tammy I would be late for my Interim trial period.

I found out while they treated me in the hospital for a concussion, broken ribs, dehydration, malnutrition, and vicious cuts, burns and contusions, the story of my rescue.

When I did not come right back from the store, Mistress June had gotten angry at my insolence. She drove there to find my motorpsycho abandoned and groceries tied to the handlebars. This confused her. She went inside but no one had seen me leave. She had promptly called my Maiden Mary and been told I was not there. Nor had I called to say I was coming. Mistress June went right to the police department and filed a missing person report when she saw drops of what looked like blood on the asphalt just next to the motorpsycho.

Dennis and Boyd came and checked out the scene but technically no one could do shit for twenty-four hours when I would officially be considered missing. Everyone waited for me to show up. When I didn't, Dennis and the others feared the thing they always thought would happen had, someone had kidnapped and murdered me. They were right.

Dennis and Boyd began to back track, even contacting Mistress Circe. She told them she had no information, the lying cunt, and tried to play dumb. Maiden Mary only knew vaguely about Master Marie. Dennis went to speak to her. Master Marie told them she had not seen me since I left to serve under Tammy. She gave them the address and the rest is history. Dennis didn't know I was there. He had only come to ask Tammy if she had seen me. When she opened the door, he heard my pleas. Dennis now had reasonable cause to push his way into the house. She was arrested and taken to jail. I was taken to the hospital and gave my deposition of the events while under heavy sedation and in much pain.

Tammy was arraigned and posted bail. She promptly disappeared. To this day she was never caught or found. Yep, she got away with it just like Julie did years before her. To this day there is an arrest warrant for her but that certainly didn't help me sleep any better. I would never be able to calm my terror when by myself in public or out in the open again. I developed agoraphobia and to this day I won't even check the mailbox without someone watching that I trust would call the cops if I were abducted.

Unfortunately, that would not prevent one in the future, but that my beauties is for another day.

I was in the hospital for another several days. Mistress June was pissed her interim trial period was being interrupted by the actions of another interim who didn't take no for an answer. She came every day to harass me about my getting out soon. I was touched by her understanding and empathetic heart, ha!

Dennis and Boyd visited several times to check on my mental health after this terrible crime. I was grateful. However, I did get several lectures from both about my lifestyle choices. I understood their concern. I of course always feared it, but it is part of the territory of being a schizophrenic.

When I had been told I had the disease when still just a kid, this was why I wanted to deny I had it. This kind of bullshit was a guarantee for a disabled, seriously mentally ill person without the protection of a constant support system. I had managed to gain a family and people who cared, but none were willing nor able to help full time. Only a Keyholder would do that.

Until I made the final submission, I was not anyone's responsibility unless they felt like it or had time. Think about that for a minute. Yeah, that is the problem. Mary and the others adored me, but they sure as shit weren't offering to take me in for good. Neither were they calling to make sure I was safe from me. Despite this latest fail, I would have to continue my path, regardless of the consequences.

My final visitor was my Goddess Linda. I still wish to this day she had decided to just stay home that day. I had been raped most diabolically, unnaturally, and unmercifully. She had no right to say what she did. Yet once someone voices something, no matter how sorry they are later, or what drove it to be said, it can't be unsaid.

I looked up to see Linda walking in looking bothered. I smiled. "My Goddess. How are you, Sister?" I was so happy to see a friendly face. I was sick of Mistress June's constant prodding to hurry up and get back to her employ.

She sat in the chair next to my hospital bed. "So one of the crazy bitches finally got to you pretty bad I hear." She glared at me.

I raised my eyebrows in surprise. "Uhm, I guess?" I didn't know what to say to that.

She shook her head. "I told you to stop jumping beds, Psycho. If you act like a whore someone will eventually assume you are one."

I choked. "Linda, you just called me a whore. Linda?"

She continued to glare. "Well, that is what it sure seems like, doesn't it? You have been with how many women this year alone? You fucked that guy at Springfields too. Psycho that is like seven females and one male in as many months. A whore is someone who does that."

I looked at the floor feeling the tears start to well. "Linda, I think you had better leave now. If you say another word, I will never be able to forgive you."

Linda growled. "Oh, is that so? I am just supposed to sit back and watch you fuck the whole town and say nothing? Maybe if I just sit back eventually you will get around to me too. Not sure I would want sloppy thirties, or fifties, or hundreds. What do you think? How many more in front of me, Psycho? Five, five hundred?"

I hit the call button for the nurse. "Get out Linda. I have heard enough. You are obviously upset, but you have no right to come here today and say this to me. If you believe I got what I deserved, then that is your right. I am used to others judging what they don't know a thing about. As it was, for your information, I was kidnapped and raped, nearly murdered because I said no. Hear that Goddess? I said no. She kidnapped me and took what I refused to give. So, get out. I have nothing more to talk with you about."

Linda suddenly realized her error. "Oh my God, Psycho. I didn't know. I don't know what got into me. I am just so jealous. I wasn't thinking. Please, I am sorry."

I glared at her openly weeping as the nurse arrived. "I know you are sorry, Goddess. Please leave now. Nurse, Linda needs to go. I am tired. Thank you both very much, but I need rest. I have another bed to hop into the next few days. This girl must gain her strength, you know."

Linda looked at the nurse but stood. "Please Psycho, I didn't mean it."

"Go. Get out," I yelled.

Linda was ushered out by the nurse, and I wept myself to sleep. Linda's words hurt more than the awful things Tammy had done to me. My unit would heal, it always did. My heart, now that was a whole different story. That was completely broken and irreparable. I now understood my Goddess was happy to judge me without even asking for the details first. That means she really saw me as a whore deep down inside. Her only problem with it was I hadn't fucked her yet. Since I was such a loose woman, my turning her down meant that she was not even good enough for the town whore. This may not be the way it truly was for her, but it is how I now would view her. It would take me many months to get over her attack that day. To this day, I still wonder, was I right in my assessment of how she really felt about me? Or was this just the green-eyed devil possessing my Goddess's soul.

I got released from the hospital and handed over right into the greedy, impatient Mistress June's hands. Tammy had already disappeared from custody. I was more than a bit afraid. I had to be restrained at night from the nightmares. When awake, every noise louder than a cricket fart sent me diving for the floor in terror. Tammy had done a number on my nerves.

To her credit, Mistress June was a good attendant to my needs. She made far too many sexual comments to a recent victim of rape, but empathy was certainly not an area she excelled at. I made up my mind that when her final day came, I would refuse her the special services of the collar. I not only was still very sore from Tammy's attack on my unit and spirit, but she was so nasty about it. I didn't think I would be able to psychologically handle her if she behaved that way when I was helpless in her bed.

Besides constant bawdy comments she chronically bitched that she had been robbed by my absences during the thirty-day period due to the kidnapping followed by the hospital stay. I told her that was not my fault, and I couldn't just make more time appear. The auction was happening September 2nd no matter what. I informed her that if she won the Key the lost days wouldn't matter anyway. She would have the Key for life if she wanted. That tended to shut her up, but only for a minute. She would start bitching again the very next day. This woman was a real pain in my ass.

School had started but it was only two weeks in when the momentous day of the end of the parade of Interims had finally come. I was having much trouble with focus but had still aced my first exams. Cherie and I were still not speaking but she had been calling Mary's house asking to have a meeting. I had refused to deal with her until after I had a stable home with the submission of my collar. One problem at a time was all I could handle.

Finally, September 1st arrived. I could barely contain my excitement at being free of Mistress June. I prayed that Master Marie would keep her promise and do what it took. I briefly thought about running away with her. Even if I didn't love her, I was no longer picky. The idea of being stuck with Mistress June for life made me sick to my stomach. I didn't want to be Nikki.

She came to me that morning demanding the special services she believed she had earned. I admitted she had earned them but. "I am sorry. I just can't, Mistress. I am still upset over the Tammy business. Please understand. You will win the Key, then I cannot deny you. Until then, grant me this mercy," I said while backing toward the door.

She shook her head walking toward me. "Oh no you don't. This is my right by contract. You already fucked me out of a week of service. I was short changed. Now you will make it up to me by providing me with the service I have waited patiently to have for myself. Psycho, now, I mean it."

I turned and ran out the door right to my Motorpsycho. I sped away never looking back. I was not going to stand for it anymore. The next day my real Master would come and all would finally be right again. I couldn't take the bullshit another day. I went straight to Maiden Mary's where Mistress Circe and I had agreed I would wait for her phone call after the auction was done the next afternoon. I hoped, despite all that had happened, Mistress Circe would still recall this agreement made long before her fall from the Green Rings.

I held my children tight that night sleeping in their room on the floor. My moments of freedom were about to come to an end. I had survived the terrors of six Interim Masters, a three-day kidnapping and rape at the hands of one, and the onset of a deep Prodromal cycle. I had found my calling, been raised to be a High Priestess, helped heal and cleanse a circle, aided in building a temple, and discovered a family. I restarted my education and became top of my college class. I had even freed my beloved Brakeman from a witch's curse. The year was only just half over and already I had lived more than some do in half a lifetime. I was tired, scared, hopeful, and above all ready to start the next chapter of my life. Mistress Circe had been selected for me in haste by someone who had abused their rights horridly. This time, I would have the Master selected by a Keyholder who wanted me dead and sold to the highest bidder. It was again, a bad moon rising no doubt.

Well, who is it going to be?

Chapter 24: Drum Roll Please, and the Winner Is
The Auction of Simon's Key
The End of Mistress Circe

The end of Mistress Circe's reign of terror had finally arrived. We knew we were beyond overjoyed. Not that her reign was not marked by many amazing wins in our bid to find our place in the society around us. It was her heartless greed and lack of human kindness that marred what could have been an amazing partnership. She just never understood that the real wealth was not in someone's wallet but in their heart. We had suffered a full year under her collar and then eight more months being tormented by her. Six of those months were under the leash of her flying monkey Interims in the most egregious misuse of the power of the Key to this date. She had even managed to select one Interim who took what she never deserved, intending to do a job Mistress Circe was too chickenshit to do herself.

We had, of course, made sure that this sort of nightmare would never be allowed to happen in the future. However, we had been very young and inexperienced in the early days of our delusion. This was a mistake, and we learned our lessons well.

So, is everyone ready to meet the woman who won the auction of our fate?

Our new Keyholder would be a force to be reckoned with. Unlike any before her she would know how to wield the power of Simon's Key to its full potential. She would both clean up our psychosis and make us wish we had just gone ahead and drove off that bridge the year before.

Until Master Jon no other would command so much of our respect, fear, and complete adoration. She would in time receive the honor of our Loyalty Dog and our heart. Too bad reality isn't our strongest suit. Her reign would end abruptly with a sudden change of her goals only two years from the day of her win that fine September day.

This Master will be plagued with a weakness of the same vein as the one before her. In love with gold, more than our silver, in time she will betray us most foul. However, not before she teaches us about trust.

Ready to meet the second most respected and beloved Keyholder we had ever known? Great. Then go ahead and bring an open mind. Don't be afraid when she brings in the ropes, it's all just an act after all. However, when she tells you to kneel you already should have been on your knees. She understands what it means to be on top. The question is, do we really understand what it means to be on the bottom?

"Sure, I am terrified Daughter Mary. I have no idea who this address belongs to. It doesn't belong to any of the six I served as Interims. With Tammy on the run, maybe it is her at a new house waiting to take me hostage again. God damn Circle. The old bat has fucked me one more time. Well, no matter. I must have faith that the God and Goddess are not done with me just yet. I will go and see who the fuck this person is, but if you don't hear from

me in one hour, call Dennis and give him this address. I usually don't ask for this, but just this once, say a prayer for me, Daughter. I don't think I can take anymore hurt."

Psycho to Maiden Mary regarding the address given to her as the winner of Simon's Key auction on September 2nd, 1994.

The morning of September 2nd threatened rain. I sat at the window watching the storm clouds gathering on the belly of the sleeping giant wondering who I would be submitting to by nightfall. Maiden Mary was in the kitchen making breakfast. I could hear all the children blathering and giggling while they enjoyed their pancakes and milk. It made me smile to know that they were growing up strong and happy with Mary's beautiful kids. Her children were as calm and gentle in nature as the Maiden herself. I did so adore that amazing woman. No person had ever been so blessed as me to know so many good souls or so cursed to know so many evil ones.

"Mother, have some coffee with me? I know you are worried. I will be honest, I am frightened to death for you. What if the next one is as bad as Circe? Is there anything any of us can do to help? Just tell us what to do for you." She handed me the cup of coffee then sat down across from me.

Her home was simple but clean. Maiden Mary didn't have a lot of money. She and Delilah ran a day care from her home. Ronnie, Circe's legal husband, did odd jobs and to his credit helped the girls out.

I never pried but it was my understanding that Mary had once been married to her children's father. The man had abandoned her for another woman. It was also my understanding that like me, she was still legally married to the creep. She and Ronnie more than most of the others understood my strange lifestyle relationships because their own was more twisted than a dogs hindleg.

"It is my burden to bear, beloved daughter. It is up to the Gods now. I only hope that somewhere in Circe's dark heart she shows a shred of compassion and lets the Key go to Master Marie or even Master Peggy. I pray it is not Mistress June." I gazed into my cup of swirling java as if trying to divine the identity of my next abuser, errrr, I mean Master.

"After what she did to you with Tammy, Mother, how can you even hope that" she said sounding disgusted.

I looked up startled by my Maiden's apparent realization of what I had already suspected. "What do you mean, Daughter? Tammy wasn't Circe's fault. The woman was nuts." I looked at the floor knowing the truth but refusing to admit to it.

Maiden Mary growled. "Mother, you are wiser than that. Circe was seeing that woman for counseling. She already knew Tammy was an abuser and you know it. She also had to know she was too poor to afford the auction. Mother, Circe denied she knew where you could be. She knew damned well where you were. She hoped you were buried in Tammy's backyard." She glared at me, appearing to demand I say that I was aware she was right.

I nodded then sighed. "Yeah, Daughter. I think Circe used Tammy to do what she wanted to do. She had to have known at the very least the girl would rape me terribly and at the worst murder me in her attempt to do the first. I was told the woman had a history of allegations of rape on a young girl under the age of ten a few years ago in Michigan. It had been a violent attack. Circe had to know that. She also had to know Tammy was broke. Tammy was Circe's revenge. I also know that just in case that failed, she had offered the Key to Mistress June. Circe knew about June's sweet tooth for forced sexual encounters. I got Circe's message (I shifted uncomfortably on the couch) loud and clear Daughter."

Maiden Mary nodded. "I am glad you see what we all do. Circe wants you dead. Now I must ask, what makes you think today she won't call with the name and address of your killer? How am I supposed to handle that?"

I smiled bitterly. "Daughter, I won't go anywhere ever again without leaving my plans or whereabouts with you or one of the Family. I learned my lesson well."

She looked at the floor. "That is wise Mother, but what if next time Dennis doesn't get there in time. I can't, I won't, imagine what you went through. It keeps me up nights."

I tried not to start crying since the images and terror was still so fresh in my mind of those horrid three days.

The pain, the fear of each attack being the final one. The knowledge that maybe no one would ever find me. The faces of my children, my Family, Mother Delleh, my Priest, Linda, everyone I had ever cared for got me through those dark days of torture. However, my soul still ached from the wretchedness of it all. It wasn't just the sexual assault, though that was more heinous than I like to admit, it was the terror of wondering if your loved ones would ever know what became of you as well as not knowing which moment would be your last.

NOTE: *When Dennis had come to the door, Tammy had stopped her raping for the first time in three days. She had managed to inflict hideous indignity almost continuously, until that last hour. As she had sat there next to me talking of her lost daughter and life before that moment, I had figured out she was working up the courage to take my life.*

I had been aware that those were likely my last moments. I closed my eyes and prayed to the God and Goddess that my children, Family, and those I truly loved would have safe and happy lives. Making peace with my maker I had been preparing myself for death.

As it was, I had gone three days without water under terrible stress, screaming, crying, and bleeding. I was not going to last much longer anyway. Tammy didn't have to lift a finger to end me if she had chickened out. The level of dehydration discovered in the hospital told the tale. I was that close to the Summerlands. Tammy intended to have her fun then kill me plain and simple.

Tammy was not the first one to try to murder me. Debbie had attempted before, and I had done a fine job at almost finishing her job for her several times. Julie had a few near misses too. So, I was no stranger to the possibility of my life ending at the hands of some monster, including me thus the Key and Collar, but it never got easier. I don't think it ever should either. This one had really shook up my existence. I was in desperate need of psychological aid or I was going to fall into terrible despair over the sexual assault and attempted murder by Tammy. Circe had indeed got her revenge but she wasn't quite done just yet.

PS: Thanks to this incident, and lack of support I received from the secular world to help me to overcome my damage, I decided that I would find a way to change the way rape and battered women were treated in these small towns. I made sure all my Temple leaders were offered the opportunity to attend classes at legitimate places of higher learning, not Circe's bullshit, on how to offer crisis counseling for victims of rape, assault, and domestic violence. I paid out of my own pocket to send Mary, Lisa, Tracy, and several other female leaders (all volunteered, by the way) to courses designed to aid the ladies when dealing with members of our community, whether Wiccan or non-Wiccan, which suffered such terrible indignities. Our Coven offered information for resources, safe houses, and legal aid when money was an issue to prosecute offenders. More than that they offered empathy, love, and a shoulder to cry on when those nightmares come in the darkness, and the monster from

291

under your bed is ready to hurt you again. To this day any member at that Coven can point a terrorized, frightened soul to a place of healing, support, and strength. In this life you can bitch about the shortcomings of the world, or you can stand up and say Let the Change Begin with Me. So Mote It Be.

I looked at her trying to seem strong. "Maiden, I may have neglected to say this but thank you for pointing them toward Master Marie. She and you are the true heroes. If you two had not lead Dennis and Boyd to Tammy's house, my children would be yours now and I would be a memory. I will never forget what you ladies did for me. I will always love you for it."

Maiden Mary nodded, tearing up herself. "You owe me nothing, Mother, but I am happy to have your love. I feel it every time we caste a circle. You really care for all of us. I think it is because we all know how hard it must be for you, yet you fight to do it for us. I sometimes wish I could be such a strong person. Then I remember those scars all over you, and I think I hope I am never tested. I think I am likely a wussy. I'd rather not find out."

I laughed. "Oh, Daughter. Not even close. I saw that lioness in you when you voted out Circe. Wow! I was shocked and to be honest, at your feet in awe. Each person has more strength inside them than they ever truly know. I am not special, my Daughter. You could and would make it if we switched places. Trust me, the spirit to survive lives in all of us. The real key is just to find the faith in yourself that no matter what, you always do your best. You will find, Daughter, you have all the tools you will ever need to do whatever it takes to get wherever it is the Gods want you to be."

She smiled at that. "I will do my best to remember that. I got a call yesterday from Summoner Johnny at Springfields. Mother Delleh says she will allow the initiations of our watchers at Mabon. She sends apologies they had to cancel Lughnasah. She is feeling better these days."

"Ah, that is wonderful news, Daughter. I was worried the watchers would have to wait for Beltane after all." I was indeed pleased to hear this news.

Mother Delleh had to cancel our planned many white cords initiation ritual at Lughnasah due to her bad reactions to chemotherapy. It turned out to be a personal blessing due to my own difficulties in August. However, tradition dictated we could not initiate during the dark half which began at Samhain. Only Mabon the second harvest and feast of bread remained before my watchers would be stuck for six months waiting for the next chance to gain their rightful place in the circle. Her allowing this most unusual event to occur so late in our year was a true blessing, and a warning.

NOTE: *I understood this was Mother Delleh's unsaid notice to me her time was running out. She obviously was not expecting to survive the winter. If she had to leave her throne the new Queen may not allow my initiates to join at all. The Queen of Green was not taking* *chances. So, it was bittersweet news. I was grateful our circle would grow, but sad to see the end of my beloved mentor and Mother coming so soon. I already suspected the cancer had spread to her brain this time. I was sadly correct. That day instead of bothering the Gods with prayers for my own happiness of receiving a decent Master, I prayed that Mother Delleh would be allowed enough time to see Circe's cup smashed and her cords cut before she began her journey to the Summerlands. To that I say the Gods heard and honored me by answering my prayers. She did survive to reign over her very last and most amazing Samhain. Blessed Be.*

Every time the phone rang that day my heart would stop in my chest. Each time it was just a Coven member asking a question or someone wanting to talk to Delilah. By three that afternoon, both my own and my Maiden's nerves were raw as a well digger's cheeks during a late Spring blizzard.

At three-fifteen the phone rang. Mary picked it up and I knew right away by her tone, the auction was over. She was writing down the address. I took deep breaths trying to calm myself. It felt like the room was closing in on me. Everything seemed to slow down. The fear was rising. Who was it going to be?

Maiden Mary hung up the phone and walked over to me looking very somber and worried. That made me even more afraid.

"Circe? What did she say? Do I need to call her to get the winning name?" I could barely eke out the words, my throat was so dry from terror.

She shook her head. "No, Mother. Circe says she never wants to speak to you again. I have the address of the winner here. Please, before I give it to you, can I try once more to talk you out of going to this person? I can try to help you, we all can try Mother."

I interrupted her. "Daughter, you are kind, but this is not something that someone can try to do. It will cost me my life if my Master fails. Now hand it over. Let me see who it is." I closed my eyes and tried to swallow while my Maiden handed me the address.

There was no name, and the address was unknown to me. I blinked and looked again. This was not right, couldn't be.

"Did she give you a name," I inquired still trying to understand why this address was not one of the five who were in the bidding war. Did one of them move?

Maiden Mary shook her head. "No. She just said your collar is there waiting for you."

I nodded. "So be it. Okay, I suppose whoever this is will be waiting. I must go. Remember, if I don't call in one hour, call the cops. No exceptions." I got up headed to the bike after handing the address back to my Maiden. It was time to end this mystery of the new Master.

Maiden Mary watched me leave with pure terror in her eyes. I am sure, like me, she assumed that would be the last time she would see me. Circe had obviously tried to kill me with an Interim once, this was likely just another attempt. Otherwise, why the secrecy?

Master Marie and Mistress June had not moved, and I knew that. It was unlikely that Master Peggy, Mistress Andrea, or Mistress Nikki had either. This was either one that Circe had rung in or Tammy, ready to finish her job. I was grateful to see it was not Linda either. So, at least I had that in my favor.

I cursed the evil witch the entire ride to this unknown address. I finally arrived in a secluded area on a backroad off the main highway. I watched the mailbox numbers for the one I was seeking. I didn't like that the homes were growing further and further apart. I also noticed the homes went from brick to wood to trailer homes. The wealth was going down with each mile. I didn't mind serving a poor Master, but one must remember Circe was selling the key to the highest bidder. A poor person would not be able to pay. Therefore, if this Master was poor, then Circe had forfeited money to punish me with something terrible. This is exactly what I expected. When I finally found the correct numbers, I stopped to look down a long drive at a single wide trailer.

Circe had indeed forfeited her funds. This person was neither wealthy nor did I believe they spent some hidden nest egg on a magical Key they had never bothered to try out first. It was now obvious Mistress Circe had chosen revenge rather than Gold. Well, at least I could find some peace knowing she had just lost a fortune over her petty bullshit. I hope that knowing she had just fucked herself financially would be enough to comfort me on the long hard days ahead. I pulled down the drive doubting it would while I suffered at the feet of some monster she had just bound me to.

I killed the Motorpsycho, got off the bike and walked back to the mailbox. I wanted to be damned sure this was the right place. It was just too hard to believe the greedy witch had given up all the dough just to stick it up my ass, hopefully not.

I saw the numbers matched. I took a deep breath then walked back. The door opened. I nearly hit the ground in sheer shock. There standing in the doorway with a huge smile was my Temple watcher Ginger in a terrycloth robe.

"Ah, Psycho. You are right on time. You have the right address. Get in here silly. I have something that belongs to you, well on you." She winked then disappeared inside leaving the door open for me.

I looked around trying to wrap my mind around this surprise. Ginger? How? What? Why? I walked into her trailer ready to demand answers to this weird situation.

She was in her kitchen hanging up the phone when I came in. "Close the door. You are letting all the flies out." She laughed while grabbing something off her kitchen counter.

I closed the door then turned to find her already standing back in the living room holding my fucking collar.

My eyes went wide. "What the fuck is going on Ginger? Why do you have that." I pointed at the circle of silver in her hands.

She laughed hard. "Oh my God, you are a riot. I told you I love that about you. I have this because I bought it. You know damn well what is going on, Psycho. Why are you playing stupid? I was told you are trained. Was the stupid bitch lying?"

I blinked, still in shock. "You bought it? From Circe?"

Ginger stopped laughing. "Uhm, yeah. Does someone else have a fucking collar with your name on it? You need to get over here and kneel. I am already tired of this bullshit. It is time to submit. I paid a lot of money for your collar. I waited since just after Litha. I also had to give up the fucking Temple over this. I am ready to get what I paid for, damn it."

I shook my head in pure shock. "You bought the collar in June. That can't be right. You never did a probation trial. The auction just happened." I sat down in one of her chairs in complete melt down.

Mistress Circe had removed my collar when she was exiled then promptly sold it to Ginger the very next day. She had already sold it but sent me to Tammy and June anyway. I was kidnapped, beaten, raped, and near killed, but already had a new fucking Master.

I looked up at Ginger angrier than I had ever been in my life. "Why didn't you call me the second you got that collar," I spit out the words to this idiot.

Her smile melted into one of her own anger. "Excuse me? Did you just raise your voice at me? Did you just question my will," she said gritting her teeth.

I smiled crazily. "Uhm yeah, sure did there, Ginger. I was beaten and raped in August by a so-called Interim Master. You had that fucking collar and you let me go. Why? I deserve to know."

She looked at me, now appearing furious. "First of all, you are one insolent little bitch. Second, I was told by Circe you had two more months left on a contract with her to finish. I was told the collar was no good until September 2nd. If one of these so-called Interims overstepped the bounds during your completion of Circe's reign that is not my problem. Take it up with Circe, Psycho. As of today, your collar is mine. Now I will not tell you again. Kneel and submit."

I looked at her realizing she had been just as fooled as I had been. Circe fucked me over and lied to Ginger. I wanted to strangle the bitch. Not that I was that surprised, just that I was incensed. I wanted a few moments to think over this sudden and surprising turn of events. I was still reeling from the understanding that Ginger, a fucking watcher from the Temple, was trying to order me around. To top that off, I had not even done a probation trial. I didn't know if I would want to submit.

I looked at her trying to shake off my daze. "Uhm, okay, okay. Circe pulled some shit. You are right, not your fault. However, this is unexpected. I have not done my probation trial with you yet. We can start that today, but I need a moment to think this shit over."

Her green eyes blazed. "I don't think you are listening. I bought your collar. There is no fucking probation trial, Psycho. You belong to me. You will kneel and submit today, right fucking now."

I stood up angry once again. "Oh no you don't. I am not a fucking slave, Ginger. You can't make me submit. You don't own me. I have the right to say no. Do you hear me?"

She suddenly broke out into laughter. "Ah, you are well trained. Yes, you are right. You are not a slave at all. You do have a choice, Psycho. You can always say no to me. You have the choice to do what I say or you can choose to be punished for insolence. I don't own you till you submit but you are going to do that right now. Because we both know that if you say no, then I will give you the choice you made, don't we?"

My eyes went wide. "What did you just say?" I recognized the meaning of those words I had not heard since the reign of Master Julie. Ginger was speaking the language of BDSM.

She smiled. "Submit now." She came toward me putting her hands on my shoulders as she forced me to my knees in front of her.

I looked at the floor stunned. This couldn't be happening. What went wrong? I heard her suddenly making promises as if she had done this very act of submitting my collar every other weekend.

She promised to protect and defend the collar till death. She promised to serve me and demanded all my services at her pleasure. She ordered both monogamy and chastity at her complete command. This means she can recall either of them at her will. Ginger demanded the title Mistress Ginger. She went further to inform me that she understood the rules of the Key, then amazingly voiced them all and agreed to everyone.

Mistress Ginger finished, then demanded I make my own promises to her collar but first demanded my Key to bind me to her. I had been listening to her, but I was feeling confused and scared. This was happening too fast. I tried to get up.

Mistress Ginger pushed me back down hard. "Oh no you don't, Psycho. Give me that Key. Make your promises now. Finish and submit."

I reached into my front pocket shaking from despair and honestly terror as the first tears of realization that this was happening struck me. I retrieved Simon's Key. Mistress Ginger snatched it from my hand quickly dropping it into the pocket of her big fluffy white robe.

"Stop crying, Psycho. I can't hear you if you are blubbering," she said sternly.

I wiped my nose with my sleeve. "I don't want to do this."

She laughed. "Of course, you don't. You don't have to do this either. You can say no, and I can punish you for it. So, up to you. I am waiting."

I couldn't bear the thought of more damned punishment after what had just happened with Tammy. Mistress Ginger seemed very, something, but I was not sure yet. I sniffed loudly, still crying as I made my promises.

She wasted no time locking the collar around my neck. I jumped back but she grabbed my shoulders and told me to be still. I heard it click and really began my crying jag as I always do.

She stepped back watching me cry like a little bitch. "Hmm, cry if you want, but this is done, Psycho. Now head to my room. Time to consummate this wedding. I have been waiting for months for you."

I looked up very upset. "Please mercy, Mistress. I just told you I had an incident not too long ago. I need more time. I also need to call my Maiden or she is going to call the police. I need more time."

She interrupted me by grabbing my collar. "I called Mary the minute you pulled up. I assumed you were smart enough to leave the address with her. I would have. You had no idea who I was. As for your incident, I am not that Interim. Do I look like that Interim? No, I don't. You will get over that bullshit right now. I didn't assault you.

302

However, if that is what you want, then disobey me again. I mean it, Psycho. You always have the choice. Mind me or suffer the consequences. We clear?" She let go of my collar.

I nodded. "Yes, Mistress." I got up and followed her down the hallway still weeping like a child.

This was my job, but I was still so upset over the Tammy business, I felt I may die. Then we got to her room at the end of the long hallway. She opened the door directing me to go inside. I did as told and almost hit the floor for the second time. On her four-post bed was an assortment of thudding devices and other implements of BDSM as well as bondage ropes.

I turned around in absolute horror to see Mistress Ginger remove her robe. She was wearing a skintight outfit made of bright red latex and leather.

She smiled at me while grabbing a crop from her assortment of thudders. "Let the games begin."

I fell to my knees covering my face wailing in terror. Circe had punished me by selling my collar to the worst possible creature on earth. Mistress Ginger was a Professional Dominatrix.

Tenth Master: Master Collar, Key and Loyalty Dog
Mistress Ginger: The Sensual Sadist Dominatrix
Reign September 2nd, 1994, until October 5th, 1996

Mistress Ginger had not expected my sudden, violent reaction to her toys.

She grabbed my wrists still holding the crop in her hands. "Get up and stop acting stupid. You have a history with this I see. Well, I had hoped Circe wasn't yanking my chain. Now get up. I want to bond you and get to business. You are only going to piss me off and make this harder on yourself, Psycho. You know that this is going to happen. So, what is it going to be? My way or punishment? Just so you know, I like to punish. Either way, I win."

I fell to my face prostrating before this cruel woman or so I thought at the time. "Mercy, please. I hate thudding. I can't take the bondage. Please mercy, Mistress."

She laughed as she told me the story of how she got my collar:

"Now that is better. I knew you were trained. No way someone so young could command so many at the Sabbat or at that Temple of yours. Only someone who knows how to submit could be that damned controlled. I knew the moment I saw you walk into the Temple Sky Clad only with your collar on that I was looking at quality submissive material. Impressive to say the least. Then you had that little psychotic fit at Litha. I got to get a better look to be sure that was indeed a professional collar and not just a misdirected attempt at jewelry. There was no denying that was a sub ring. I asked around to see who you answered to. I was told about Circe being your Crone and put two and two together when they said you lived with the old bat. I decided to visit to get the scoop you know. When Circe told me your collar was up for grabs, I did whatever it took to have it. Now here you are. You may not like what I like, but that is tough shit. I don't like having to clean up drool or go months while you are in the fucking hospital sleeping off a crazy attack. That is the way it works. You know that. You have been doing this a long fucking time just like me. We are two sides to the same coin. I will do what you need, and you will repay me with what I need. Now get your ass up and do your fucking job, Psycho. Enough of this bullshit."

I heard her words realizing she was fucking right. This was what I was trained to do. I hated her for saying the truth. I would require a lot of defending, protection, and she would have to go long periods without any attendance when I flew off to Mars or when I was too psychotic to do my services correctly (right Master Jon). I would have to pay her back in any way she deemed fair. Even thudding and bondage was not off the table. I got off the floor back to my kneeling position wiping my eyes dry.

"What do you need me to do, Mistress. I apologize for my outburst. It won't happen again." I looked at the floor hating my life, hating her, hating the world again. So much for that incredible healing Mother Delleh helped me with, eh? Ah not so fast, give it a few days. I need to adjust just like everyone else. This was sudden after all.

Mistress Ginger was a sensual sadist. This means she liked edge play but not the kind where you nearly kill your sex partner. This kind of sadist likes to torture their partner by pleasuring them to the point of pain. How does that work? Simple. they either make the partner orgasm until they are so sensitive it hurts – multiple orgasms one after another hurts like hell – or they do like she enjoyed, bring the partner to the point of orgasm then back off, repeatedly. This Mistress would not allow me to reach my ecstasy by her hand but would bring me close over and over till I was practically mad from it. She, of course, didn't want this sort of torture for herself. When it came to her pleasure, she expected to receive it without fail. Failure resulted in thudding. So, I made sure to never fail.

She was also into thudding, bondage, and humiliation. Lucky me. Now on the note of humiliation. That is a hard thing to do with one such as myself. She did her best to find ways to cause indignity but often failed to find something that could embarrass me. I am schizophrenic, pansexual, and a lifestyler. I take over churches dressed like a witch, walk into crowded rooms without my clothing or a wig, dance like a loon anywhere, dress like a ghoul, and fucked my Priest while people watched. Yeah, was tough for old Mistress Ginger to find something that would get under my skin and cause it to turn red with shame, plus Simon owns that one.

Her first attempt to humiliate me was an order to finish myself off while she watched. This was only after she had taken me to the brink several times. She was most dissatisfied when that failed to upset me. Hey, I was ready to get my fucking orgasm. She had been teasing for hours, I do mean hours. I wouldn't have given a shit if all of you had been there watching me. I was getting to the top of that mountain and yodeling one way or another. Okay, that was too much information (nurse, I need meds, someone please get me some help over here).

Now as for the thudding. Unlike Master Julie or even stupid old Mistress Circe, Mistress Ginger was trained. She knew how to make it hurt without cutting me all to shit. She did bruise and leave stripes but those heal. She also knew to allow healing time between session and understood the no strike zones such as back, kidneys, shoulders and stomach or chest. She never struck me on the head with tools unless it was a well-placed backhand with her bare hands.

NOTE: Before you judge Mistress Ginger let me tell all of you this: These types of behaviors were unfortunately for me her pleasures. I was always allowed to refuse any of them. It would of course result in a punishment far worse than what she was asking in the first place, but I did have the choice to refuse any or all service requests. I may not have enjoyed this shit, but it was the price I would have to pay for the amazing service this Mistress would provide in return for the next two years. Under her rule I would come to accept, then embrace, my nature as tightly as I had embraced my spirituality during Mistress Circe's.

Mistress Ginger would teach me to not be ashamed of being a schizophrenic. She also would help me accept that I am a person with a powerful and healthy sexual appetite. She managed to undo all that Debbie and her apes had done. Mistress Ginger would cure my hatred of all things sexual and help me understand it was okay to find pleasure wherever I can and however I can. She managed to break through the ice that had stopped up my flow of sexual drives, by rocking my world to its foundation. Want to see how? Stick with this one. She will surprise you. Never judge what you think you know or see, listen till you decide.

Once the Mistress was finally sated, and I was black and blue from her lustful thudding, she finally cut me loose from my bondage. I provided her with bath service and attended to her meal needs. She retired to her favored place on a large, overstuffed couch and ordered me to eat at her feet while she watched. She began to lay down the rules I would follow for the next twenty-eight or so months. These were non-negotiable laws of the household.

I was to eat three times a day. If I lost weight that was not ordered, I would be thudded for every lost pound. She ordered that any cut, bruise, or abrasion that was found on my unit she did not put there I would be punished without question. Self-abuse was forbidden. Mistress Ginger made it a directive that I would not make any threats or attempts at violence against others or suicide towards self. If I dared, she would have me immediately put into inpatient treatment without argument or apologies accepted.

She demanded to see all my prescriptions after we had eaten. Mistress Ginger examined them and made fresh directives. She would purchase a pill reminder box the next day. I was to take this with me everywhere I went. She would not tolerate my missing doses of my medications. At night I would be questioned every day about timing and if taken. If I lied or had missed a dose I would be punished, no questions asked, no excuses granted.

Mistress Ginger liked to be clean and everything she owned clean too. I would bath daily, wash my wig weekly, and again, no quarter given if I failed in my duty. I was ordered to bath her every day, then I would also bath without fail on her heels. I was also informed the next day she would purchase clothing for my unit that she found pleasing. I was ordered to change outfits daily and wash all clothing (hers, my children and my own) on Tuesdays without fail or else.

Her final commands that night was that I would finish my own housing and reunite my family. She would allow me to move into my house. She would come to live in my home, after I prepared it to her liking, and she would aid in the care of my children. Mary could still babysit but she believed the children should be with their mother as often as possible. Last, I would grant her guardianship immediately taking it from Mistress Circe. Mistress Ginger would contact legal counsel to see how to free me from the tyranny of my Work Master payments, or at least how to keep my income funneling back into my own household.

I was released by Mistress Ginger to return to my children and Maiden Mary's home. She had ordered me to return by six the next morning for wake-up service since it was a Saturday. She informed me that she would work out a schedule to ensure I served her household and personal needs but allowed for my employment, education, and own family needs until we could get everyone under the same roof.

I left her trailer that night feeling very frightened. I was very sore from her overzealous games. I was wondering how the hell my train had just jumped the track without my even seeing it coming. I had expected Mistress Circe to pay me back for my standing up to her and ending her greed, but this was beyond terrible. I had become so prodromal I didn't even recognize that Mistress Ginger was doing her job. She had managed to address, fix, and take control of my out-of-control situation. All I could understand about this new Mistress was that she was a sadist who wanted to beat me to get her rocks off. I already hated her a great deal. I couldn't believe I had ever thought she was good looking once. Now all I could see was ugly.

I pulled in to find a very worried Mary pacing her porch. She ran over to hug me overjoyed that I was not kidnapped and dead in a ditch somewhere. I held her off thanks to my bruised unit not willing to take anymore touching for a while. This confused the sweet Maiden, but she honored my request to back off.

She watched me wincing as I painfully got off the bike. "Oh no, Mother. Are you okay? Did the new Master hurt you? Who is she? She called and told me not to call the cops. She said you were safe, but you were gone so long I almost called Dennis."

I groaned. "Daughter, this Mistress is the worst. She is a pushy broad, has a nasty temper, and to be honest if I had a gun, I would likely do something I would regret later. Circe really fucked me royal on this one. No matter, she will get hers at Samhain. I need to rest. Can I borrow your couch? I must go deal with this stupid bitch again by six in the morning."

Maiden Mary's eyes got wide. "Oh Mother. If she is horrible, don't go back. You can stay here as long as you want. I will call the woman tomorrow and tell her you want her to leave you alone."

I nodded at Mary. "I just need some time to think, Daughter. There must be some way out of this without betraying the collar. I know who to ask. I will get back to you on it."

Maiden Mary looked at the ground. "You are wearing the collar again, Mother. Why did you let her put it on you? It is disgraceful."

I chuckled. "You weren't there, Daughter. This idiot wasn't going to take no for an answer. Look, I will see what I can do. Stop worrying. Have some faith, I told you, it will work out the way it is meant to. It always does."

Mary looked at me hard. "You will talk to Simon, right? That is the guy Circe caught in the jar. He is the real Master. I remember that is what Circe said. He can fix this?"

Her question startled me. "Yeah, Simon will decide what to do. Daughter, please never say his name again. He is my business. I am sorry that Circe brought him to everyone's attention. That is private, okay?"

She nodded. "Of course, Mother. I just wanted to be sure he wasn't still in Circe's jar. I know he will help you do the right thing."

Mary went into the house leaving me there rubbing my sore backside wondering if I could even get Simon's attention. I was not always able to contact him, but this was an emergency. I called for him, then took a seat on the porch to wait to see if he would come.

I had almost given up hope he would appear. Then suddenly in the darkness I heard him whistling some ditty I had never heard before.

"Simon? Is that you," I called out.

"None other. Did you call?" He came into the light of the porch smiling and smoking as usual.

He sat down next to me. "So, I take it you don't like the new Mistress, Ginger, right?"

I nodded, starting to tear up with both despair and anger over the events of the day. "I hate her, Simon. She is horrible. She beats the unit. Tied us up and wants to beat us for everything. If we look in the wrong direction, she said she will beat us."

He started laughing which made me angry. "Psycho, stop being a baby. She doesn't want to beat us. She is trying to help us. You don't listen, and you know it. This Mistress is being fair. You don't mind the rules, you get punished for it. That is life. You mess up, bad things happen. End of story."

I growled. "Bullshit. I don't get beaten at work when I mess up, Simon. She is just like Master Julie. She wants to hurt us for pleasure. This is very bad. Can't you see that?"

Simon put out his smoke and took a deep breath. "Oh? Did she break the unit anywhere? She stopped before it was seriously hurt, didn't she? She is offering to do the job we need in a Master, and you are pissed because she likes to spank us? Really Psycho? Grow up. If she wants to thud, and doesn't leave scars or cuts, who cares? We are tougher than that. We get to have a real home, protection from the courts, and she is offering to bring our children to live with us and our Master. You are being childish. Do your job and she will do hers."

I groaned. "I don't want to be hurt anymore, Simon. Nothing is worth pain. Nothing." I was now whining like a little bitch.

He stood up, appearing angry. "Stop it. I mean it. We are getting sick. We need help, Psycho. Deal with it. I am not kidding. You mind this Mistress and there will not be much pain. This is up to you. You have a choice, so make it."

I glared. "Punishment or do what you are told is not a fucking choice, Simon."

His eyes went wide. "It isn't? Really? Okay, so don't take the pills. Get the collar cut off, throw away the Key. Go psychotic. Get locked up. This time get killed."

I was confused. "What? Why would I want to do that?"

He chuckled. "Exactly. You take the pills and have a fucking Master because you made the same choice this Mistress offers. You can stop the pills, but you will be psychotic. You don't have to follow my Key or orders, but you will die. You choose to comply rather than be punished. This is our life. She understands our world. Mistress Ginger said it well. Two sides to the same coin. She is the side we don't have, we are the side she desires. It is a perfect union. This is the Master I have been waiting for. Mistress Ginger is going to do what no other has done. She will save us from us. Do what she tells you. Follow her orders. No matter what she wants, deal with it, Psycho."

I cowered at his words. I must do what Simon wants me to do. He is me, and I am him. Like it or not, he had ordered us to mind this red-headed nightmare. I nodded that I wouldn't argue any further. I knew better. Simon can be a real bitch when angered. I had pushed him far enough to realize he wasn't going to allow us to back out of the collaring. We were now fully submitted to Mistress Ginger, right or wrong, this was now our rightful Keyholder. Simon had said so.

We spoke a bit regarding her knowledge of backing out of the Coven on her own. She was wise enough to realize she could not both lead and follow any more than we could. We had judged this Mistress too quickly. Mistress Circe was trying to punish us with the nightmare of our world, but she had backfired yet again. Mistress Ginger may be exactly what was needed to help us fill the last gaping hole in our world, the cycling psychosis. It was going to cost us pain, and humiliation for her pleasure, but likely not more than we would do to ourselves if not put under strict control. At least this way our hands, tongue, and life were not in danger of being severed from us. Just our dignity and we never could hold on to that for long anyway. Oh well, sucks to be us.

The next morning, I arrived to perform wake up service to my new Mistress. I knelt next to her bed calling for her gently until she opened her eyes. She had already given me a key to her front door.

NOTE: *It may seem interesting that Key holders trust me so much so quickly. When one takes possession of my Key and Collar, they already know I will defend my territory and my Master to the death. That is what submission is all about. It is an allegiance of honor. I would never steal, harm, or otherwise molest one who controls my destiny if I am lucid. Usually when I get psychotic most Keyholders are smart enough to take precautions to protect me and themselves. Mistress Ginger still had a few months before she would have to deal with my demon schizophrenia. For now, she was safe as a baby lamb in the middle of Fort Knox.*

She allowed me to perform all my services without interruption. Mistress Ginger just sat there while I dressed, groomed, and attended her needs for the day. When I was finished brushing and fixing her hair without being told I knelt at her feet waiting for further instructions.

She smiled wide. "Very nice. You are indeed trained. Old school too I see. Aren't I the lucky one? If only

Dungeon Master Paul could see this. He would bust a nut. He thought all of you were gone from the Earth, and to find one so young and pretty. Female to boot. Ah, I will have to call and brag. He will never believe it."

I looked at the floor. "I don't understand Mistress. Forgive my ignorance. What is you pleasure?"

Mistress Ginger sighed. "Well, I plan to go shopping to fix your look today. I am proud of who I am. You will learn to find pleasure in your own too. I would have never known had it not been for that damned collar. I don't like that collar. I am getting one made that is more streamline, less obvious and easier to lock. This shit here is more of a slave manacle. You are no slave. You are something rare and special. You deserve a collar that demonstrates that. So, I suppose I want breakfast first, then maybe a quickie. Then off to the shops. What do you say to that?"

I kept my gaze down. "As you wish Mistress. Thank you for your kindness and mercy."

"You are released. Finish and bring my food to the couch. I am going to call my friend Paul. Be quiet as possible while you cook. I have left a menu for you on the stove. Follow it. It should be done within the hour." She waved her hand to release me.

I nodded. Then got right to work on my tasks as commanded. I almost forgot my medication, but suddenly recalled her thudding tools. I was heading to serve her breakfast, but quickly returned to her kitchen and took the pills. I didn't want to get any more thuds than she already had planned for me. She was a professional dominatrix, so I was aware her types of punishment could be very nasty. I decided not to ever find out what they were. I would not give her trouble if I could help it.

She saw my correction. "Ah, I was so hoping you would forget your meds, Psycho. I was really going to have some fun with that." She laughed as she hung up her phone.

I had overheard her speaking of me to someone. She was very pleased with my behavior. I noticed she left out my initial refusals to submit and was bragging to someone of her most rare type of submissive. I didn't know what that was or meant but I assumed at some point she might tell me. I wasn't going to ask. If I did, she may think I was ignorant. My whole life was a joke worth laughing at. No reason to give her another reason to chuckle at me.

I nodded. "As you wish Mistress. If your pleasure is to have fun at my expense, it is not for me to deny it." I handed her the tray of food.

She smiled. "Now you are behaving the way you were trained. Nice. I can see this is going to be even better than I had hoped. However, I didn't see you make yourself any food, looks like I get to punish after all." She seemed very happy about that.

Her face fell when I reached into my front pocket and pulled out several packages of sliced turkey. "I apologize Mistress. I didn't want to foul up your meal with my disgusting food. You told me to eat at your feet but if I am in error, then I will happily accept your choice of correction."

She shook her head. "No need. Sit on the floor now and get to it. I have decided to call in special services of the collar after we shop. I have something in mind for later. After that, we will go to your house and see what needs to be done to make it comfortable. I am anxious to get out of the sticks and back into civilization, even if it is only that shitty little town."

I sat down to eat. "As you wish Mistress. I will transfer the guardianship first thing Monday morning. I will need to give you my schedule for classes and court ordered appointments."

She nodded. "Yep, give me all your important documents and records as well. I need to see what I am dealing with here. Your Maiden called me late last night. She told me you are going acute. From what I saw at the Litha celebration, I agree with her. I will need to set up a safe place for you to go when your time comes. She has made arrangements with me to keep the kids when you are going inpatient when I can no longer control you."

I stopped eating and looked up at her in terror. "Mistress? Why? I won't need to go into the hospital if you keep me from doing stupid things."

Mistress Ginger shut me up with a hand command for silence. I stopped speaking immediately. "Oh no you don't. I am just a human being, Psycho. When you go full on insane you could hurt yourself, me, hell anyone. When that time comes, you will go into the local mental hospital. I want you close so I can make sure those rat bastards treat my girl as decently as possible. Make no mistake, you will be going at some point."

I shook my head. "But Mistress, I don't want to go to the hospital. Please mercy."

She commanded silence with her hand again. "Do you want to argue with me about this? I am happy to hear you voice your displeasure with my decision. Then when you are finished, we can correct your talking back to me when I know what is best for you. You will learn to trust my judgement or we can correct yours. I seem to recall you are wearing the collar and I have your key. Not the other way around. Understand?"

I looked down. "Loud and clear, Mistress. As you wish." She had me dead to rights.

I had granted her the right to make all my decisions by my submission to her collar. She was holding my trust and Will. It was true I would not always like what she chose. I no longer had the right to argue unless she did something that caused or would cause me damage. I couldn't be trusted. I knew that but I sure as hell didn't have to like it. I went back to eating while cursing her silently in my mind. She may be able to keep me from talking back using my words, but I sure as shit could do what I wanted in my head.

After breakfast was eaten and cleaned up, we left for her shopping trip. I was told to drive. It was pretty apparent this Mistress intended to use every single service I provide. I wondered if she would even make a few up.

She had me take her to several shops. Her taste was very obviously fetish and BDSM. I was to wear only black, which made me very happy, and was told I could keep my makeup look. However, she added chest/breast harnesses, latex, netting, heavy corsets, chain belts, rivets, spikes, O/D rings, and even leg/arm harnesses to my already very gothic looking wardrobe. She bought several thudding outfits for her bedroom pleasures. If you don't know what that looks like go and do some sexual explorations on your own. It is okay, I won't tell anyone.

I was a bit more than angry that she was going to require me to wear this shit out in public to advertise to the fucking world I was involved in a damned D/s relationship. Mistress Ginger noticed my pouting about it.

"What's wrong, Psycho? Don't like your new clothes?" She laughed as I drove back to our town to show her my home.

I shook my head. "Forgive me Mistress, but you would have me run around hillbilly land looking like I escaped from a fucking BDSM dungeon? What are you thinking? The townspeople already hate me enough without adding this shit. Punish me if you must but I cannot sit here and not say a thing. Remember, you asked me," I growled.

Mistress Ginger dropped her head backward emitting a deep laugh. "Oh, you are killing me, Psycho. Let me get this straight; you run around wearing a witch's outfit, come to church naked, look like a ghoul wearing a long black duster in the middle of summer, and a chest harness bothers you? You think the townspeople who already think you are a whore, know you are schizophrenic, and a High Priestess, can think less of you? I am not telling you to wear a fucking ball gag in the street, Psycho. Get over yourself. You will wear what I tell you to wear and be grateful for it. Stop trying to hide. Who gives a shit who knows? They are never going to accept you. So, be you. Fuck them, understand?" She was still laughing.

I nodded. "As you wish Mistress. I will not deny you. However, if our house catches fire from the town's folk trying to burn out the lesbian, BDSM, Wiccan, weirdos, I will say I told you so," I said bitterly.

Mistress Ginger laughed even harder. "First of all, I am not a lesbian any more than you are, Psycho. I am pansexual, just like you. I don't care what gender or color the partner is long as they can do what makes me cum. Second, the only arson fires in this town that I have ever heard of are alleged to have been set by a certain submissive, High Priestess, schizo that wears a silver collar and takes offense when she is mistreated."

I flashed her a hateful look. "That is a lie, Mistress. I don't know anything about any fires."

She smiled, still chuckling. "Sure, you don't, Psycho. Look, people who disrespect the collar get what they deserve don't they? I am aware of what will happen to me if I fuck up with Simon's Key. I know of a witch that has been exiled, a family that was burned out. There was another one that went to ICU with a broken pelvis, and another that held that collar of yours currently on the run from the law for the rest of her life. The only one I know of that went to rest in peace appears to have treated you right. You will never have a reason to punish me like you have the others. Don't bother to deny it, I know what you did. I respect that. I hear you loud and clear. I will watch my ass, of that you can be sure."

I just kept my eyes on the road. "Why Mistress I have no idea what you are talking about. I always treat my Masters right. I provided all of them the equal service for the service they provided me. I believe you have been listening to idle gossip. You should not believe everything you hear."

She stopped smiling, appearing very serious. "I hear just fine, Psycho. Equal service for equal service told me all I ever will need to know about those rumors I have heard. I am sure the service they got they earned honestly. Now turn on the radio. Find something rock-n-roll. I can't wait to see our new house. This is going to be the best years of our lives, Psycho. Finally, I have found a submissive powerful enough to match my Dominance. A perfect circle of silver at last. We will be an unbreakable team. You will see, you and me forever." She began to dance to music only inside her head.

I turned on the radio as she commanded. "As you wish Mistress. Forever is exactly what I had in mind."

Wow, right there the whole time. That Mistress Circe was a sneaky bitch. Mistress Ginger had been duped too, as had all those Interims. This made me even more sure that Tammy was sent to end my life, but alas she was never found to ask if she and Circe has made plans together.

In the next two years under the rule of Mistress Ginger there is a lot of Lifestyle stuff, sexual fetishes (discussed, not that I am involved in all of them so get those minds out of the gutter; okay put them back in. I was just kidding), as well as Wiccan rules, beliefs, and other religious stuff in play. I have not been holding back because readers want the real and raw story. If you are okay with my openness about sex, abuse, assault, and off beat religions then you will need to purchase the next book in the series.

Mistress Ginger is all about sex, and I am about to reach a point that will bring more alternative people's sexual and belief styles into the next book.

This is my real life, my memories, my journey. It was far from pleasant or kind. I cannot shut out the sights, sounds, or knowledge so writing it doesn't bother me one bit.

To be continued in book four of the 27 Masters Series: The Professional Dominatrix

About the Author: Alexandria May Ausman

Alexandria May Ausman in her 16th year was diagnosed with Schizophrenia. She was quickly abandoned by her foster parents. While still only a teen, she was forced to battle this devastating illness alone.

Alexandria has struggled with lack of a support system, numerous psychotic episodes, exploitation, homelessness, and an uncaring mental health system.

Alexandria raised two healthy children. After obtaining her bachelor's degree in psychology she worked as a child abuse investigator and became a diagnostic psychologist while acquiring her Master's in psychology. Alexandria never forgot the experience of 'slipping through the cracks.' Her life's goal is to help people suffering abuse and/or mental illness have access to necessary services. By accident, she became a model of 'gothic attire' and the World Goth Queen.

She began writing a fictionalized account of her life experiences after a catastrophic return of psychotic symptoms. Today, Alexandria is retired, and homebound due to crippling symptoms of Schizophrenia. She currently lives in Tallahassee, Florida, with her loving husband and a loyal support dog.

www.ingramcontent.com/pod-product-compliance
Lightning Source LLC
Chambersburg PA
CBHW071406090426
42737CB00011B/1370